JACK THE RIPPER
A PSYCHIC INVESTIGATION

JACK THE RIPPER
A PSYCHIC INVESTIGATION

THE COMPELLING PARANORMAL SEARCH FOR
THE KILLER'S TRUE IDENTITY

By Pamela Ball

ARCTURUS

Published by
Arcturus Publishing Limited
For Bookmart Limited
Registered Number - 2372865
Trading as Bookmart Limited
Desford Road, Enderby,
Leicester, LE9 5AD

This edition published 1998

Printed and bound in Finland

Text and illustration
layout by Blue Design
Cover design by Paul Ashby
Project editor: Tessa Rose

© Arcturus Publishing Limited
1-7 Shand Street, London, SE1 2ES

ISBN 1 900032 13 9

CONTENTS

PREFACE

The Ripper murders have attracted many controversial theories since they were committed in autumn 1888. The intention in writing this book was not to add to the barrage of argument and counter-argument that has steadily flown back and forth, but rather to see whether a different approach to the conundrum, using psychic tools of investigation, would shed new light on the mystery.

I came to the subject with no preconceived notions or ready-made suspects. This has given me a tremendous advantage over other writers on this complex subject, because I have had nothing to prove. I gathered material for the book purely to find out as much as I could about the key players in the drama (victims, suspects and investigators) with a view to answering as many as possible of the questions that still haunt this compelling tale. This approach has allowed me to wander into all sorts of highways and byways, largely unconstrained by other people's theories and unpressured by the thought that I had to 'solve' the case.

The information that came to me and that I explored with my team is by its nature unique. Only as I neared the end of the investigation did I realize that I had been privileged to explode a few myths; to offer evidence of some suppositions, and concurrently to reveal facts which have hitherto remained hidden. I have become very excited by these findings, despite the realization that I have not been able to support my conclusions by offering indisputable 'proof'.

In the beginning I had nothing concrete with which to work psychically. In many ways I was starting with a clean slate, because a great deal of the tangible evidence available has been lost or destroyed during the passage of time. Only towards the end of the investigation was I able - through the generosity of several distinguished Ripper experts - to examine important artefacts: a knife said to have been left by the side of Annie Chapman's body, a diary thought to have been kept by James Maybrick and a shawl long believed to have belonged to Catharine Eddowes at the time of her murder. I tend to view with suspicion objects that are said to have a 'history'. As in other respects, the tangible seems to have the greatest propensity for leading us up blind alleys.

There are those who will find the methods used suspect, to whom I would reply that I did my best to act with responsibility and integrity; there are those who will disbelieve me, to whom I would simply say I have recorded what happened as faithfully as I could; and there are those who will call me mad - that is their privilege. The Jack the Ripper saga will always create controversy. For a few people one of the most controversial aspects of this book will be the use of channelling or mediumship in pursuit of information. There are many who may feel that working in the way I have done for the purposes of this book is both dangerous and foolhardy. The gift of channelling is one which carries with it a great deal of responsibility. It is not simply done for fun or 'kicks'. Such contact is only made with the consent of the spirit or entity concerned. Any other type of connection would be akin to low magic and the art of the magician - that of using spiritual energy for one's own purposes and for invoking spirits.

In my thirty years of working with the spirit world, I have used 'evidential' mediumship only to bring comfort to my sitters, to give information from the spirit world, and to assist a spirit entity to move on. The investigation was undertaken on the strict condition that at no time would I expose myself to evil. I brought to it an open mind but also an understandable sense of fellow-feeling for the women involved. It would be arrogant of me to assume that others have not tried to bring comfort to the victims of Jack the Ripper. In my sessions with them, I hope I was able to bring them clarity. As far as the killer himself was concerned, I personally felt that reaching an understanding of him was an important - and valid - part of the investigation. In addition to understanding his motivation, it might also be just possible to allow him some peace within his soul.

I trust that readers will accept this book in the spirit in which it was written, purely and simply as a record of a psychic investigation. I hope they will concur with my feeling that it adds to our understanding of the Ripper himself, and, more importantly, to his victims, the period and the mystery that make up this enduring saga.

THE TOOLS OF THE INVESTIGATION

The tools used in this investigation were chosen by me as the most appropriate to yield results in the circumstances. Another psychic may have chosen a different yet equally valid set of tools, so it would be wrong to regard this investigation as one which follows a set pattern according to established groundrules. As far as I am aware, few psychics cross disciplines in the way that I do by, for example, using astrology coupled with psychology as an investigative technique. These additional tools allowed me continually to cross-check or test information I received at different stages of the investigation.

As with any experiment, I did my best to devise a method that was as scientifically rigorous as possible. I undertook most of the astrological work and contact sessions; the latter were set up in order to open the door to another dimension, allowing me to communicate with those in the spirit world. Initially I left my two assistants, Fiona and James, to complete the conventional research. As far as possible I was purposely kept in ignorance of their findings, particularly while the sessions were under way. This was done to guard against the danger of the information received by me psychically being contaminated by prior knowledge. Inevitably, as the investigation progressed I became increasingly aware of information they had unearthed. It was at this point that my 'secondary skills' really came into their own.

The principal 'alternative' skills we brought to this investigation were astrology, channelling, psychometry and dowsing. We had very specific reasons for employing these particular tools. Below are explanations of how they were used and to what purpose.

ASTROLOGY

While many descriptions exist of both the victims and the suspects, we felt that the information available was sufficiently sketchy to warrant further investigation. We wanted to know about the everyday lives of these people, how they handled what life had to offer; in short, what made them tick. Astrology is as much an intuitive art as it is a science. We have used astrology to assess the characters of the main players in the Ripper case and brought intuition to bear in sensing the vibration of each of them.

We knew where and when both victims and suspects were born, although not the precise time of birth. This gap in our knowledge meant that we could not be entirely accurate in our astrological assessments. So far as the victims were concerned, however, we felt that it would be possible to paint a broad picture of the types of women they were, and perhaps to glean what aspects of their characters might have turned them into victims. Could the infamous killer, we wondered, possibly have been drawn to them for other than the obvious reason that they all appeared to be what in those days were called 'unfortunates' (prostitutes). The charts would hopefully tell us if there was a victim type or profile.

Similarly, wherever possible we have scanned the astrological charts of the suspects to help us to interpret what was going on in their lives at certain times, and to ascertain their potential for murder. Where practicable we have also scanned their charts in the month of the murders for evidence of stresses that could have led any of them to commit such heinous crimes.

Astrology is unique in that it gives us an opportunity to assess the significance of specific moments in time. The precise moment at which a person is born decides what influences will be at play throughout the rest of his or her natural life.

The planets represent different cosmic forces that affect the individual's basic character traits and changing urges and needs. They provide the dynamism which makes each of us what we are, and decide how our physical, emotional, mental, and intuitional systems will develop. These planetary energies are utilized according to the planet's position in the zodiac (which sign they are in), and by its relationships (aspects) to other planets in the heavens. For the purpose of our investigation aspects are classified as difficult or easy.

Planets fall into three groups according to how long it takes them to complete one cycle.

The first group of planets - these are called the Personal Planets, since they affect each person in a unique way - takes less than two years to complete a full cycle. They are the Sun, Moon, Mercury, Venus, and Mars.

The key characteristics they represent are:

Sun	Identity, purpose (individuality)
Moon	Feeling, responsiveness (personality)
Mercury	Intellect, communication (mentality)
Venus	Attraction, harmony (affection)
Mars	Energy, assertiveness (initiative)

The second group includes the planets Jupiter and Saturn, which take about 12 and 20 years respectively to complete a full cycle. Their effects are felt more as long-term inner urges rather than immediate conscious needs. These urges determine how the individual views the world in which he or she lives. The qualities associated with these planets are:

Jupiter	Enthusiasm, adventurousness (expansiveness)
Saturn	Caution, restraint (conservatism)

The planets in the third group move so slowly that their energies influence entire generations in essentially the same way by setting the social or cultural tone of an age. We hoped the transpersonal planets would help us to understand how victims and suspects alike would have reacted to the 'prevailing wind' of their times.

Uranus makes a full cycle in about 84 years, a full lifetime, while Neptune and Pluto take about two centuries (164 and 247 years respectively). The characteristics of these transpersonal planets are:

Uranus	Independent, intuitional (originality)
Neptune	Inspirational, mystical (sensitivity)
Pluto	Regenerative, obsessive (control)

The influences of the transpersonal planets will vary among individuals, depending on how they relate to the other planets of the horoscope, and how they fall into a person's natal house. Often, for instance, the position of Neptune can indicate a sensitivity to drink or drugs - those substances that bring about a change of consciousness.
(Fuller explanations of the planets are given on pages 163-166.)

THE PSYCHIC SKILLS

The so-called psychic - or intuitive - skills, of which there are several, develop as part of the spiritual quest to discover one's own truth. One of the better known skills is the ability to link into the future - popularly known as fortune telling - and to decide what actions may be appropriate. Many people use the art of the clairvoyant to assist them to make the best use of their lives.

Part of understanding the future, however, lies in being able to 'read' the past in the light of the person's character and to understand what has brought an individual to a particular point in time. Astrology also allows us to 'read' this moment in time through a person's natal chart. Many people recognize that psychics and clairvoyants have the ability to 'read' past events and give information which may not be accessible to the layman. What the psychic or clairvoyant accesses is a record of the past, present and future of all our lives (called the Akashic Records). He or she is able to view this record in the same way that an ordinary person would watch television or a video, and by so doing gains a greater understanding of the life that is under scrutiny. Using astrology and the psychic skills together gives a kind of cross-referencing that is helpful in establishing contact.

Channelling

I used the technique known as channelling, or mediumship, to consult the Akashic Records. I used it also in the contact sessions with the spirit dimension. If one believes in the principle of life after death, then it is possible to communicate with an individual who has died and to find out if they are at peace, have left behind the problems of this life, and understand - in part - the life that they have led.

The contact sessions were structured so that three people were present on each occasion. It helps the medium if someone there is used to her way of working; this function was fulfilled by my assistant, Fiona. The third person present then acts as a kind of objective observer, so that supplementary questions can be asked. In addition, I felt it might be appropriate to have, occasionally, at least one other person present who would be able to give their own view of the proceedings.

Each session took place in the same surroundings in order that conditions be as similar as possible on each occasion. This helps me to feel secure, and also makes it easier for me to re-orientate myself at the end of each session. Familiar noises can be accommodated and ignored, though at times intrusions from the outside world did occur. In one session, for example, the noise of a plane disturbed the conditions before a proper link had been made. There used to be a belief in old-style spiritualism that the time at which each session took place was important, because this helped to raise the level of vibration. Our sessions generally took place around the same time each week, but this tended to be for the benefit of the people taking part rather than to accommodate the spirit entities.

Working psychically involves the use of a great deal of electromagnetic energy, and this can affect even modern-day technology - tape machines or computers, for example, can malfunction as a result of this interference. Contrary to popular belief, this is not due to the work of spirit entities. That said, there were times during this whole

THE TOOLS OF THE INVESTIGATION

investigation when obstacles seemed to get in the way of communication.

When making contact with the spiritual realms, particularly when dealing with something as 'dark' as the Jack the Ripper mystery, a degree of protection is required from the energies that may be stirred up. Our protection took the form of a simple prayer, said before each session, in which we asked that the participants in the sessions, the place where they occurred and the motives for the enquiry be both protected and understood.

Dowsing

We used a technique called dowsing with a pendulum to try to fill the gaps in our knowledge - for example, to ascertain birthdates where they were unknown or there was some doubt - and to verify some of the information received through channelling. The question put by the dowser must be unambiguous to elicit a 'Yes' or 'No' answer. For the author, the answer 'Yes' is signified by a clockwise circular swing and the answer 'No' by a backwards and forwards movement. The movement differs from person to person; see the impromptu training session with the pendulum that occurred during the Mary Kelly contact session for an example of this (page 125).

Psychometry

Psychometry is the art of being able to sense the vibrations of an object and thus to tell its story; the clairvoyant holds the object and using his or her intuition allows the object to 'speak'. With its use it is possible to give dates which are often verifiable, to describe emotions which were occurring at that time, to discover whether assumptions made are true or to give information about the owner of the object.

* * *

A word of warning to the curious. It is unwise to 'play' with any psychic tools unless one is competently guided initially. Anyone who chooses to do so should be prepared to take the consequences of their actions. The author will accept no responsibility for what may happen if any reader is so foolhardy as to ignore this advice.

THE RIPPER PHENOMENON

There is a part in each of us which is fascinated by the grotesque and ghoulish. However hard we may try to deny it, it is that part which causes us to have nightmares, thrills at the horror film and screams on the fairground ghost train. That part is usually held very firmly under control by our rationality - that ability to explain what is going on in life. Once we have an explanation and a neat conclusion, we are able to file each happening tidily in some corner of our mind and leave it there.

It was the ferocity of the attacks and mutilations attributed to 'Jack the Ripper' which fascinated and repelled the Victorians in 1888. Multiple murders were rare, and those that occurred did not carry such grim hallmarks. There was a killer on the loose; no-one knew who he was; no-one knew when he would strike again. The escalation of violence that each fresh killing represented struck terror into the hearts of most Londoners, and particularly those living in the Ripper's domain, the East End of the city. The fact that the killings were committed in a short time frame of ten weeks gave them added impact. No sooner had the public got used to one atrocity than another was committed, only worse. Victorian Londoners would have had no conception - and thus no understanding - of modern psychological techniques aimed at explaining such a phenomenon. The tendency, especially among the God fearing, would have been for them to blame themselves for such a curse of almost Biblical proportions being meted out to them.

There are still too many loose ends trailing from the saga of Jack the Ripper to allow us to forget about it. Although many serial killings committed since then have been both more violent and more numerous than those of Jack the Ripper, these particular murders continue to haunt the imagination. One of the main reasons we have not managed to accommodate them is because a real identity has not been assigned to the murderer. We spectators need to be able to project our horror onto the individual responsible. We need to know that he or she is human, is flesh and blood and, like ourselves, can be made accountable. These fundamentals are reassuring, enabling us to file the information we have about the guilty deep in our memory, safe in the knowledge that they will be physically shut away for their crimes or that their lives have been terminated, either by their own hand or by those to whom we have given authority, such as the police, or, in some instances, the judicial system. But Jack the Ripper has not been brought to justice. We have not been able to stand him up in front of us and accuse him, let alone execute him.

We have not been given the choice of exercising mercy or demanding retribution.

The police officers assigned to the case may have come to their own conclusions about the identity of the Ripper, but we are not able to prove for ourselves who he was. Many suspects were interviewed and rejected at the time, and equally many have been suspected since. The psychic and clairvoyant Robert Lees is believed to have led the police to the killer, but we have no proof. Everything about this case goes against our innate belief in justice, and leaves us with the uncomfortable suspicion that evil may have been allowed to triumph over good. The passage of time has not allayed the feeling that we have failed to put right a wrong.

Every good suspense story has within it an element of conflict. Whether that conflict is an internal one or one which is apparent to all, as in the fight between good and evil, does not matter. What does matter is that conflict should be resolved, and in the Ripper story this does not happen. The 'poor unfortunates' who became the victims are abandoned without an understanding of what adversity they experienced and what disharmony took them to the depths. The suspects who have been put under the spotlight have no way of vindicating themselves. The police, who should have been in a position to cast the light of truth onto the proceedings, are left to seem, at worst, somewhat fraudulent and, at best, incompetent. Jack the Ripper himself remains as the brooding, anonymous face of evil, with no trace of the internal conflicts which may have led him to commit the killings and the frenzy of mutilations that followed. Over one hundred years later the motives behind the crimes are still not clear.

Oddly, the whole phenomenon of Jack the Ripper seems to have mirrored the doubts, fears and prejudices of the average Londoner, and it needs to be looked at within the framework of the 1880s, a period of economic uncertainty and increasing class tensions. The concept of the individual pitted against collective authority was never as acute as in Victorian England. Although in theory many of the socially aware would work for the good of humanity, in practice this was not always so. Many aspects of the case highlight the conflicts and upheavals which had to occur if inequalities arising out of the process of economic growth were to be rectified.

How to begin to understand this phenomenon? We took as our starting point the area in the East End of London where the murders were committed.

JACK THE RIPPER'S LONDON

Our first psychic experiment took place on 8 July 1997 when we ran a test session to ascertain how easy it would be to orientate within the time-frame and the environment of the investigation. I wanted to sense what it would have been like to live in Whitechapel in 1888 or thereabouts. At the same time I wanted to establish how easy - or otherwise - it would be to make contact with the Ripper's victims.

Because this session was a spontaneous experiment and I, for one, did not expect to get much from it, we did not audiotape it (all other sessions except one are on tape). In the event I am not sure that a tape would have made more sense than the notes taken by my assistants at the time. The session was particularly fragmented, with snatches of seemingly disparate information being received. As will be appreciated, the medium has no control over this, and is largely a recorder of the sensations and impressions that come through.

Contact work is similar to other pursuits in that practice makes perfect. I had not had the benefit of practice in this context and so I chose a technique that would enable me to gradually go back in time and gather information that subsequent research would be able either to verify or contradict. Going back in time too quickly can also be a shock to the system, without a degree of objectivity, and at this early stage in the enquiry I wanted to avoid negative experiences that might shake my confidence.

SENSING THE ATMOSPHERE

I began the session by telling myself that I wanted to go back in time by periods of ten years, and allowing through visualization the pages of a calendar to turn back by the requisite number of years. I trust that when the pages stop turning the information I receive will be relevant.
The pages stop for the first time ... Looking at the atmosphere Pam has the overall feeling of 'red'. This seems to be a type of pollution. It seems to have been more polluted than it is now. Pam seems to be near Tower Bridge in the 1920s.

When questioned as to why the 1920s, Pam replies that she feels this was the biggest period of change in Whitechapel; it feels unstable - there is an unpleasant feeling.
The pages stop again, this time in the 1910s. It is smelly, due to the poor sanitation.

16

When she reaches the 1900s, Pam asks whether modernization occurred in Spitalfields around 1904-5. *(Subsequent research proved this to have been the case.)*

In the 1890s conditions feel very damp and nasty.

When Pam links in to the 1880s, London feels empty; there are few people about. The roadways as such are poor. There are muddy paths - pavements, but no highways, possibly alleyways. The basements are damp. It is very hot and smells strongly of spices.

(Interestingly, when we visited the Old Operating Theatre Museum and Herb Garret at Guy's Hospital, later in the investigation, this smell was recognizable. Research revealed that in the Whitechapel area at this time there were many manufacturing establishments including a manure works, a vinegar factory and a brewery.)

It is not a good time; there is a strong need to get away, to get out of where you are. Pam says she can understand why many East-Enders went hop picking in the summer.

Pam mentions Sheldon Street. *(Research would reveal only a Shelton Street in Covent Garden near Seven Dials. We have not been able to ascertain whether there has ever been a Sheldon Street in Whitechapel.)*

The feeling is of a very strong community spirit, although men and women seem to inhabit separate communities. Men are more like protectors than pimps, but they can not stop girls from being prostitutes.

People get together for company. There is a sense of duality - sharing, but also keeping what is yours. People are not alone much. Conditions feel very cramped and there is a lack of space and light. Pam experiences, for the first time, the sensation of her skin crawling.

At this point Pam links in with the victims. All of them seem very independent. There is an acceptance of behaviour, of life. No improvement is expected.

THE BACKGROUND

By the mid 1880s the East End had become a powerful symbol of poverty. In Whitechapel alone 39.2 per cent of the population were living on or below the poverty line. In the minds of most people living outside the area, East London equated with not just poverty but also degenerative behaviour, depravity and law-breaking. This ghettoization was reflected in the attitudes of the East-Enders themselves who were deeply prejudiced against foreigners, Jews, the police, and upper class society.

The arrival of foreigners at the docks caused resentment, the East-Enders anxious that 'English' jobs were being lost to the flood of newcomers. There was an increase in popular anti-semitism, particularly because 90 per cent of the 60,000-70,000 Jews in London - half of them born in the country - were living in the East End. The success of the Jews caused animosity. Charles Booth, a well-known social reformer, noted that periods of unemployment, bad food, and overcrowding '... seem to leave unhurt the moral and physical fibre of the Jew.' He also stated that Jewish inhabitants of the East End tended to rise in the social scale when others were falling. The animosity directed at Jewish people is evident in the Ripper case. At one of the inquests, the coroner, Mr Wynne Baxter, described the killer as using 'Judas like approaches'. Will Cross, the carter who found the mutilated body of Mary Nichols (see page 33), supposedly pointed at the nearby Jewish cemetery and said the murder was 'probably some sneaking yid who wouldn't pay for his fun.'

Overcrowding was a major problem, as the figures given in the following census for 1871 show.

	MARRIAGES	BIRTHS	DEATHS	BIRTHS MINUS DEATHS
IN EAST LONDON	52,200	155,100	115,000	40,100
IN WEST LONDON	68,200	239,300	62,000	177,300

The policies of the government and of middle-class reformers helped to exacerbate this problem. Prince Albert himself turned his mind to improving conditions for the poor in the East End, and in 1885 the R.S.A. held a competition to enable young architects to win a prize of £2,000 by designing new dwellings for the area. (It says a great deal that the full prize money was not paid out, though several of the better plans were published.) Often the rents for the new apartments were too high for the previous tenants of the slums to rent. In 1891 55.5 per cent of the people in Whitechapel lived with more than two persons per room in dwellings with fewer than five rooms. Rents in the West of London rose by only 11 per cent between 1880 and 1900, whereas those in the East End jumped by 25 per cent. The total rateable value of property in 'West' London was £5,000,000 - in the 'East' it was not half that; the average rateable value of a house in the West was £70 as compared to £24 in the

East. In the West there were on average 13 houses and 106 people per acre, in the East the figures were 18 and 144 respectively; 7 individuals resided in each house in the West but 8 in the East.

To give some sort of picture of what these figures represent, a typical East End household would have comprised father, mother and five or six children - and possibly grandmother - sharing two rooms if they were lucky. There would be little or no sanitary control (often the privy was not even connected to the main drainage). Contrast this with the typical home in the West End, consisting of mother, father and two or three children, a maid and a cook. Somewhat romanticized as this picture may be, it is nevertheless a fair reflection of the contrasting conditions to be found at the time in East and West London.

The Poor Rate (the sum paid to paupers) in the West was 1s.3d while in the East it was 3s, reflecting the greater need of the people there. In the West there were three paupers to every 100 compared to five to every 100 in the East. There were 7,000 inmates of workhouses in the East, 3,000 more than in the West. In the West there were 30,000 professionals and in the East End fewer than 10,000.

Despite the greater poverty in the East there were 500 agencies for relief in the West, and 300 in the East. In the West there were 95 Church of England Churches and 214 clergy, while in the East the figures were 65 and 128 respectively. This worked out at one church for every 5,200 souls in the West, whereas the East had to get by on one church for every 10,000. Clergy such as the Reverend S. Barnett, the Vicar of St Jude's in Whitechapel, had an extremely hard job. His wife at one point wrote of her distress at not being able to do more to assist their parishioners.

One final note to highlight the discrepancies in provision is that the Charity Organization Society dealt with 4,000 cases in West London at an expenditure of £5,300, while in the East it dealt with a mere 1,500 cases at an expenditure of £1,200.

Making Ends Meet

As in the area of housing cited earlier, sometimes attempts to improve the lot of the poor made matters worse. Social reformers did not allow the people of the East End to know what was best for them or what changes were necessary. The social purity movement, for example, thought that by changing the 'traditional social and sexual habits of the poor' they would be bettering the conditions of women in the East End. These 'habits' included casual prostitution, which was used by many women to supplement their or their family's income. The purity group's misguided attempts often had the effect of leaving families without visible means of support. In 1887 alone, 200 brothels in London were closed as a result of government and purity group actions. Coming shortly before the outbreak of the Ripper murders, these closures left thousands of women homeless, more vulnerable and therefore open to attack.

For many people in dire straits the seeking of poor relief was a last resort. In the workhouse 'all the necessities of life are provided and yet they are unavoidably given under such conditions as are distasteful to most recipients'. This and other extracts from *The Handy Book for Visitors of the Poor* of 1874 make it clear that the poor were viewed with suspicion and not a little disdain by their betters. Many women chose to live without assistance, in their own way. The following article, 'The Needlewomen of the East-End' from the *Pall Mall Gazette* of 18 July 1884, gives an insight into the lives of working women in the East End.

Yesterday, at No. 8 High Street, Shadwell, there was witnessed the first beginning of an enterprise which, if supported as it deserves, will do much to lighten the lot in life of some of our working women. At that address a philanthropic lady, of unbounded energy, but alas! of delicate health, has started what is hoped will be the first of a multitude of Working Women's Co-operative Associations, where the public will be able to enter into direct communication with the needle-women, so as to obviate the intervention of middlemen or sweaters. At the simple little shop in Shadwell High Street Mrs Heckford sells articles of dress made on the premises by needle-women, none of whom are required to work more than eight hours per day, in a healthy workroom at a decent wage. The small capital of £500 needed to set this modern establishment going has been supplied by some friends interested in the lot of working women, and the success of the experiment will be watched with the keenest interest by all who are acquainted with the sad and often terrible condition of the East-End needle-women.

How many women there are in the East-End who live by the needle, I do not know. Mrs Heckford told me yesterday that from where we were standing you could go, east, west, north and south, and in almost every house you could pass you would find at least one needle-woman. In all London, according to the last census, more than a quarter of a million women were returned as making their living by that means - an army of working women more numerous than any other class, excepting those engaged in domestic service. The more's the pity that their lot should be so hard. In face of a general and most indisputable improvement in the condition of labour, it would seem incredible, if it were not only too horribly true that the condition of the needle-women is even worse than it was when the "Song of the Shirt" stirred the nation's heart. That song of woe might have been composed yesterday and every word of it might be applied to the needle-women, thousands of whom are crowded together in that solid block of misery, the centre of the East-End. If in Hood's time the needlewomen were chastised with whips, they are today chastised with scorpions. Should there be any who doubt this is so, let them take the train from Stepney to Bow Road, and plunge into the endless mass of low red-roofed houses which are spread to the left and right as far as the eye can reach; and miles further down to the river banks. In most of these miserable abodes the needle-women are at work. Any time, any season will do; they know no holiday, except that involuntary one when there is no work to be had and when grim death itself is their guest, death of starvation. But it is perhaps better to go on a grey wintry day, for when a reflection of the sunlight falls into the dens, they are almost too ghastly a picture to look at. And this is how they live and their work is done. They begin early, as early as possible, for a day's work with them means fourteen or fifteen hours stitching if they mean to earn a shilling a day. The work is done for large London firms, but before Mrs Heckford's courageous experiment there was no direct communication between employer and employed; it is almost all done on the "sweating" system. A "sweater" ("I'll call them middlemen, it's more polite," says a gentleman the other evening at a meeting of the Women's Provident and Protective League, but "sweater", though less polite, is a term more to the point) receives a quantity of work from the employer which he has to deliver at a certain time and for a certain price - a moderately good price, I hear; he gives the work out either to the women themselves or to another "sweater". It is often the case that the second "sweater" sublets the work again and the third once more, each of course profiting by the process. Can it be surprising then, that the wages of the poor women are low? They received 1s 6d for a dozen shirts, 9d for a dozen petticoats, 4 3/4d for a pair of trousers, which last sum is divided between the machinist and "finisher", and 3d for a braided knickerbocker suit. How pretty they look in the show windows, the airy lace-trimmed children's fancy frocks and aprons! A worker who with trembling fingers stitches them together can earn 1s a day by them, 1s 6d if she works from 8am to midnight. No wonder her thin fingers tremble with haste, with weakness and with the constant fear that her work may get soiled or that some little part of the work is not done exactly as prescribed. Woe be to her if the latter be the

case! For a walk to the shop to deliver her work means the loss of
half a day; often it means a precious penny for the loan of a pair of
boots; and at times when she is too weak to walk, the sum of
fourpence for riding; and if there is the least fault in one of the
articles, the whole dozen - they are usually taken in dozens - comes
back and has to be returned by the worker. And let her beware of
coming to her destination an hour later than ordered: "Drilling" is
then her share; "drilling" means waiting for days, and waiting means
starving. Sometimes in the case of married needle-women the
husband earns something towards a living, and then the misery is
not quite so great. The fact, however, is that in the East-End
thousands of men are always out of work, and if not out of work
many of them in the class which live with poorer needle-women are
"in trouble" caused by legal authorities, which trouble compels
them to leave their homes and set up in other quarters.

What has been said above, applies only to the "honest" needle-
woman. There is a way by which she can escape poverty and hunger
and it is, alas, followed by the majority. "Life in the streets"
provided the girl has any personal attractiveness, is more
remunerative; it pays so well that finery can be bought instead of
rags, and idleness and ease may take the place of toil or worry. No
wonder they fall; the temptations are strong. Here for instance is a
little low room. A sewing machine stands before the window. In
front of it sits a tall pale girl, with large beautiful eyes full of brilliant
light. The girl is in a decline. By her side sits an old woman, also busy
with her needle. "She cannot always do the machine sewing now,
she faints away so often" the old woman says, looking at her
companion. "She goes to the hospital, and they say she must have
nourishing food; but all last week we had nothing but bread. How
can we buy nourishing food?" she adds, with a humble smile. There
is one way of supplying that need, but the girl would rather die. It is
no phrase, but a stern reality. She is dying now, one among
unnumbered examples of the silent heroism of the East-End, the
un-noticed martyrdom of the abject poor.

I have said before that their work never ceases. There is, however,
one exception. When the shops are "taking stock" - which happens
twice a year - work is slack, and it fares hard with the workers;
otherwise good needle-women have not many difficulties in
obtaining work. Of trade unions they know nothing, and even if
they did they would not dare to join them, partly from fear of
exciting the ill-will of the employers, or rather of the "sweaters" and
also because there would be plenty of people willing to take the
work for as low and even lower wages, should they attempt to strike.
They are hungry and they cannot wait, but must take what they can

get. The introduction of sewing machines is greatly lamented in the East-End. Before their time pay was incomparably better; the women could earn a living by their wages then, now they barely exist. Work which cannot be done by machine is no better paid because it is done by hand. In one case - anybody willing to go to the East-End is free to enquire about the correctness of this statement - two women are sewing soldiers' kits; it cannot be done by machine, and by eighteen hours of labour the women are enabled to earn each 11 1/2d a day. Why, I ask, in the name of wonder are there still so many women engaged in this work while domestic servants are always wanted? Because, I am told in reply, to become a domestic servant a girl must at least have some idea of decency and order; before she can lay a table she must know what it is to sit at a covered table; and before she can make a bed, she ought to have seen something else than a ragged palliasse [a straw mattress], or, worse still, a bed filled with dirty rags, the only bed of many of the poorest. This is said to be the case with many. But there are many well skilled in the domesticities who nevertheless starve as seamstresses. It is the commonest resource of the female unattached. Nearly everyone can sew, the work can be taken up and dropped as the case may be, and it is a handicraft to fall back upon.

* * *

The Business of Prostitution

The prostitution system in London operated in three main forms. At the top end of the trade were the introducing houses where clients met carefully selected girls who travelled to the brothel especially for the assignation. The procuress handled all the financial arrangments and would regularly send notes to clients inviting them to meet the latest personality from France or wherever. Beneath the surface of this service to the well-to-do, there was, of course, an undercurrent of perversion. The procuress catered for all tastes and, of course, knowing her girls and her clients, would become very skilled at matching them up. It is more than probable that it is this type of establishment that first attracted Mary Kelly, the last of the Ripper's victims (see page 45).

The introduction houses, however, supplied only a very small part of the London sex market. Traditionally, most girls sought their custom on the streets. They used 'dress houses' where they paid an exorbitant rent for food, clothing and lodgings. They were in perpetual debt to the owners of these houses and lived in virtual slavery. By the same token there was tremendous comradeship among the girls, and they were protective of one another.

Other prostitutes freelanced, taking their pick-ups to the 'accommodation' houses which were everywhere throughout the West End - often these were shops or coffee houses which openly displayed notices worded 'Beds to be had within'. The client rented the room as well as the girl. Police evidence suggests that by the 1880s dress houses were on the decline and this freelance trade made up the biggest section of the industry.

The lowest form of prostitution was found in the East End, where it was common to work the streets and alleyways for the price of a bed in a lodging house - fourpence in 1888. The connection between common lodging houses and prostitution in London was extremely close. The two flourished hand-in-hand in the East End, particularly in Whitechapel, which in the 1880s contained 63 brothels, 1,200 known prostitutes and 233 common lodging houses capable of sheltering 8,500 people. Lodging houses were the only accommodation available to many in the East End. These places were highly profitable for their owners but degrading and debasing for their boarders. In such houses it was often difficult to distinguish between the honest poor and the criminal. Indeed, the police frequently did not make a distinction between the two.

Whores and Mothers

The debate about prostitution reflected the fears of many people concerned about the spread of industrialization and the migration of increasing numbers into the cities and large towns. The problem was that the legislation of the time reinforced existing patterns of class control and male domination. In the Victorian years women were expected to fit one of two archetypes, that of mother or whore. Within the home the middle-class husband cosseted and adored (or completely ignored) his wife. She was either an adornment to his household or a drudge to be used in whatever way he saw fit. The prostitute was there when his appetites became too gross for this paragon to cope with, or when she was pregnant or had just had a child. This double standard allowed the men access to 'fallen women' while at no time censuring them for it.

The prostitute and all her bawdiness became an integral part of 19th century fiction. Her story was reflected in the attitudes of society, which considered any woman who had transgressed in this way beyond redemption. Society required an atonement for her sins, which could be achieved only through death. The feeling of the time was 'once a prostitute always a prostitute'. According to contemporary literature a 'fallen' woman would ultimately be reduced to 'the most abject poverty and wretchedness; subjected to the most loathing and painful diseases, their fate could only be premature old age and early Death'.

This condemnation came not from the woman's peers but from those above her on the class ladder. The lower classes tolerated deviant sexual and social behaviour whereas the middle classes seemingly found them impossible to understand. Victorian attitudes to sex split along these class lines.

Violence and the Urban Poor

In the East End assaults of men on women occurred frequently, often arising out of drunkenness. George Sims, an investigative journalist and author, stated that people in the East End were so used to the sounds of violence that few would stir to see what was the matter. This point was highlighted in the murder of Mary Kelly when witnesses said they had heard a cry of 'Oh, murder' but took no notice. In the higher echelons of Victorian society such attacks were thought to be very rare, though one suspects that, as now, much marital violence in that stratum remained hidden from public view. For example, Annie Besant, the social reformer and eventual leader of the Theosophical Society, left her clergyman husband because of his mistreatment of her. The violence evident in the Ripper killings confirmed the prejudices of many middle-class Victorians, who were convinced that such behaviour was confined to foreigners or the lower classes. If the killer were English, then he was most likely a member of the dregs of civilization and living in the East End.

The people of the East End, by contrast, were initially thrown into a panic by the killings and looked among their own kind for a suspect, although there was a widespead feeling that no-one from the area who was not foreign or insane would perpetrate such crimes. Despite their antagonism towards the police, many showed great willingness to pass on information that might help capture the killer. Subsequently they came to believe that the culprit would be found beyond the narrow confines of their class and condition. Indeed, the notion that Jack the Ripper was of a higher class than his victims or the known suspects was widely accepted by East Enders.

Those in the front line offering help to the needy, such as the Reverend Barnett, recognized that violence was woven into the fabric of daily life. In his opinion even the slaughter houses, which he described as an 'open peepshow of cruelty to animals' had 'moral consequences, especially for the children of the poor'.

Riots were a relatively common phenomenon in East London. As time went by and the calls for social reform grew stronger, they began to take on a more obviously political hue. The so-called 'Black Monday' riot of 8 February 1886, which forced the resignation of the then Metropolitan Police Commissioner, Henderson, arose from a meeting organized by the Social Democratic Federation. This outbreak of violence, in which windows were broken and shops attacked, was allegedly instigated by people from the East End. The East End was perceived by the authorities as a powder keg waiting to explode. This notion was supported at the time of the murders by Sir Charles Warren's order that the message scrawled on the wall near the scene of the Eddowes murder - 'The Juwes are the men That Will not be Blamed for nothing' - be erased. In his report to the Home Office Superintendent Arnold explained that '... a strong feeling existed against Jews generally ... I was apprehensive that if the writing were left it would be the means of causing a riot.'

Throughout the 1880s, the plight of the East End was seen to inflame class tensions and, perhaps, anarchy. Prior to the Ripper murders, in the summer of 1887, a large number of homeless, unemployed vagrants began to camp in Trafalgar Square. Many in the East End wished to make the 'toffs up west' aware of their plight and used Trafalgar Square as a place to sleep. That summer was a warm one, and relief agencies got used to taking assistance to the people in the square - it became almost a way of life. The police were reluctant to move the vagrants on. Then, on 'Bloody Sunday', 13 November 1887, the Metropolitan Federation of Radical Clubs, a socialist movement, organized a series of marches and demonstrations to protest at the government's policy of coercion in Ireland. On the instructions of Sir Charles Warren, the Metropolitan Police commissioner, the police violently dispersed the marchers before they reached Trafalgar Square and in the process cleared the square of its vagrant population, killing one man. This action exacerbated tensions between East and West, fanning the flames of class hatred and distrust.

To people in the West End the Whitechapel murders revealed the extent of the rot in the East. Their anxiety was that this rot might spread. The fact that Whitechapel lies next to the City of London, the financial heart of the nation, made the threat from the killings seem greater. The East End and the anonymous murderer were synonymous as a boil waiting to be lanced.

It is perhaps no concidence that the dock workers' strike of 1889, the year after the final murder in the Ripper series, was staged without bloodshed and that it changed irrevocably the structure of working life, bringing better wages and better employment conditions.

THE WHITECHAPEL WALK

Our own investigation into the area began with our version of the Jack the Ripper walk (today a well known tourist activity) to see whether psychic information could be gleaned or contact made by sensing the atmosphere at the various murder sites in the East End. Not surprisingly, given the passage of time and the changing needs of the area, we discovered that many of the old names and street configurations have been changed or are in the process of regeneration. Former landmarks such as pubs have also been pulled down or radically altered. Pockets of old buildings are now dwarfed by the necessities of modern-day life such as supermarkets and new flats. Our walk, therefore, could in no way be a trip back in time to the London of 1888. This situation was guaranteed to make it very difficult for me to categorize correctly the information I received on a vibrational level. We set off, therefore, more in hope than expectation.

We began our walk at Durward St, formerly Bucks Row; as with several of the sites where Ripper murders occurred, its name has subsequently been changed. Durward Street turned out to be one large building site, and there, proudly in the middle, stood the old Board School, in the shadow of which Mary Ann Nichols had met her death. The building itself was in the process of being refurbished, presumably to be used as flats. No marker showed where Mary was murdered, and no cold chill or uprush of emotion gave any indication of the horrific crime that had been committed there.

However, as if to show that the area still clung to its roots of poverty and community spirit, a poignant scene unfolded which could just as easily have been enacted in the 1880s as now. Sleeping off his excesses of the night before was a gentleman of the road whom we shall call George. Two people, a man and a woman, were trying to wake him, concerned that he might be arrested if the police found him in that state. George had been turned out of the rehabilitation centre and 'needed to get his head down for a couple of hours'. The couple directed him to the local Salvation Army centre which, we later discovered, has been in existence since the time of the murders.

We continued, crossing Vallance St (formerly Baker's Row) into Old Montague Street. A crudely hand-painted notice saying 'Beware,

Vice Area' jarred slightly with the relatively new multiple dwellings flanking the street.

In the Ripper's time, Thrawl Street and Flower and Dean Street were known for their lodging houses, which were used by the girls. The ethnic mix of the area is distinctly different from what it was in the 1880s, with the many small shops previously run by Jewish tailors now owned predominantly by Asians.

Turning into Hanbury Street, we found the brewery which now stands on the site where Annie Chapman was murdered. The only psychic link that occurred here was a strong sense of resignation, a feeling that I also experienced in the contact session with Annie (see page 106).

We planned to have lunch at The Ten Bells pub, which has become famous for its association with the Ripper - at one time it was called the Jack the Ripper. We were both amused and dismayed to discover that the 'fayre' on offer today includes exotic dancers. A visit to The Ten Bells is considered a must because several of the victims and at least one of the suspects are known to have drunk here. True to the spirit of modern-day capitalism, there are many 'Jack' mementos on show and souvenirs for sale. There is said to be a good deal of psychic activity here, although it was conspicuous by its absence on the day of our visit. Apparently one bedroom is haunted, legend has it, because Jack the Ripper may have hidden there at some point, escaping through a window. Certainly the window has been known to blow out rather more often than is comfortable, and many people have experienced weird happenings in the place.

Disappointed, we continued to the area which once contained Millers Court, where Mary Kelly was murdered. This is now flanked on one side by a car park and on the other by offices. It was so curiously devoid of atmosphere that we wondered whether we were in the right place and asked a workman. He did not know the name of the street, but knew of its connection with Jack the Ripper. A weak link was established with Mary Kelly, my first contact with her. I experienced a feeling of nausea and strong pressure on the shoulders, a sensation that I experienced in contact sessions with other victims. I had a strong sense of the presence of a small moustachioed man.

We turned into Crispin Street, passing the women's refuge where Mary Kelly is thought by some to have trained as a domestic. In Goulston Street we were unable to locate the spot where the infamous message 'The Juwes are the men That Will Not be Blamed for nothing' was written. We later discovered that the site had been demolished.

We then went to Mitre Square, in which it seemed the only original items left from the late 19th century were the cobblestones. We could not agree on the exact spot where Catharine Eddowes met her messy end. The actual site of her murder is probably covered now by an ornamental flowerbed. An almost palpable sense of brooding seemed to inhabit the whole square, despite the brilliant sunshine. Its history before the 1880s might account for this. Mitre Square is reputed to be troubled by the fatal argument between two canons of the Holy Trinity Priory in the 12th century, although this story is said to be complete myth.

The buildings surrounding Mitre Square are modern and it was incongruous to be there picking up the vibrations of the past while others were doing everyday things such as picking up their children from school, having a cigarette break, and taking calls on their mobile phones. Despite the many changes in the intervening years, I felt many perceptible traces of the existence of Catharine Eddowes. One spot I perceived to be particularly unstable. I felt very strongly that the murderer came at her from St James' Passage and left via Mitre Street. It would be interesting to find out whether other evil deeds have occurred there since 1888.

We succeeded in getting lost in the various underpasses on our way to Henriques Street, formerly known as Berner Street. The site of Dutfield Yard is now part of a school playground. Again I failed to make what could be considered a meaningful contact. This begs the question as to whether a good medium actually needs the vibrations of the place concerned to make contact. Certainly, in my own case, more success was had in the proper contact sessions, through the circumstances of the various deaths.

THE MURDERS

VICTIMS	PLACE FOUND	BORN	DIED
Martha Tabram	George Yard	10 May 1849	7th Aug 1888
Mary Ann 'Polly' Nichols	Bucks Row - now Durward St	26 Aug 1845	31 Aug 1888
Eliza Anne 'Annie' Chapman	Hanbury St	2 March 1841	8 Sept 1888
Elizabeth Stride	Berner St - now Henriques St	27 Nov 1843	30 Sept 1888
Catharine Eddowes	Mitre Square	14 April 1842	30 Sept 1888
Mary Jane Kelly	Millers Ct (between White's Row and Brushfield St)	1 April 1863	9 Nov 1888

Opinions differed at the time of the murders as to who were actually Ripper victims. The press ascribed as many as fourteen murders to the Ripper. Emma Smith, for example, was originally identified by them as a victim, but the probability is that she died at the hands of the Old Nichol gang, one of several gangs operating in the East End at the time. The police authorities credited the Ripper with five victims: Mary Ann Nichols, Annie Chapman, Elizabeth Stride, Catharine Eddowes and Mary Jane Kelly. The only other possible Ripper victim considered by the police was Alice McKenzie, who was murdered and mutilated on 17 July 1889. However, police surgeons Phillips and Bond disagreed over whether she had been dispatched by the same hand responsible for killing the five recognized Ripper victims, and so she has remained only a possibility. McKenzie's murder occurred some eight months after the final recognized killing, and for a killer with such an appetite for blood lust one feels this is too great a gap.

We have followed the police view in all but one respect by including Martha Tabram in our list of six victims. Apart from the last victim, Mary Kelly, Martha was the only one to be killed indoors. She died of multiple stab wounds, and was not mutilated as the others were. The manner of her dying convinced the police that she could not have been killed by the Ripper. Tabram would have been the Ripper's first victim, and it is possible that through the experience of her murder he refined his murderous desires. Tabram fits the tight time-scale of the murders - hers took place on 7 August 1888, the final killing on 9 November 1888. Subsequent information revealed that she played an intrinsic role in the case.

In this section we present two different strands of our investigation. First, in chronological order of the murders, we look at the known facts about each of the victims. Secondly, we will try to assess the types of people they were at heart.

7 AUGUST 1888
MARTHA TABRAM

Martha Tabram was born in Southwark on 10 May 1849. Her maiden name was White, and she was the youngest daughter of Charles and Elizabeth (née Dowsett). Charles died in November 1865. He was lodging alone at the time of his death, apparently separated from his family, although it seems that movements were afoot to effect a reconciliation. On the night he died, his wife was visiting him for the first time since their separation; another daughter, Mary Anne, was also visiting. Later that evening he died suddenly from what was called syncope (lack of oxygen to the brain). No-one can judge the effect this turn of events would have had on the 16-year-old Martha, coming on top of the separation of her parents. It would almost certainly have destabilized her at a time when she should have been learning to make successful relationships.

Looked at from a spiritual and psychic point of view it would have made her highly sensitive to what was occurring around her. She would claim later that she was prone to 'hysterical fits' which meant that she would be taken to a hospital or a police station. Whether these fits were a form of epilepsy or were caused by drink is not known for certain. She married Henry Samuel Tabram on Christmas Day 1869 after living with him for a time and bore him two sons, Frederick John in February 1871 and Charles Henry in December 1872. The marriage does not seem to have been happy, and by 1875 it had failed. Henry had left her, ostensibly because of her drinking. In common with many other men in similar circumstances, he paid Martha an allowance until she took up with another man, when he reduced it from 12 shillings per week to 2/6d.

This man was a carpenter named William Turner. Martha was to live with him on and off for twelve years. She was reputed to spend any money that she was given on drink. By 1888 Turner was out of work, and Martha was earning money selling trinkets and small necessities. They had left their lodgings owing money, though Martha later returned the key under cover of darkness. Turner left her - apparently because of her drinking - about three weeks prior to the murder. He last saw her on the Saturday before she was killed when he gave her money. He is a shadowy figure in Martha's life, somewhat unprepossessing, and, one suspects, unable to handle the forcefulness of her character.

Martha seems to have been a woman who had a lot of time for other people. Like others of her ilk, she loved a good time, and one can picture her taking great pleasure in the small things that made up life in the East End. It has always been assumed that she supplemented her income through prostitution, although it is not known for sure that she was a prostitute. A prostitute known as 'Pearly Poll' testified at Martha's inquest that she and Emma (as she knew her) had been drinking with two soldiers on the night of the murder, and that Martha had taken a guardsman up into George Yard at around 11.45pm. Police Constable Barrett said that he had spoken to a young Grenadier Guardsman in Wentworth Street (near George Yard) at about 2am who claimed to be waiting for a friend. At 3.30am a cab driver returning home noticed what he took to be a sleeping form on the first floor landing of George Yard Building. At 4.50am a dock labourer on his way to work discovered Martha's body in a pool of blood.

The Evidence

An examination of Martha's body showed that the attack on her had been frenzied. There were 39 stab wounds, all but one of which could have been inflicted by a penknife. The breasts, stomach and genitalia seemed to have borne the brunt of this attack; death would have occurred approximately 2 hours prior to the examination, which took place at 5.30am. These timings would suggest that the murderer probably only just escaped detection.

One oddity surrounding Martha's death is the behaviour of Mary Ann Connolly, the real name of the prostitute known as 'Pearly Poll'. Despite being given more than one opportunity to do so, she would not positively identify the soldiers who had allegedly been drinking with herself and Martha on the night of the murder. She disappeared prior to an identity parade she was supposed to attend, and then wrongly picked out two Coldstream Guardsmen as the soldiers in question. The police then realized that Pearly Poll was not going to help them. With hindsight, one cannot help wondering whether, having initially decided to help, she was not then intimidated by someone who persuaded her not to cooperate with the police.

31 AUGUST 1888
MARY ANN NICHOLS

Mary Ann Nichols (known as Polly) was the daughter of a locksmith, Edward Walker, and his wife Caroline. Born in Dean Street off Fetter Lane in London, she would have grown up well aware of the contrast between the affluence of the City and the poverty of Whitechapel. She married William Nichols when she was nineteen, in January 1864. The couple had their own lodgings for a short while before moving in with her father in Walworth. It is thought they lived with Edward for some ten years and then moved to Stamford Street off Blackfriars Road. The marriage finally broke up in 1880, by which time Polly had had five children by William.

Polly's family claimed that an affair her husband had with a nurse tending her during one of her confinements contributed to the breakdown. William Nichols neither confirmed nor denied this, simply saying that he 'had a certificate of his boy's birth two years after that'. This would strongly suggest that his affair actually took place during the penultimate pregnancy, in 1877; their last child was born in 1879. He claimed that Polly had left him on several occasions; probably when she became so disenchanted with her life that she went off to try to make changes. His unfaithfulness seems to have soured his relationship with Edward Walker, although the family remained on good enough terms for Edward John Nichols, the elder son, to be living with his grandfather at the time of his mother's death. The other children were living with their father.

Polly was thirty-five at the time of the final break-up and may well have felt that she had missed out on life. She is known to have been a drinker, and again one feels that this was her way of escaping from the mundane. Her astrological chart shows her to have been such a free spirit and yet in protesting against perceived restrictions at home, Polly would ultimately find herself hoisted by her own petard. Records of the time depict both Polly's father and her husband as conventional yet kindly types. Her father said of her, 'I don't think she had any enemies, she was too good for that'. Despite having lost contact with her for some years, Nichols was much affected by her death.

After leaving William, Polly spent long periods living in various workhouses. For nine months in 1880-81 she was in Lambeth Workhouse, returning there in 1882-83, when she spent time in both the Workhouse and its infirmary, and again between April and May 1888. At some point in 1881-2 she went to live with her father. By this time she was drinking heavily and after a quarrel she left again. Her father later heard that she was living with a blacksmith called Thomas Stuart Drew in Walworth. In June 1886 Mr Walker saw his daughter for the last time, at a family funeral, when Polly's circumstances seemed markedly improved.

In April 1888 Polly found herself a position as a domestic servant, and wrote full of hope to her father about her new position. In July, however, she absconded, taking with her some clothes belonging to her employer. She found herself sharing a room with a woman called Ellen Holland in a lodging house at 18 Thrawl Street, which she did for about six weeks. This woman was probably the last person to see Polly alive.

Polly had been seen at about 11.30pm on 30 August walking along Whitechapel Road. About an hour later she left The Frying Pan public house and made her way to the lodging house in Thrawl Street. At 1.20am the deputy turned her away because she did not have the requisite fourpence for her bed. She did not seem particularly downcast by this, and by 2.30am she was drunk and staggering around. About this time she met Ellen on the corner of Osborn Street and Whitechapel Road. Ellen suggested that they go back to the lodging house, but Polly always preferred to pay her way and she refused to accompany her, boasting that she had earned her doss money three times over that day - and spent it. An hour and a half later she was dead.

Charles Cross and Robert Paul found her body at approximately 3.45am in Bucks Row (now Durward Street). Unsure as to whether she was dead or not, since the body was still warm in places, they sent for assistance. This came in the shape of three police constables. Police Constable Neil, on whose beat the murder occurred, sent his colleagues for the doctor and the ambulance while he stayed with the body until his inspector arrived. Dr Llewellyn pronounced the woman dead and ordered her removal to the mortuary shed at Old Montague Street Workhouse. The body was eventually identified by an inmate of Lambeth Workhouse after the police traced a laundry mark on Polly's petticoat to that establishment.

The Evidence

Polly was a small woman, 5 foot 2 inches tall, with delicate features, grey eyes and high cheekbones. At some time she had had an accident, indicated by a scar on her forehead. She obviously tried to look after herself. Just prior to her death she is said to have expressed great pleasure in the fact that she had acquired a new bonnet. Dr Llewellyn, who conducted the post-mortem, remarked on the cleanliness of her thighs.

Polly Nichols was the first Ripper victim to be deliberately mutilated, but it was only on the arrival of her body at the mortuary that the extent of her injuries was appreciated. In his testimony Dr Llewellyn described her injuries thus:

> Five of the teeth were missing and there was a slight laceration of the tongue. There was a bruise running along the lower part of the jaw on the right side of the face. That might have been caused by a blow from a fist or pressure from a thumb. There was a circular bruise on the left side of the face, which also might have been inflicted by the pressure of the fingers. On the left side of the neck, about 1 in below the jaw, there was an incision about 4 in in length, and ran from a point immediately below the ear. On the same side, but an inch below, and commencing about one inch in front of it, was a circular incision, which terminated at a point about 3 ins below the right jaw. That incision completely severed all the tissues down to the vertebrae. The large vessels of the neck on both sides were severed. The incision was about 8 in in length. The cuts must have been caused by a long-bladed knife, moderately sharp, and used with great violence. No blood was found on the breast, either of the body or clothes. There were no injuries about the body until just about the lower part of the abdomen. 2 or 3 ins from the left side was a wound running in a jagged manner. The wound was a very deep one, and the tissues were cut through. There were several incisions running across the abdomen. There were also three or four similar cuts running downwards, on the right side, all of which had been caused by a knife which had been used violently and downwards. The injuries were from left to right, and might have been done by a left-handed person. All the injuries had been caused by the same instrument.

8 SEPTEMBER 1888
ANNIE CHAPMAN

Annie Chapman was born Eliza Anne Smith in Paddington, London on 2 March 1841. The family moved to Windsor in 1856. Annie is thought to have come from a better class than most of the victims, although there is little evidence to support this. She married a relative of her mother's, John Chapman, in Knightsbridge, in 1869. They continued to live in West London until 1881, when they moved back to Windsor, where John had a job as a coachman. It is said that John was dismissed from this position because of Annie's thieving. The couple had three children: Emily Ruth born in 1870, Annie Georgina (who would later travel with a circus in France) in 1873 and John (a cripple) in 1881.

Just before the death of Emily, in 1882, Annie abandoned the family; some sources cite her drinking and immoral habits as the cause of the split. However, this version of events seems incomplete, given that John's death in 1886 at the age of 44 was from cirrhosis of the liver and dropsy, evidence that he too must have been a drinker. According to her friends Annie went to pieces after her husband's death. At some point in 1886, she lived with a man who made sieves and because of this became known as Annie Siffey or Sievey.

She supported herself by hawking around her crochet work and artificial flowers, and most of the time would probably earn enough to keep the wolf from the door. About a week before her death she complained of feeling unwell; the post-mortem report would show that she was suffering from a form of tuberculosis. (In the July test session I felt that one of the girls had emphysema or a lung problem, giving a severe cough, and this later proved to be Annie Chapman.) She was also very badly nourished and was told off more than once during the days before her death for purchasing drink rather than food. Yet one must have some sympathy for her. If she was feeling ill, drink would have gone down more easily than food.

At about 1.50am on the night of her murder she was turned away from the Dorset Street lodging house where she normally slept and went off to find herself some money for a bed elsewhere. We do not know if she was murdered on her way to or from the lodging house, but she was found at the back of 29 Hanbury Street, about a quarter of a mile away, at six o'clock in the morning. There was usually much coming and going in the early morning since many of the residents had market jobs. It is known that prostitutes used the passageway at the side of the building to ply their trade. John Richardson, the landlady's son, claimed to have cleared the area of vagrants from time to time, but not on the night in question. John Davis, the carman who rented the attic room at No. 29 for his family, discovered the body as he left for work. He had apparently been unable to sleep, and yet had heard nothing out of the ordinary. On finding the body he called two packing case makers who worked further along the street. Inspector Chandler was called to the scene and he then summoned Dr George Bagster Phillips.

The Evidence

Annie had, it is thought, been dead for at least two hours by the time Dr Bagster Phillips arrived at the scene. It seems that there were few bloodstains on her clothes. Her black jacket was stained around the neck, but had only some spots on the left arm. There was some blood on the skirt, as if she had lain in it, but other clothing - consisting of two bodices and two petticoats - was relatively unstained. A pocket which she wore under her skirt was empty and had been torn.

As in the case of Polly Nichols, when the body was taken to Whitechapel mortuary it was washed and prepared for examination before it had been properly viewed. This meant that clues may have been lost.

Dr Bagster Phillips was reluctant to reveal the full extent of the injuries at the inquest, but, after an adjournment of six days, he revealed them in their full horror. (The press in their wisdom censored his evidence as being too horrible to publish.) Dr Phillips' reluctance may have been because police believed that they were close to making an arrest, and did not wish to scare the perpetrator into running away. Coroner Baxter, however, was acting within his legal duty by insisting that the evidence be made public.

The following is an extract from Dr Phillips' inquest deposition:

> I found the body of the deceased lying in the yard on her back, on the left hand of the steps that lead from the passage. The head was about 6 in. in front of the level of the bottom step, and the feet were towards a shed at the end of the yard. The left arm was across the breast, and the legs were drawn up, the feet resting on the ground and the knees turned outwards. The face was swollen and turned on the right side, and the tongue protruded between the front teeth, but not beyond the lips; it was much swollen. The small intestines and other portions were lying on the right side of the body on the ground above the right shoulder, but attached. There was a large quantity of blood, with a part of the stomach above the left shoulder... The body was cold, except that there was a certain remaining heat, under the intestines, in the body. The stiffness of the limbs

was not marked, but it was commencing. The throat was dissevered deeply.
I noticed that the incision of the skin was jagged and reached right round
the neck.

It has been established that there was bruising to the face and shoulders, some old marks received in a fight with another lodging house inmate over a bar of soap. Thus Annie had been partially suffocated, probably to silence her before her throat was cut, and death occurred through loss of blood to the brain. The mutilations occurred after death. Part of the belly wall, including the navel, the womb, the upper part of the vagina and the greater part of the bladder, were all missing. It was this that led to the growing belief that the killer must have some anatomical knowledge.

It seems that Annie's rings, made of brass, had been forcibly removed, and the contents of her bag, including possibly two farthings, had been laid out beside her. Many feel that there was some ritualistic intent in this, and that this points to a magical or Masonic involvement. One cannot help wondering whether the killer simply wished to indicate that he wanted one thing and one thing only, the symbol of her womanhood. Remembering also that at that time women were not allowed access to Masonic knowledge, but in some lodges the power of the Goddess was recognized, the way in which Annie had been mutilated may simply indicate, albeit in a very perverted and twisted fashion, that she was unfit even to be a woman.

Discounting the Masonic theory leaves us with the possibility mooted at the time of the murder that Annie had been killed in order to procure a specimen of a woman's uterus. It had been known that an American was attempting to obtain specimens of that organ, and this would link with the possibility that that individual was Francis Tumblety (see page 87).

Annie Chapman was by all accounts an insignificant person. Descriptions put her at about 5 feet tall, stout, with a thick nose, blue eyes and dark hair. Reports in the press that her teeth were missing were proved inaccurate by the post-mortem report. Already sick, and not coping, death must almost have seemed like a welcome relief. Dr Phillips times her death at around 4.30am, yet at about 4.45am John Richardson had checked the yard for security and swore that there was nothing there then. At about 5.30 a neighbour heard a commotion, a woman's voice saying 'No' and the sound of something falling against the fence. Was this the actual moment of her death? Where did she spend those last hours of her life?

30 SEPTEMBER 1888
ELIZABETH STRIDE

Elizabeth Stride was born Elizabeth Gustafsdotter in Torslanda, Sweden, near Gothenburg, on 27 November 1843. Her mother was Beata Carlsdotter. By 14 October 1860 she was working in Carl Johan Parish, Gothenburg, as a domestic. In February 1862 she was working in Cathedral Parish, Gothenburg. It must be assumed that things did not go well for her, because in March 1865 she was registered as a prostitute in Gothenburg. On 21 April of that year she gave birth to a still-born baby girl. Later that same year she was treated at Ostra Haga for venereal disease.

In 1866 she came to London with a foreign gentleman, ostensibly to experience different cultures, and was registered on 10 July 1866 as an unmarried woman. Three years later, on 7 March 1869, she married John Stride at St Giles-in-the-Fields. After their marriage the couple ran a coffee shop in Poplar between 1870 and 1875.

She was later to claim that she had lost her husband and two of her children in a steamship disaster. There is proof that there was indeed such a disaster in 1878 when the steamship *Princess Alice* was sunk with the loss of 527 lives, but no proof that any of those lost were related to Elizabeth. (Her husband actually died in 1884 in the Poplar Union Workhouse.)

After receiving treatment for bronchitis at the beginning of 1882, she went to live at Flower and Dean Street Lodging House, where she stayed on and off until 1885, when she took up with Michael Kidney. Her life with Kidney was punctuated by their spending short periods apart. He claimed that her drunken binges were responsible for taking her away from him. The couple are known to have quarrelled in the days prior to her murder. (However, Michael himself liked a drink, so although he claimed drink took her away from him there had to be other reasons as well.) More likely her drinking habits were a way of escaping from a sense of constriction.

In May 1886 and again in September 1888 she is known to have applied for alms at the Swedish Church in London, and in the meantime (March 1887) to have charged Kidney with assault, although she failed to turn up for the hearing in April. In September 1888 she returned to Flower and Dean Street again, saying she had had an argument with Michael Kidney. She had not been there for about three months. It was here that she is said possibly to have met Thomas Barnardo when he was trying to persuade prostitutes to give up their children so that they could achieve a better life.

Elizabeth (or Long Liz, as she was known) was, in fact, quite small, being only 5ft 2in in height. She had dark reddish curly hair, a pale complexion and grey eyes. She appeared much younger than her forty-five years, despite the fact that she seems to have lost the teeth in her lower jaw. She supported herself by taking in tailoring. In addition to her mother-tongue, she spoke both English - allegedly like a native - and Yiddish. Those who knew her spoke highly of her and of her character.

The circumstances of her death are these. On the evening of 30 September 1888 she was paid sixpence for some charring she had done for the deputy head of the lodging house at Flower and Dean Street. Later that evening she was met by two friends. She gave one of them a large piece of green velvet for safekeeping, and asked to borrow a clothes' brush from the other.

At about eleven o'clock she was seen kissing and cuddling with a man near the Bricklayers Arms. He was described as short, with a dark moustache and sandy eyelashes. Three-quarters of an hour later she was seen by William Marshall in Berner Street talking to a man in a short black cutaway coat and a sailor's hat. A man called Matthew Packer later claimed that, at midnight, he sold Elizabeth and her partner a stalk of grapes, although this evidence has since been largely discounted. At 12.35am Police Constable Smith noticed Stride and a young man opposite the International Workmen's Club. The young man was said to have been about 28 years old, with a dark complexion and a small dark moustache. He was wearing a black diagonal cutaway coat and a hard deerstalker hat.

At approximately 12.40am a man called Schwartz witnessed an argument with a woman close to the gateway of Dutfield's Yard, where the murder took place. Schwartz saw two men at the scene, although he was not sure whether they were together. The first was described as about 30, height 5ft 5in, with a fair complexion, dark hair, a small brown moustache; he had a full face, was broad shouldered and wearing a dark jacket and trousers and a black peaked cap. The second man was aged 35, height 5ft 11in, had a fresh complexion, light brown hair, light brown moustache, and was dressed in a dark overcoat and an old black hard felt hat with a wide brim. He was holding a clay pipe. (This description most closely matches my perception, picked up during the contact session, see page 102.) Schwartz spoke little or no English, and was very frightened because the second man, whom he may have recognized, appeared to be in pursuit of him. This man shouted the word 'Lipski' - at that time an anti-Semitic insult arising from the killing of a fellow lodger by a man called Lipski.

At one o'clock Louis Diemschutz drove his pony and cart into Dutfield's Yard, where he hired a stable. His pony shied at an obstacle on the ground, which initially he took for a bundle of old clothes, then a drunk, before he discovered the body of Elizabeth Stride.

The Evidence

At the inquest on 3 October Dr Phillips described the injuries thus:

> Cut on the neck; taking it from left to right there is a clean cut incision 6 in in length, incision commencing two and a half inches in a straight line below the angle of the jaw. Three quarters of an inch over undivided muscle then becoming deeper, about an inch dividing sheath and the vessels, ascending a little, and then grazing the muscle outside the cartilage on the left side of the neck, the cut being very clean, but indicating a slight direction downwards through resistance of the denser tissue and cartilages. The carotid artery on the left side, and the other vessels contained in the sheath were all cut through save the posterior portion of the carotid to about a line of 1/12th of an inch in extent, which prevented the separation of the upper and lower portion of the artery. The cut through the tissues on the right side was more superficial and tailed off to about 2 in below the right angle of the jaw. It is evident that the haemorrhage, which will probably be found to be the cause of death, was caused through the partial severance of the left carotid artery.

30 SEPTEMBER 1888
CATHARINE EDDOWES

Kate (Catharine) Eddowes was born on 14 April 1842 in Wolverhampton. She was one of the 11 children of George and Catherine Eddowes who were married at Bushbury, Wolverhampton on 13 August 1832. George, who worked in the tinplate industry, took his family to London soon after Kate's birth. William, the youngest child, died within five months of his birth in 1854, and a little over a year later, in November 1855, Kate's mother died of tuberculosis.

This effectively dispersed the family. The two eldest children were already in domestic service and, although Kate moved to live with the family of first an aunt and then an uncle, she did not settle. Kate met and moved in with Thomas Conway. She bore him three children, and stayed with him for the next twenty years, though there is no record of them having married. She had the initials T.C. tattooed in blue ink on her forearm.

The couple separated in either 1880 or 1881 - the reason for their separation variously given as the other's drinking. In that year Kate met and 'took up with' John Kelly. They are reputed to have got on well and had a mutual concern for one another. Kate seems to have been liked by many and was described by the deputy at Cooneys, a lodging house where she usually stayed, as a 'very jolly woman, always singing'. Her sisters, Elizabeth Fisher and Eliza Gold, said that she was good natured and cheerful.

Kate Eddowes was 46 at the time of her murder in the early hours of 30 September 1888. She was of slim build, about 5 feet in height, had dark auburn hair and hazel eyes. Her clothes were old and dirty. The amount of clothing and nature of her belongings showed that she had to be a vagrant or someone who frequently stayed in lodging houses. It was not until 2 October that the police discovered her identity. On that day John Kelly, Kate's partner, walked into Bishopsgate Police Station, saying that he thought he knew the woman. She was Kate Conway, also known as Kate Kelly, with whom he had been living for the last seven years at the lodging house known as Cooneys. He is said to have been astonished by the news that his common-law wife was the latest murder victim.

His story was that they had been hop-picking together, but had not done well and had decided to come back to London. On the night of Friday 28 September they had separated in order to find lodgings for the night. Kate went to the casual ward at Shoe Lane, Mile End, while Kelly slept at Cooneys. The next day they met and Kate pawned a pair of Kelly's boots. This enabled them to buy breakfast. After breakfast they decided that Kate would visit her daughter in order to ask for some money. According to Kelly, that was the last time he saw Kate alive. Catharine did not find her daughter; she had moved without leaving a forwarding address, probably in an attempt to avoid her mother's scrounging. But by 8.30 that night Catharine was completely drunk, having obtained money from somewhere.

She was locked up for her own safety, not being sober enough to give her name, though she later owned to Mary Ann Kelly. This is now believed to be the name of John Kelly's former wife. When she was released, at about one o'clock in the morning, she commented that she would get a 'damn fine hiding'. Some forty-five minutes later she was dead.

At approximately 1.35am someone fitting her description was seen at the Dukes Place entrance to Mitre Square, talking to someone with whom she seemed familiar. About ten minutes later Police Constable Watkins found her body in the south-west corner of the square. The doctor, named Sequira, who was summoned by the constable's colleague, also timed his arrival at 1.45am. The police surgeon, F. Gordon Brown, was sent for by the station inspector and arrived at the murder scene just after two o'clock.

The Evidence

It is interesting that Catharine is the only victim to have been killed within the jurisdiction of the City of London police force. Records show her belongings to have been meticulously listed. She wore no drawers or corsets but had plenty of undergarments: a grey petticoat, a very old dark green woollen skirt, an old blue skirt and a white chemise. Her outer clothes comprised a black straw bonnet trimmed with green and black in velvet with black beads; a handkerchief of red gauze silk; a black cloth jacket with imitation fur edging around the collar and sleeves. She also wore a dark green chintz skirt, which was patterned in Michaelmas daisies and golden lilies with three flounces; a man's white vest; a brown linsey wool dress bodice with a black velvet collar and brown metal buttons down the front; a pair of brown ribbed stockings, mended at the feet; a pair of men's laced boots; and a piece of old white apron.

Her belongings consisted of a large white handkerchief, one blue striped bedticking pocket and two unbleached calico pockets; a white cotton pocket handkerchief; 12 pieces of white rag, a piece of white coarse linen, blue and white shirting, 2 small blue bedticking bags, 2 short clay pipes, 2 tin boxes (one containing tea and the other sugar), a small-tooth comb, a white-handled table knife, a metal teaspoon, a red leather cigarette case with white metal fittings, an empty tin match box, a piece of red flannel containing pins and needles and a ball of hemp. There is a theory that the cigarette case may have been dropped by her murderer and erroneously listed as belonging to her.

Here is a shortened version of the post-mortem report:

> The throat was cut across to the extent of about six or seven inches. The sterno cleido mastoid muscle was divided. The cricoid cartilage below the vocal chords was severed through the middle. The large vessels on the left side of the neck were severed to the bone, the knife marking the inter-vertebral cartilage [in other words, her throat was cut]. The sheath of the vessels of the right side were just open; the carotid artery had a pinhole opening; the internal jugular vein was open to the extent of an inch and a half - not divided. All the injuries were caused by some very sharp instrument, and pointed. The cause of death was haemorrhage from the left common carotid artery. The death was immediate. The mutilations were inflicted after death. We examined the abdomen. The walls of the

abdomen were laid open, from the breasts downwards. The cut commenced opposite the ensiform cartilage, in the centre of the body. The incision went upwards not penetrating the skin that was over the sternum; it then divided the ensiform cartilage. The knife was held so the point was towards the left side and the handle toward the right. The cut was made obliquely. The liver was stabbed as if by the point of a sharp knife. There was another incision in the liver, about two and a half inches, and below, the left lobe of the liver was slit through by a vertical cut. Two cuts were shown by a jag of skin on the left hand side. The abdominal walls were divided vertically in the middle line to within a quarter of an inch of the navel; the cut then took a horizontal course for two and a half inches to the right side; it then divided the navel on the left side round it - and made an incision parallel to the former horizontal incision, leaving the navel on a tongue of skin. Attached to the navel was two and a half inches of the lower part of the rectus musela of the left side of the abdomen. The incision then took an oblique course to the right.

There was a stab of about an inch to the left groin, penetrating the skin in superficial fashion. Below that was a cut of three inches going through all the tissues, wounding the peritoneum to about the same extent. There had not been any appreciable bleeding from the vessels.

Under questioning at the inquest Dr Brown confirmed that the cause of death was the cut in the throat, probably with a sharp pointed knife that was at least six inches long. Dr Brown thought that Catharine was probably on the ground when the wound was inflicted and that the organs removed could be of no use for professional purposes. Someone used to cutting up animals would have known how to reach the kidney. Dr Brown also felt that the act would probably have been performed by one man. The injuries would have taken about five minutes to inflict, and there would have been no time for the victim to cry out.

A kidney sent to Mr Lusk, the president of the Whitechapel vigilance committee, was thought by some to be that of Catharine Eddowes. Information I received during the 8 July test session has convinced me that the body part was not Catharine's.

Kate is said to have believed that she knew who the Ripper was, and on the night of her murder it would seem that she might have been on her way to meet someone. Her contact session showed a sense of urgency - see page 99.

9 NOVEMBER 1888
MARY JANE KELLY

Mary Kelly is widely agreed to be the last Ripper victim. Very little is known about her, and what information exists is suspect or contentious. The stories we have of Mary Kelly are those which she herself told to Joseph Barnett (her lover at the time of her death) and her friends in the East End. None of the information about her life which she claimed as fact has been proved, and it seems that Mary was a past mistress at concealing her true history. Recent research has shown that Mary Jane Kelly was probably born in Limerick on 1 April 1863; it is this date which we have used for our astrological assessment of her character (see page 179).

The facts according to Mary Kelly are that she moved to Wales in early childhood, and that her father worked in an iron foundry. She is said to have had six or seven brothers and one sister. Mary claimed to have been married at sixteen to a collier called Davies or Davis who died in a pit explosion two or three years later. To date, no record of the marriage, or of any children born to it, has been found. After her husband's death, Mary moved to Cardiff to stay with a cousin, and at this point in her life became a prostitute. It can be deduced that she went to London, probably in 1884, where she is supposed to have worked in a high class West End brothel. Mary spoke of having gone to France with a client 'but came back because she didn't like it'. (It is known that at this time there was contact between high class brothels in the major European cities and that a type of 'cultural exchange' occurred in which star performers were borrowed to service wealthy clients.) This French connection gave Mary the opportunity to call herself Marie Jeanette, the name by which Joe Barnett knew her. She was Mary Jane to others of her acquaintance.

It is not known with certainty how Mary came to be living in the East End, but the assumption is that on her return to London from France she could not return to the West End, presumably for fear of retribution. Our contact session with her (see page 125) shed a disquieting light on her motivation for shifting 'down market'. However, according to one of her landladies, she did manage to retrieve some fashionable dresses from an address in Knightsbridge, presumably that of the brothel where she had formerly worked. Those who knew her said that Mary liked to maintain a good image, and their testimony is supported by the astrological chart we cast for her (see page 179).

Mary moved initially to the western end of Ratcliff Highway

(notorious for its street prostitution), near St. Katharine's Dock, and by 1886 she was living with a Mrs Carthy at Breezer's Hill in the same area. According to Mrs Carthy, Mary left to live with a man who wanted to marry her. It is thought that this man was a plasterer called Joseph Flemming, with whom Mary was still on good terms at the time of her death. He would give her money when he could. Why they split up is not known, but when drunk Mary was said to become 'very quarrelsome and abusive' and it is possible that Flemming could not handle her drinking.

Mary Kelly and Joe Barnett (see page 76), a Billingsgate fish porter, met on Good Friday, 8 April 1887. A few days later they met again and decided to live together. This may have been a purely practical move on Mary's part. Despite her continuing friendship with Joseph Flemming, Joe Barnett seems to have spoilt Mary and looked after her up until the time he was dismissed from his job, for an unspecified reason, in August 1888. Their relationship was highly volatile, and shortly before her murder Mary broke a window pane during one of their frequent arguments. Kelly and Barnett finally separated on 20 October 1888. He was to claim that she had resumed prostitution and that he could not stand the fact that she was allowing other prostitutes to stay in their room. It is open to conjecture whether the reason she asked these women to stay was in order to protect herself from Barnett's now unwanted advances.

One of the prostitutes so befriended was Maria Harvey. Mary is known to have spent the afternoon before her death with Maria in the latter's new room at New Court. Mary also spent part of the early evening with another friend, Lizzie Albrook. It was this young lady whom Mary warned against going onto the streets as she had done, and to whom she had spoken about returning to Ireland. Joe Barnett visited Mary between 7.30 and 8pm at Millers Court. Later that evening, Mary was seen in the company of a shabby, blotchy-faced man who had a carroty moustache and a billycock hat. He was carrying a quart pail of beer; she was drunk and said she was going to sing. Between midnight and 1am several witnesses heard her singing 'Only a violet I plucked from my mother's grave'. This was the last positive identification of Mary alive.

The Evidence

Mary Kelly's body was discovered at ten o'clock in the morning by her landlord's runner, who had gone there to collect the several weeks' rent that was owing. Receiving no reply to his knock on the door, he looked through the broken window and saw the horror within. Due to a lack of communication permission from Sir Charles Warren, the Metropolitan Police commissioner, to use bloodhounds in the search was not given and the room was finally forcibly entered at 1.30pm. Inside the room the police found the remains of what had obviously been a fierce fire in the grate - some of the ashes were still warm, and the spout of the kettle in the fireplace had melted. Women's clothing had also been burnt; this was later identified as belonging to one of the women who had been staying with Mary.

As many question marks surround Mary Kelly's death as they do her life. Certainly there were discrepancies between newspaper reports and the inquest depositions. At the inquest, a Sarah Lewis claimed to have recognized a man who had accosted her and a friend the previous Wednesday in Bethnal Green Road. She had seen the same man, accompanied by a woman, near the Britannia pub as she came towards Dorset Street on the night of the murder. This same story was attributed by the press to a Mrs Kennedy who was said to be visiting her parents nearby. Sarah Lewis said she saw a man standing in the doorway of Millers Court, whereas Mrs Kennedy admitted to no such thing. To this day, it has not been clarified whether Sarah Lewis and Mrs Kennedy were one and the same person.

George Hutchinson, a friend of Mary's, came forward after the inquest and said she had asked him for sixpence at about 2am. He had been unable to oblige and watched her proceed to pick up a client near Thrawl Street. He claims to have waited outside Kelly's room for some 45 minutes, during which time no-one left. It seems odd that Hutchinson's statement only came to light after the inquest and after Barnett had given his evidence.

According to Dr Bond, who assisted Dr Phillips in the post-mortem examination, death was estimated as occurring at about one or two o'clock in the morning. The fact that the body was not as cold as would be expected was explained by the heat from the fire. However, a report of cries of 'Oh, murder' from the direction of Kelly's room shortly before 4am would lead one to believe that she died later; these cries were disregarded by residents of Millers Court, because it was not unusual to hear such screams. Dr Phillips put the time of death at between five and six in the morning.

One theory is that Mary Kelly wanted to disappear and that the body found in Millers Court was actually that of Winifred May Collis, who was sheltering with Mary at the time because she was pregnant. This is supported by an inexplicable piece of evidence given by Caroline Maxwell, the wife of a lodging house deputy, who claimed to have seen

Mary Kelly at about eight o'clock in the morning, several hours after the estimated time of her death. According to Caroline, Mary had spoken of being unwell and 'having the horrors of drink upon her'. Until more information comes to light, it must be assumed that Caroline was lying, possibly to cover up for some misdemeanour of her own or someone else's. Our own investigations lead us to believe that the victim was indeed Mary.

At the post-mortem, Dr Bond had made a series of notes which later went missing and did not resurface until 1987, when they turned up in a bundle of documents returned anonymously to Scotland Yard. They are stamped 10 November 1888, and seem to be the first authentic record of Mary's injuries. These show that:

> The face was gashed in all directions, the nose, cheeks, eyebrows and ears being partly removed. The lips were blanched and cut by several incisions running obliquely down to the chin. There were also numerous cuts extending irregularly across all the features.
>
> The neck was cut through the skin and the other tissue down to the vertebrae, the 5th and 6th being deeply notched. The skin cuts in front of the neck showed distinct ecchymosis [bruising].
>
> The air passage was cut at the lower part of the larynx through the cricoid cartilage.
>
> Both breasts were removed by more or less circular incisions, the muscles down to the ribs being attached to the breasts. The intercostals between the 4th, 5th & 6th ribs were cut & the contents of the thorax visible through the openings.
>
> The skin & tissues of the abdomen from the costal arch to the pubes were removed in three large flaps. The right thigh was denuded in front to the bone, the flap of skin including the external organs of generation & part of the right buttock. The left thigh was stripped of skin, fascia & muscles as far as the knee.
>
> The left calf showed a long gash through skin & tissues to the deep muscles & reaching from the knee to 5 inches above the ankle.
>
> Both arms & forearms had extensive & jagged wounds.

There were other wounds which indicated that Mary may have attempted to defend herself, by using her hands. Her heart had been taken away and could not be found.

The inquest was conducted with almost indecent haste and lasted less than half a day, allowing only enough time for the first part of Dr Phillips' evidence to be given. This established that death had occurred as a result of severance of the right carotid artery. The jury had been directed by the coroner to ascertain only the cause of death and to leave further investigations in the hands of the police. Such a course of action, though not wrong, went against normal procedure; this being that all evidence needs to be heard. It was assumed that the rest of Phillips' evidence would be made public at some later date, but this did not happen. The rationale behind the decision would appear to have been fear of what the press would make of the horrific injuries sustained by the victim. If the degree of mutilation were exposed to media attention this would serve only to cloud the issue and possibly hamper police enquiries.

Another bone of contention appears to have been that the inquest was held in Shoreditch although the murder had occurred in Whitechapel. When a juryman questioned the conduct of the inquest procedure, he was quickly and firmly silenced by the coroner, who told him that jurisdiction resided in where the body lies not in where it was found. The coroner's behaviour was thought odd by the press at the time, and this laid the foundations for many conspiracy theories.

At the same time a free pardon was offered by the government to 'any accomplice, not being a person who contrived or actually committed the murder, who shall give such information and evidence as shall lead to the discovery and conviction of the person or persons who committed the murder.' This was simply a sop to public opinion.

It may have been that the police had a suspect in view and were afraid of scaring him into flight. Alternatively, it could be there was something to be covered up and their suspect was to be protected.

Mary Kelly continues to create controversy even in death. When we set up our contact session with her, we experienced a degree of duplicity that was difficult to understand (see page 125).

ASSESSING THE VICTIMS

One question that is frequently asked in any serial killing is, 'Why these particular victims?' The life stories of each of the Ripper's victims seem to follow a familiar pattern. The hard facts of these women's lives reveal them to have been mostly middle-aged, down on their luck, possibly prostitutes, and all with a drink problem. The flat or solar astrological chart that we devised for each of the women gives a more rounded portrait of how they would have reacted to their circumstances and what was going on around them. The two crucial pieces of information needed before a solar chart can be calculated are a birth date and a place of birth. We obtained this information initially from secondary sources which we then double-checked against official records. Only two of the victims proved problematic in this respect.

Mary Kelly's origins proved impossible to trace with any degree of certainty. She seemed to have come from nowhere and invented a fund of stories about herself, none of them reliable. We followed several leads without success. The likelihood was that a strong element of fantasy would appear in her chart, and this was not the case with any of the charts cast. We were beginning to despair when new information emerged in a Ripperana magazine, giving a possible birthdate of 1 April 1863. This time the astrological profile fitted the known personality in all its complexity. We hope that further research will prove beyond a shadow of doubt that the birthdate we used is indeed the correct one.

Annie Chapman was difficult to trace for a different reason. Her real name is believed to be Eliza Anne Smith. As can be imagined, there are thousands of Smiths and to have obtained birth certificates for all the likely candidates would not have been feasible. In her case we have opted for the information given by what we consider to be the most reliable sources.

The full astrological charts can be found at the back of the book. At this juncture we will explore the major features of the personalities revealed in the charts.

Astrological Profiles In Brief

Catharine Eddowes and Mary Kelly have the Sun in Aries, giving them an up-front me-first type of personality.

Martha Tabram had Saturn in Aries. This placing tells us how she would have handled the men in her life (rather selfishly), beginning with her father. She also had Uranus (the planet of sudden happenings) and Pluto (the planet of transformative energy) in Aries, indicating that she was suspicious of most men unless unexpectedly disarmed or she thought she was doing something for the common good.

Annie Chapman had Venus (the planet of femininity) and Pluto conjunct in Aries, which means that in her relationships with men she would ideally have needed to be adored and cosseted; without this confirmation, she would tend to wither up.

Polly Nichols also had Uranus and Pluto in Aries, although in her case the influence probably indicated her need to be part of the changes taking place on a generational level. Her foray into Trafalgar Square to be part of the campaign against homelessness would be indicative of this.

The charts of Elizabeth Stride and Catharine Eddowes also show a generational influence in that both had Pluto in Aries. Elizabeth Stride is thought to have shown great concern over the state of the East End in a conversation with Thomas Barnardo. Catharine would have undergone some profound change in her life at around the age of four, possibly to do with the death of a member of her family. Mary Kelly had Neptune in Aries close to her Sun, which indicates that her life from about the age of seven would have been one of fantasy or fabrication. Incidentally, Arian women are accepted as being the only group of women who can exist without a partner if they have to.

Another sign that is prominent in some of the women's charts is Taurus. This sign is ruled by Venus, the planet of beauty and femininity, and would give a sensuousness and tactile approach to life. With three planets in this sign, Martha Tabram particularly would have been a lover of fine things. In her younger days she would have been quite beautiful. Polly Ann Nichols had Jupiter in Taurus, which would give an expansive personality, one which would have wanted everyone to be happy and having a good time. Elizabeth Stride was atypical among Ripper victims in that she had no planets in Taurus. Catharine Eddowes had both Mars and Venus in Taurus, which would suggest that she was sensuous and sensual; in some individuals this configuration gives a liking for role-switching and what some might regard as deviant sexual practices. Mary Kelly had both Venus and Pluto in Taurus, which again suggests some aspect of a Beauty and the Beast scenario, and the need to be constantly reassured of a lover's devotion.

Pisces, which can make the individual dreamy and not properly connected to reality, is also prominent in Martha Tabram's chart, with Neptune in its own sign and Mars as well. This would make it hard for Martha to believe in any sort of reality, and she would have wished to escape from and deny her own validity in some way.

Annie Chapman with the Sun and two other planets (Uranus and Mercury - the planet of communication) in Pisces would also have had difficulty in holding on to reality, and would have been de-stabilized by sudden shifts and changes in her fortunes. (It is more than possible that her problems stemmed as much from lack of worldliness as from alcohol. She simply had difficulty in handling real life.)

Elizabeth Stride and Catharine Eddowes had Uranus in Pisces. Both women would have had opportunities come their way out of the blue, only for them to disappear just as suddenly.

Mary Kelly had Mercury in Pisces, giving her a somewhat roundabout way of expressing herself. In its most negative manifestation the individual uses innuendo and suggestion. She also had Chiron (the sign of the healer) in Pisces, suggesting a person who would lend a sympathetic ear in times of trouble. In Mary's case, however, this faculty would be blocked by her emotional make-up.

In simple terms, the individual layouts show the following:
Martha's planets are mostly in one quadrant of the sky, indicating that she would have been fairly intense but not a needy individual.

Annie Chapman would have been a dreamer, but would have 'led with her chin' and landed up in fights that were not necessarily of her making. She needed to feel that life was worth living.

Polly Nichols would have been very conscious of rights for women, and the need for self-improvement. She may have come across to others as something of a witch, while personally acknowledging a dislike of men.

Elizabeth Stride had a stellium (a group of four planets all within three degrees of one another), which suggests that she had a need to be up-front and 'out there'. It is interesting to speculate whether she had been on the stage at any time; she may well have considered that high class prostitution was her stage. She would have enjoyed creating fantasy for others.

Catharine Eddowes may have been the sort of person to create a happy atmosphere in which other people could recharge themselves while she ended up exhausted, having been pulled in different directions.

Mary Kelly would have been continually trying to deal with an excess of energy, and all the frustrations that can bring. Her life would often have seemed like a treadmill from which she could not escape.

First Contacts

I first linked with the women in the course of the 8 July test session (see page 16). They presented themselves both as a group and as individuals. What came across was that prostitution was simply a job, a means to an end, and for most of them that meant drink and enjoying themselves. Prostitution supplemented their income and their lives; it was not their main way of earning. At one point I experienced strong feelings of despair. I discovered that Catharine Eddowes was not a natural prostitute and that she had problems with her daughter. Martha Tabram looked after women; she was a cleaner; she had a hip problem; and she liked a good time. She also did not seem to be a prostitute. She had a 5-year-old child around her - possibly a grandchild. Mary Kelly, it appeared, had run away from home.

I felt that Catharine Eddowes was already seriously ill and would have died a short time later, possibly from a heart condition. (Subsequent research did not support this feeling about Catharine, although Annie Chapman was, in fact, seriously ill.) I asked if one of the girls had a stutter, or some other speech impediment. (It was discovered that Annie Chapman slurred her words more than was normal while in drink, and Elizabeth Stride had lost her teeth in her lower left jaw.)

The women had little concept of danger, although Elizabeth Stride, in particular, found what she did dangerous. None of them was warned about the danger, despite the individual - ie, the Ripper - being known in the East End. (Interestingly, Mary Kelly was known to have been fascinated by the Ripper stories in the newspapers; some sources suggest this was because she was terrified of what might happen to her. Her astrological chart shows an aspect which might be called 'the need to know'.)

Victim Profile

Based on the evidence we have gathered, the Ripper's victims were women who enjoyed having a good time no matter what the circumstances; who had a strong sense of their own individuality; who had grown up in the school of hard knocks; who had had children or were motherly types, and who had gone about as far downhill as it is possible to go. These women were not fools, except when they had been drinking, and they would have cared little for the rules of society.

If they were all prostitutes, each of them would have had very different reasons for being so. Martha Tabram, Annie Chapman and Polly Nichols would have been prostitutes only out of necessity. Most of the evidence concerning Catharine Eddowes and prostitution is circumstantial, in that she had no money one minute but then seemed to find money for drink from somewhere. She would have used prostitution as part of a repertoire of party tricks. In Elizabeth it would have been an expression of her natural flamboyance. Mary Kelly would have used prostitution because it was something she was good at.

There is something else, at a deeper level, that seems to draw these women together. The impression is that it is concern for their collective lifestyle. Astrological placings can give an idea of how one reacts to belonging to a group, and they can also define what influences a whole generation. In the previous chapter we looked at the prevailing social conditions in Victorian London and the attempts of reformers to improve them. These reformers, it could be argued astrologically, were acting in accordance with this cosmic pull. The actions of all the women except Mary Kelly (who was only 25 at the time of her murder) would have been influenced by the need for change shown astrologically at around the age of 40-45 in their individual charts.

In the Victorian era women in general identified quite strongly with the image of the mother figure epitomized by their Queen; just as many women today identified with Princess Diana and her struggle for self-expression. All women - even those at the bottom of the social pile - knew what it was like to have had children, and then to have lost them - through death or separation of some kind. The huge loss or privation this represented took the individual into a dark area of her being. Today it is recognized that most women eventually emerge from it as stronger and more able people, often because they have given their energies to an interest or a cause outside themselves.

Women are in general more open to radical change and will agitate until it has been achieved. The women of the East End were no exception to this. Many would have felt in their bones that something had to be done to improve their lives. It is known that Polly Nichols and Elizabeth Stride were separately involved in this movement for change. Like many in the East End who fell on hard times, these women had to get by in the best way they knew, but only the small and insignificant Annie Chapman can be painted so 'unfortunate' as to have been incapable of massing for action - psychologically if not physically - as part of the 'monstrous regiment'. To believe that they were incapable of wanting to right perceived wrongs is to misunderstand both the nature of the women's lives and the women themselves.

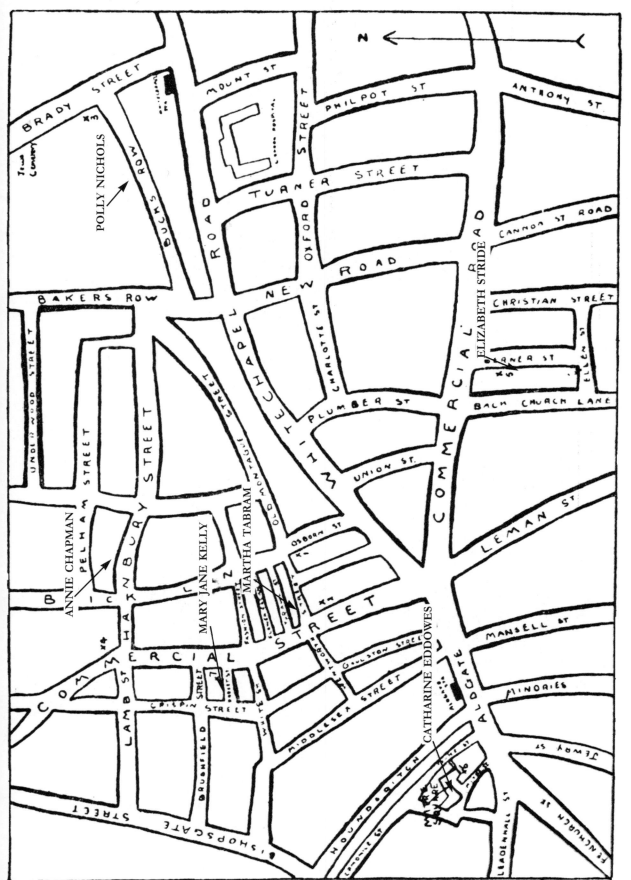

A simplified map of the area in which the murders were committed, showing the individual sites. When connected the sites closely conform to the shape of an arrow.

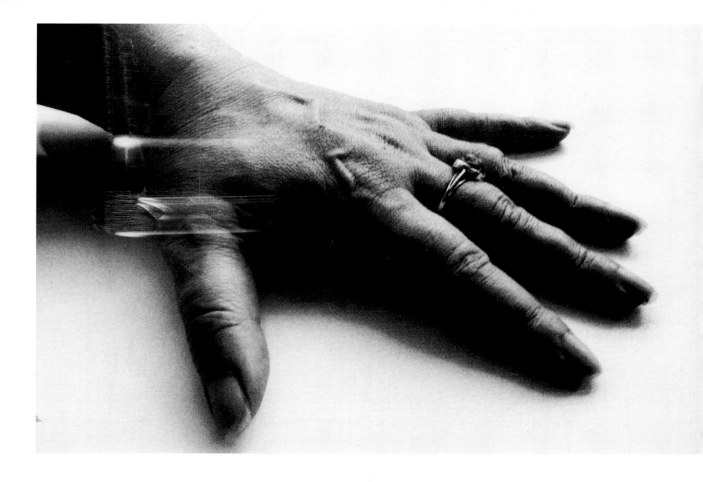
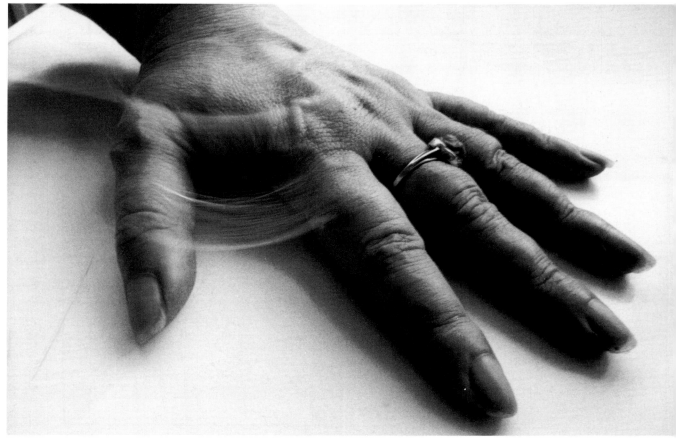

Opposite page: Taken at a slow shutter speed the images of the hands show the pendulum swinging (top) backwards and forwards for a negative response, and (below) circling for a positive response. The pendulum used (left) was a quartz crystal ring suspended on a simple chain.

Below: A contemporary photograph of the heart of Whitechapel, showing the junction at which Whitechapel High Street meets Whitechapel Road.

A typical East-End dwelling, c. 1900: one room for a family of seven.

The policy of slum clearance improved the housing stock but often at new rents the poor could not afford

A row of working people's cottages in the East-End in the 1880s.

Lodging houses such as this were the refuge of many of the urban poor, including several of the Ripper's victims.

THE NEMESIS OF NEGLECT.

"THERE FLOATS A PHANTOM ON THE SLUM'S FOUL AIR,
SHAPING, TO EYES WHICH HAVE THE GIFT OF SEEING,
INTO THE SPECTRE OF THAT LOATHLY LAIR.
FACE IT—FOR VAIN IS FLEEING!
RED-HANDED, RUTHLESS, FURTIVE, UNERECT,
'TIS MURDEROUS CRIME—THE NEMESIS OF NEGLECT!"

THE WHITECHAPEL MURDER — THE CRY IS "JACK THE RIPPER"!!

Left: Punch *magazine's view of the East-End fed middle-class fears and prejudices.*

Above: In early 1889 news of the murders was still filling the pages of the Illustrated Police News.

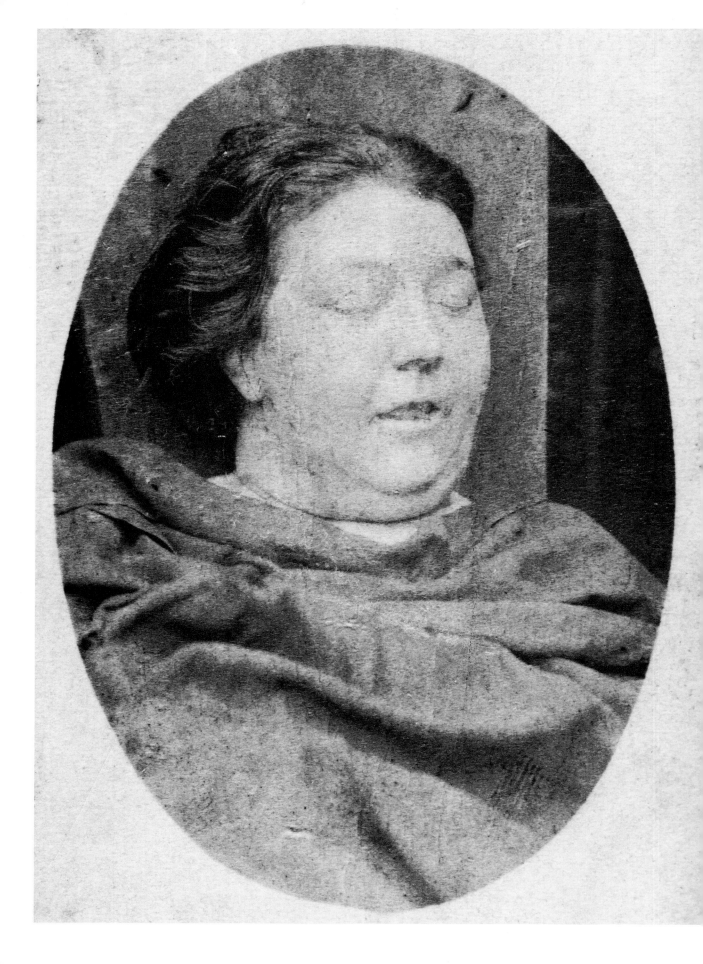

Opposite page: Martha Tabram was not officially classified as a victim of the Ripper at the time. Psychic research, however, revealed surprising information and she became a key figure in our drama.

Below left: George Yard buildings (now demolished) where the body of Martha Tabram was found.

Top right: The Board School in Durward Street (formerly Bucks Row) is close to the spot where Polly Nichols was murdered. It is seen here before its renovation.

Below right: Newly renovated as a block of private flats, the Board School, like many other buildings in the area, is losing obvious traces of its past.

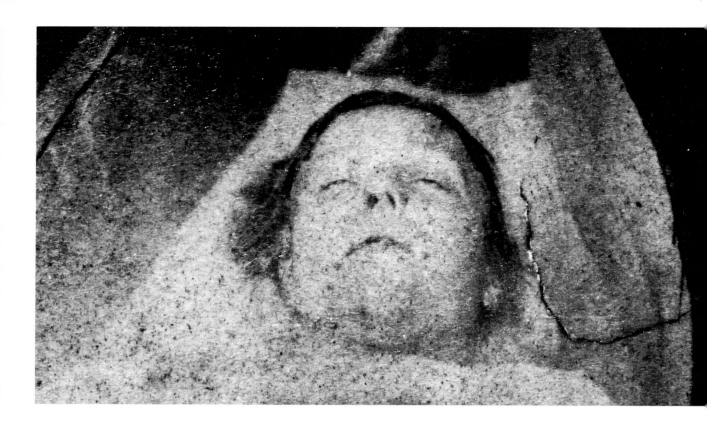

Top: Polly Nichols. The contact session with her revealed a great deal about the personality of the murderer and the manner of her death.

Above left: A 1960s shot of Bucks Row (later renamed Durward Street by public petition), where Nichols was murdered.

Right: 29 Hanbury Street in 1967. In 1888 the door on the left would have led to the back yard where the body of Annie Chapman (opposite page) was found.

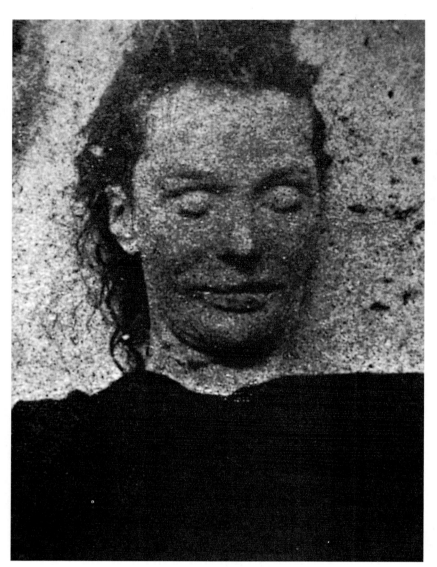

Left: Elizabeth Stride, a death made possible by anger and carelessness.

Below left: The site of Stride's murder, Dutfields Yard (in Berners Street, now Henriques Street), has been a school since 1909.

Opposite page: Catharine Eddowes — the knowledge she had may have become her death warrant.

Below right: A view of Mitre Square, the site of Eddowes' murder, taken almost on the spot where the greatest psychic disturbance was experienced (see page 29). We think her body lay almost where the flowerbed is today.

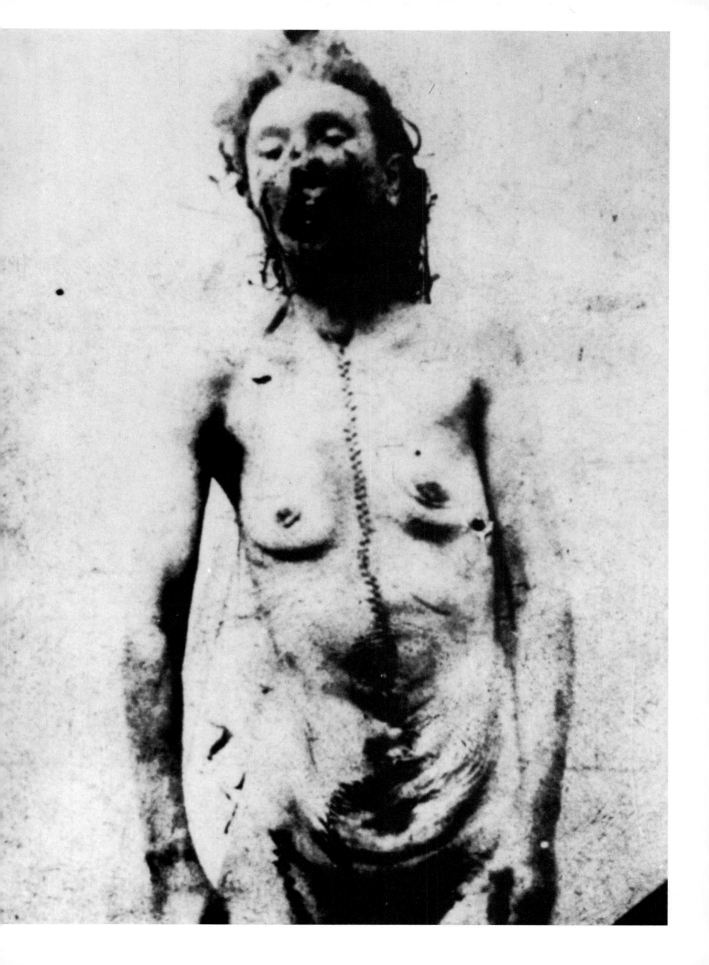

Above: Mary Jane Kelly, the last of the Ripper's victims and an enigma from the beginning of her short life to its brutal end.

Right: Millers Court, where Kelly was murdered. The last positive identification of her alive was a few hours before her death when she was heard singing 'Only a violet I plucked from my mother's grave'.

The type of 'jolly new bonnet' of which Polly Nichols boasted shortly before her death.

Hat decoration. The session with Annie Chapman revealed that she may have partly earned her living by decorating hats.

A fashionable dress of the time. Mary Kelly allegedly attempted to recover such garments from an address in Knightsbridge.

Cutaway coat and wide awake hat - the type of clothing sometimes associated with Jack the Ripper.

The Bloody Sunday Riot of 13 November 1887 fuelled unrest among London's poor and generated mistrust of the police.

Special constables, pictured here undergoing training, were drafted in by Warren to help quell the riot.

Right: Sir Charles Warren, Metropolitan Police Commissioner, whose ban on public meetings in Trafalgar Square triggered the Bloody Sunday incident. He was accused by many of mishandling the Ripper case.

CATCH AS CATCH CAN:
THE POLICE INVESTIGATION

London's Metropolitan Police Force had vast powers at its disposal to enable it to solve the Whitechapel murders. It could, in theory, have investigated every shop, public house and every lodging house in the huge area of London - excluding the one square mile of the City of London, which was policed then, as now, by its own force. There were, however, large areas even within the immediate vicinity of the murders which were not combed for evidence, though there is no rhyme or reason as to why they should not have been. Areas where suspects had been sighted or the bodies found - such as in the immediate vicinity of Bucks Row (now Durward Street) and Berner Street (now Henriques Street), Mulberry Street, Plumbers Row, The Minories, Sion Square and Greenfield Street - were ignored. Instead, as a contemporary noted, 'arrests were made by the score, principally of the low class who inhabited the locality of where the murders were committed'. Action, it seemed, had to be seen to be taken, never mind that it had no genuine focus. The uncertain start was perhaps indicative of the inexpert skill and low morale of the fledgling department whose responsibility it was to apprehend the murderer.

Police Politics

The Metropolitan Police had been in existence for 59 years when the first Ripper murder occurred in August 1888. Even by this time objections to the idea of a police force could still be heard. In 1842 a Detective Department consisting of two inspectors and six sergeants had been formed. The Department was greeted with suspicion by the public and aroused jealousy in some powerful quarters within the Metropolitan Police itself, and for these reasons expansion of the force was restricted. This situation changed in 1868 with the appointment of Colonel Edmund Walcott Henderson as Commissioner. He expanded the 15-strong department (out of a total police force of some 8,000) in an attempt to counter the rising crime rate. However, morale was dogged by grievances over pay, leading to a strike in 1872, and revelations of corruption. According to Chief Inspector John Littlechild, writing in 1894, in addition to dynamite conspiracies, explosions, the Whitechapel murders, 'perhaps no matter has been of such great importance at Scotland Yard as the discovery of the Great Turf Frauds of 1876.' As part of the move for change instigated in the aftermath of this scandal, Henderson decided that a study of the very efficient French Sûreté should be carried out and measures taken to run the Metropolitan Detective Department along similar lines. It was recommended that the Department should be independent of the uniformed branch and have a direct line of communication to the Home Secretary. These recommendations fuelled existing animosities between the Detective Department and the regular police. The seal was set on the reforms by a change of name, in 1878, to the Criminal Investigation Department. Howard Vincent, the man who had undertaken the study of the Sûreté, was appointed to lead the revamped department. Vincent soon resigned - it is believed from boredom - and was replaced by James Monro. The latter was well-liked by everyone, including the rank and file, although he was an inflexible and highly principled man.

Henderson was forced to resign as Commissioner in 1886 after criticism of police handling of rioting. He was replaced by Sir Charles Warren, a soldier and committed Christian, who took up the post on 29 March 1886. Despite an excellent record as a military man, Sir Charles knew little about policing methods or how investigations were conducted. He made an immediate enemy in James Monro. Warren initially agreed to Monro's proposal that Sir Melville Macnaghten, a friend of Monro, should be brought in as assistant head of CID, which would allow Monro to carry out the dual role of Assistant Commissioner (CID) and Secret Agent, but then he reconsidered and decided against the appointment. Monro appealed to the Home Office and eventually resigned. He was then given the task by the Home Office of heading the Secret Department, an intelligence unit working against the Fenian movement.

The identity of his successor (Doctor Robert Anderson) was not made known immediately and this delay led to 'sinister rumours' circulating among CID officers, who were already demoralized by what was perceived to be unfair treatment of their former head. According to Anderson, Monro was 'not an easy man to follow ... things might have settled down - for all the officers knew and trusted me. But for some occult reason the matter was kept secret, and I was enjoined not to make my appointment known ... I had some difficulty in preventing CS Williamson from sending in his resignation ... Then again I was at that time physically unfit to enter on the duties of my new post ... And so, after one week at Scotland Yard, I crossed the Channel.'

When the murders began, Charles Warren was on holiday in France, Anderson was on sick leave in Switzerland, Chief Superintendent Williamson was ill and Superintendent John Shore was taken up with other matters. Overall responsibility for police activity during the Ripper investigation was given to DCI Swanson. The senior officer closest to the ground on the investigation was DI Frederick George Abberline.

The Hunt Begins

The modus operandi of Jack the Ripper was established in police minds with the murder of Annie Chapman, the second victim by their reckoning. From the outset the police were not well equipped to cope with the case. Their experience of other murder enquiries was of no help because these killings were unlike any others. The phenomenon of murdering to a pattern and targeting a particular section of society was unheard of. This killer's seemingly insatiable thirst for victims, together with the ferocity of his methods, was uniquely disturbing. Jack left few, if any, clues behind him. He seemed to strike at random. No woman - especially ladies of the night - felt safe, and no man was above suspicion. Even Queen Victoria was not remote from the concern generated by the murders. At the height of the scare she received a petition of four thousand signatures from women in the East End which had been organized by the wife of the Vicar of St Jude's in Whitechapel. In a memorandum the Queen referred to 'the first murder', and she took a personal interest in the case; it was she who suggested that the police might question drovers coming in on the cattle boats from the continent.

In October 1888, after a fourth victim had been claimed and the police were no nearer to finding the killer, the Home Secretary, Henry Matthews, called for a progress report on the investigation. A report sent to the Home Office on 19 October 1888 by Swanson reveals that 80,000 handbills had been distributed, house to house searches conducted, 200 lodgers questioned, and enquiries made of sailors on the Thames, Asians in London opium dens, Greeks, Gypsies, and cowboys from a US exhibition being held at the time. Furthermore, '300 people were questioned as a result of communication from the public ... including 67 butchers and slaughterers.' Other occupations suspected were bootmakers, cork cutters, sailors or servicemen on leave - indeed anyone who may have possessed a knife, for legitimate purposes or otherwise.

The Rumour Mill

In the absence of any firm leads, rumours about the killer's identity were rife. The Ripper murders were constantly in the news, and newspapers played a particularly important part in disseminating information about them. The newspapers, especially at the popular end of the market, also helped to increase anxiety among Londoners and contributed to Jack's crystallization in the public imagination as a figure of fear.

In early October it was suggested that the Ripper used 'peculiarly Eastern methods' and that the killer acted when he was 'primed with his opium, or bang, or gin and inspired with his lust for slaughter'. On 6 October the *Times* printed a telegram from an English sailor then in New York, stating that the previous August a Malaysian cook had told him that 'he had been robbed by a woman of bad character and that unless he found the woman and recovered his money he would murder and mutilate every Whitechapel woman he met'. The case of a Jew charged with the mutilation of women in 1884 in Austria led to rumours in the East End that a Jew could atone for the sin of sexual relationships with a Christian woman by mutilating her.

The publication in the press of several letters purporting to come from Jack the Ripper - disclosed in the hope that someone might recognize the handwriting - helped only to increase police confusion and the Ripper's notoriety. In one of these letters, 'Jack' is said to have talked of a larger number of victims than the five attributed to him, and with scare-mongering rife his tally was boosted in the public imagination to as many as twenty.

For a time people became more vigilant and more suspicious, and this led, hardly surprisingly, to a contagion of false alarms. The police acted on information received and investigated most leads as best they could. Some suspects were arrested and questioned more than once. Others attracted attention to themselves by displaying bizarre behaviour. A tale is told of a Dr Holt, who, while playing the amateur detective, had blackened his face in an attempt to catch the Ripper, only to be attacked by a crowd who mistook him for the miscreant.

Many men were suspected on the flimsiest of evidence. The murders seem to have awakened an archetypal evil and anyone even approximating to this evil was immediately suspected. A butcher who had accidentally stabbed himself received undue attention, as did a customer of The Prince Albert pub in Brushfield St. Mrs Fiddymont, the landlady, had him followed because it was noticed that he had bloodstained hands.

One story which illustrates the mistrust the Ripper murders generated within the East End community is that of a man called John Pizer. Nicknamed 'Leather Apron' from the working garment he wore, Pizer came under suspicion and was questioned by the police. By all accounts a very timid, sickly little man, he could not be positively identified by witnesses when he was brought before them. He gave a good account of himself and could provide what would today be considered a cast-iron alibi. Even so, on his release from police custody he was so afraid of the reaction of his peers that he went into hiding and for some time afterwards he was regarded with great suspicion by members of his community.

Encouraged by press reports that some doctors associated with the victims' inquests and post-mortems felt that the perpetrator might have anatomical knowledge or some skill with a knife, the belief took hold that the killer had to possess certain surgical skills and instruments. The two main theories were either that the killer was a religious fanatic intent on ridding the world of prostitution or a medical doctor. One myth concerned a Dr Stanley who was said to have turned killer because his son had been infected by prostitutes with venereal disease. A commercial reason for the killings was also posited - it was commonly believed that there was a market for the organs removed from the bodies of the victims. Some people said the uterus could be used magically, for instance to obtain invisibility (see page 67). For some time no doctor was above suspicion in the East End, nor was anyone who carried a black bag.

Slaughtermen also came under suspicion, especially Jewish ritual slaughterers or Shochtim. A Shochet was almost certainly a learned man, and the idea was born that the killer might have read some mad interpretations into the various Talmudic denunciations of harlots and gone out to do God's will. The police did actually arrest two Shochtim, but both had alibis. This did not let the Jews off the hook. The double murder of Elizabeth Stride and Catharine Eddowes at the end of September led to more finger-pointing in their direction. Elizabeth Stride's body was found opposite the International Workmen's Club, an organization which had mainly Jewish members who seemed determined to preserve their culture and practices. After questioning everyone from the Club, the police eliminated them from their enquiries. However, they came away with a description of the man they were looking for: 'Age, 37, height, 5'8". Rather dark beard and moustache, dark jacket, vest and trousers, black scarf and hat; speaks with foreign accent'. This description was not helpful in that it fitted thousands of Jews. And then there was the message scrawled in Goulston St, near the scene of the murder of Catharine Eddowes (see page 26), with its peculiar spelling of the word Jews (Juwes). Significance was attached to this and the opinion formed that it must be quasi-Hebrew and therefore written by a Jewish hand.

Sir Charles Warren wrote to the Chief Rabbi, whose response was swift and dismissive. He stated that in no language he knew was 'Jews' spelt in this way and he suggested that it was more likely to have been written by an illiterate Englishman. The press were unaware of this correspondence. The actual message was erased - and this led to the belief that someone, somewhere, was covering up for the Jews.

Jill the Ripper

The theory has been expounded fairly frequently in Ripper literature that the murderer was a woman, possibly a midwife but more probably an abortionist. This is feasible, in that she would have had the knowledge to commit the mutilations, she would have been able to move around the streets at night without attracting comment, and she would have been able to explain away her bloodstained clothing.

One variation on this theme is that Jill the Ripper killed in order to cover up her bungled attempts at abortion. In seeking an abortion a woman lost the protection of the state and often put herself in the hands of people with little or no medical expertise. Although maternal deaths as a result of bungled abortions were not uncommon, and fear of prosecution was great, this idea does seem somewhat far-fetched. It is possible that the women knew of, or were involved in, some such bungled attempt. Mary Kelly is thought by many to have been three months' pregnant at the time of her death. However, the idea that all the murders may be attributed to one ham-fisted abortionist is too improbable to be taken seriously.

The midwife as murderer theory has been given one ludicrous twist too many by the suggestion that a pram was used to transport the victims, this mode explaining the lack of blood on the streets at the sites of the murders.

One murderer-as-woman theory has at its centre Olga Tchkersoff, if she ever existed, who is said to have borne a grudge against Mary Kelly for leading her sister into a life of prostitution. Olga is said to have told two friends of her involvement in the murder of the last two victims (Eddowes and Kelly). This would tie in with another theory that Catharine Eddowes, who sometimes used the name Kate Kelly (Kelly being her partner's surname), was mistaken for Mary. Unfortunately, no firm information on Olga is available and so we were unable to make an astrological assessment to ascertain the likelihood of her involvement in the murders.

Scapegoats

The public's concern and disquiet was not helped by a press that was largely antagonistic towards the police and widely publicized their failures and shortcomings. *Punch* magazine showed a satirical cartoon

60

which depicted a thoroughly confused blind-folded constable, while other newspapers railed against the lack of progress. Mistakes were made almost from the outset of the investigation. In the Nichols case, for example, confusion and ignorance are apparent in the immediate aftermath of the murder. Evidence was destroyed, perhaps inadvertently, by a local resident who, despite the presence of a police constable, had washed away much of the blood by the time Police Inspector Spratling arrived at the scene. Further evidence was destroyed at the mortuary where the body was stripped and washed - despite claims of instructions to the contrary - before the post-mortem was conducted.

Sir Charles Warren became a scapegoat for police failure to apprehend the killer. He was lampooned mercilessly for introducing changes to the police force and blamed unfairly for some operational errors. His idea to employ bloodhounds in the tracking of criminals was sound. However, the attempt to introduce the dogs in the Ripper case was farcical. Aware that their use was innovative, the police on the ground delayed breaking into Mary Kelly's room to wait for them. Unfortunately, no-one was cognisant of the fact that the dogs' owner had withdrawn them from trials because payment had not yet been ratified. Our perception of Warren is that, although stubborn, he was much maligned, and regrettably in November 1888 went like a lamb to the ritual slaughter of resignation. He was replaced by his arch-enemy Monro, who finally had his way in that Macnaghten was brought in as assistant head of CID.

It is interesting to note that four years later, in 1892, in the case of the Crown versus the serial murderer Thomas Cream (see page 70), the CID would demonstrate how much improved their investigative techniques were. Unlike the Ripper case, as a result of painstaking detective work they would gather enough cumulative evidence to convince a jury that Cream was guilty of poisoning four prostitutes and thus bring a complex case to a successful conclusion.

THE PSYCHIC DIMENSION

The evil of the Jack the Ripper murders can still have a profound effect on individual psyches. All of the team were made aware that we were becoming highly sensitive to the information we were party to. This sensitivity proved to have quite long tentacles, even extending beyond our immediate circle. Shortly after the first contact session, a friend became concerned about me and continually had the phrase 'she has come to harm' running through her head. What struck her - apart from the anxiety she was experiencing - was the old-fashioned ring of the phrase, 'She has come to harm'. It is not the sort of expression she would normally use, nor indeed would anyone at the end of the 20th century, but it is language appropriate to the Ripper era.

As the investigation gathered pace I experienced many lurid dreams and coincidences which could be said to be directly connected with the case. After one contact session in particular, I had a dream in which I appeared to be a composite character of all the women, confronting some unspeakable difficulty. I do not believe that at that point I was linking with the girls, but with my own fears and doubts as to my abilities. However, although I interpreted the dream on a psychological level, its effects stayed with me for some days afterwards. I was thankful that I possessed enough knowledge, not to mention effective techniques, to be able to deal with the situation. This was not the case in the 1880s.

Psychism in the 1880s

Knowledge of psychism and psychic techniques was largely still in its infancy at the end of the 19th century. Occultism and magic had always been available to those who cared to delve for them, of course, but by and large the average man in the street knew very little of such practices. This hidden dimension had been first held up for ordinary people to view in the 1840s when the Fox sisters of Hydesville, New York were said to have developed the ability to communicate with the spirit realm. Here was another dimension of being which seemed prepared to communicate with certain individuals; information which could not have been 'known' by conventional means, became available. There was then - as there is now - the necessity to suspend belief in previously cherished ideals and to accept the manifestations of this other dimension.

The nearest phenomenon to which spiritism can be likened today is crop circles. As with these mysterious occurrences, interest started slowly then increased in complexity until many different theories were expounded. Unfortunately, as the movement grew apace, it also grew fashionable, and while in some people contact with spirit led to an appreciation of spirituality and to a greater awareness of the wider world and of philosophical and social issues, in others the new techniques were used simply for fortune telling and parlour games. A few unscrupulous practitioners led to an element of charlatanism creeping into the movement, and the histrionic behaviour that became associated with spiritism - some of which may have been genuine, given the sensitivities of the people involved - inevitably gave the whole movement a bad name. The valuable work in honing techniques and skills was done in home or development circles held all over the country. Indeed these were often the training ground for mediumship. The early psychic ability shown by Robert Lees, for example, was developed at prayer meetings run by his father.

Psychism was used quite early in the Ripper investigation, albeit on an ad hoc basis, with people up and down the land holding sittings to see what they could discover. *The Echo* newspaper of 8 October 1888 reported one such event in Cardiff, held to enquire into the murder of Elizabeth Stride. The information received was that the murderer was a middle-aged man who lived in Commercial Street, or Road, and was part of a gang of twelve. At another sitting, held in Bolton, the killer had 'the appearance of a farmer, though dressed like a navvy, with a strap around his waist and peculiar pockets. He wears a dark moustache, and has scars behind the ears and in other places. He will [says the medium] be caught in the act of committing another murder'. The quality and standard of mediumship then, as now, was variable, and depended on the understanding and discipline of the medium concerned. Usually the presiding entity, or chief spirit communicator, was given a name by which it could be recognized. Lees, for example, was said to have a spirit guide called Myhanene, and the spirit entity with whom final decisions seemed to rest went by the name of St Clear.

One of the problems with any psychic experience is that it is entirely subjective and often occurs in the absence of witnesses. When presented with psychic information from one of these amateur mediums, the police must have experienced great difficulty in deciding what was genuine and what was not. This understandable lack of expertise was probably the reason for such credence being given initially to the story recounted by a certain Mary Malcolm.

Mary Malcolm claimed that on the night of Elizabeth Stride's murder she had received what the *East London Observer* called '... an occult warning of her sister's death'. She claimed to have been lying awake in bed when she felt pressure on her breast and heard three distinct kisses. This is supposed to have occurred at about the same time as the murder. The *East London Observer* says: 'It was more than probable that, Judas-like, he first betrayed his victim with a kiss and the pressure on the breast is what would naturally occur as he knelt over to cut her throat'. The paper then goes on to suggest that if the account is true, the circumstances may have only come to mind after she had heard of her sister's death, and that if in fact she had spoken of her presentiment prior to the news having reached her it would be a worthwhile case for investigation by the Psychical Research Society. In actuality Mary Malcolm was not Stride's sister, but merely someone seeking to capitalize on the murder. It is nowhere stated that Mrs Malcolm was mediumistic, and it was later proved that her story was concocted from newspaper reports she had read.

There were many people who had dreams and experiences supposedly identifying the murderer. A Mr B Barraclough wrote a letter saying that the house at 20 Wurt Street, Whitechapel, should be watched. Apparently his children had been experimenting with 'table rapping' (a form of psychic communication) and it had identified the killer as Tom Totson of 20 Wurt St, Whitechapel. The communicating spirit had said that the police should be warned by telegram. One particular case is of interest in that a man of the cloth had his report of his dream countersigned lest he be thought mad. In this dream the clergyman received the information that a Pat Murphy and Jim Slaney would walk past 22 Gresham Street at 4.10pm on 28 November. The assumption was made that these individuals - who were unknown to the clergyman - were in some way connected with Jack the Ripper.

The Genuine Article - Robert Lees

Although described by the police as a madman, Robert James Lees was the one indisputably genuine psychic involved in tracking the Ripper. Lees was born in Hinckley, Leicestershire on 12 August 1849 and brought up within a family of Salvationists. Largely self-educated, he is said to have shown psychic powers almost from infancy. At the age of thirteen he was allegedly consulted by Queen Victoria in her search for solace after Prince Albert's death in 1861, but refused to become her personal medium on the grounds that he was too young for the responsibility. This story is not supported by written evidence in research done for biographies of Queen Victoria. However, even thirty years ago when the author first worked in the spiritualist field, convention demanded that the privacy of clients be strenuously protected no matter what their status. Given the social and political climate of the time, it is more than likely that no record would have been kept by either party and that a thick veil of discretion would have been drawn over any consultations between the young Lees and his monarch.

Lees married in 1871 and for a time worked for *The Manchester Guardian*. In 1886, in response to a realization that there were large numbers of men and women who did not attend worship, he determined to develop a course of lectures to widen people's spiritual knowledge. This led eventually, in 1893, to the formation of the People's League, which he would run for six years. At the time of the Ripper murders in 1888, Lees is believed to have been living in Peckham, south London.

Lees' view of the role of a medium or clairvoyant is expounded in a booklet he produced to explain how his books were written; according to Lees, all of these were dictated to him through his spirit guides. Lees considered that 'we are in duty bound to leave the initiative in their [the spirits'] hands and reverently give them an opportunity to prove their case upon their own lines.' He described his part in the transaction as that of a recorder.

At the beginning of October 1888 Lees wrote in his diary that he had offered his services to the police, presumably in connection with the Jack the Ripper saga, and had been turned away. Eventually, he contacted Scotland Yard direct, who promised to write to him. It seems that he had received random clairvoyant flashes which had given him information about the murders.

On three separate occasions, Lees is said to have 'received' information relevant to the murders. In all three instances Lees probably felt the presence of evil. On the first occasion he is believed to have clairvoyantly seen one of the murders being committed and was able to describe the clothes the man was wearing - a dark tweed suit and a light coloured overcoat. This experience is thought to have disturbed him so much that he had to go abroad to recover from its effects. The uninitiated might regard this as an irrational reaction; and yet for someone whose psychic faculty may have seemed to be becoming unmanageable or spasmodic, rest and recuperation would have been very necessary. Clairvoyant flashes can seriously disturb the equilibrium and have considerable emotional impact. In Lees' day the psychological implications of such a shift in perception were not well understood. It is little wonder that he should have been viewed with such suspicion or that he should have had difficulty in coping with the effects of his psychism.

On the second occasion Lees was riding on a bus with his wife. He is said to have dismounted from the bus when he felt that he could identify a particular person as the murderer. His claim was treated with some derision by a policeman and by the time he had convinced an inspector of his concern the suspect had disappeared. The third 'sighting' was when Lees followed a psychic trail which led the police to the home of a well known physician.

Lees' role in the Ripper saga was not made public until 28 April 1895 when the Chicago *Sunday-Times Herald* newspaper revealed the story of this third psychic trail and the fact that the physician - 'believed to be a Dr William Withey Gull' - was subsequently incarcerated in an Islington asylum under the pseudonym 'Thomas Mason, Inmate 124'. The alleged source of this information was one of the doctors who had sat on the panel of the informal commission of lunacy which had examined this miscreant's state of mind. The doctor thus named - Dr Benjamin Howard - issued a strong denial of the 'facts' presented in the article.

Robert Lees himself appears neither to have denied nor to have authenticated the story. It is only hearsay that he did follow a psychic trail which led to the home of an eminent doctor whose wife held a post at the royal court. At no time did Lees name the physician. He did say that the doctor in question had a young son. Lady Gull made reference to a visit by a medium and a policeman who had asked 'impertinent questions', but to this day it has not been proved beyond doubt that this man was Lees or that the man followed was Gull. Lees would say no more than that he had obtained authority from Queen Victoria herself to assist the police in their enquiries. Lees' family believed that he received some kind of a pension in payment for his participation, and it is accepted that he left the country for some time after his part in the investigation ended.

Lees eventually retired to Ilfracombe, where he died in 1931. His obituary notice of 23 January - which, incidentally, was written by a friend - hints at a cloud hanging over him in later years. The notice states that he lived for 26 years 'being denied the solace of love and sympathy' and that he had lived in the 'cold shade of disapproval and animosity'. Other reports, however, indicate that he continued to use his talents to great acclaim for many years.

We experienced great difficulty initially in obtaining information about Lees and it took a trip to Stansted Hall, the home of the Spiritualist National Union, to gain some insight into the man behind the myth. When we tried to contact him psychically it seemed as though we had to prove our credentials in order to work with him (see page 135).

Black Magic

The idea that the Jack the Ripper murders are in some way linked to black magic was widely publicized by Aleister Crowley in his memoirs, which were first published in 1969. Crowley is most remembered - and perhaps feared - for the occult practices he used in order to gain power over his women followers. He has been condemned for this and also his credo, 'Do as thou wilt', although in fairness to him this sentiment could more positively be read as 'Take responsibility for your actions'. It is more than probable that Crowley's claim of a black magic connection was an effort by him to take credit for something that had already been revealed by the Earl of Crawford in an article published in the *Pall Mall Gazette* in 1888.

Crawford's theory was that when a line is drawn between the various murder sites the shape represents either a four-armed cross or a five-pointed star, a magical symbol called a pentagram. I subscribe to the view that the murder sites more closely conform to the shape of an arrow which points in the direction of the seat of government, but readers must decide for themselves. For the figure to be an exact pentagram both the first and the fifth murder would have had to have taken place elsewhere. For the figure to be a cross the fifth murder (or sixth if counting Martha Tabram) would have to be discounted as not belonging to the series.

Crawford's article also fuelled the belief that spirits can be evoked when fat from the human body and certain parts (presumably the uterus) of a harlot are used in combination in a magical ritual. A secondary theory was that a degree of invisibility could be achieved by the use of magical ritual. This theory might hold water were it not for the fact that the uterus was not removed in every murder committed by Jack the Ripper. There was also a belief that the murderer, in order to refine his rituals, would need to progress from the uterus to other parts of the human anatomy.

Among our suspects only Robert D'Onston Stephenson is known to have dabbled in the occult, although whether in black or white magic is not known. If his pseudonym - Tautriadelta - is any indication, he must have been recognized as a very powerful magician. Stephenson did not explain this magical name but others have taken it to mean the 'Crossing of Three Triangles'. The Tau cross symbolizes the highest form of perfection, beyond the sacrifice of the human body. Each of the three triangles represents one level of existence, and the formation of the three in a 'delta' triangle affords the individual maximum protection on all levels of existence. In later life Stephenson wrote a critique of the gospels called *The Patristic Gospels* which he claimed to have penned with the 'undeniable guidance of the Holy Spirit'.

We tried to make contact with Stephenson but he did not make himself available for comment. At the test session conducted in July I felt there was no connection between the murders and the occult, nor indeed did I feel that they had religious significance.

MINOR SUSPECTS

One remarkable feature of this case is the lack of both hard evidence and unanimity about who the Ripper was. Even the origin of his nickname is disputed. Among the East End fraternity people were often known by a nickname (e.g., Leather Apron, Long Liz, Dark Annie) and it is possible that it was simply coined by them to give an identity to the mystery killer. Initially it was thought that Jack might be a member of a gang, though this idea was later discounted. The likelihood is that he worked alone or possibly with one accomplice.

In the previous section we looked at some of the general theories regarding the identity of the killer. Here we begin the examination of evidence against many of the individuals who have been named as suspects at various times. We regard all of the following as minor suspects, because for one reason or another none could have been Jack the Ripper. None of the crimes committed by Chapman, Cutbush, Deeming or Ostrog display characteristics resembling those perpetrated by the Ripper. In the case of Cream, a poisoner, even if he had been inclined to change his modus operandi, it would have been a physical impossibility for him to have been in Whitechapel at the requisite times. The case against Pedachenko is very weak, as is the notion that Stephen could have been directly involved in the killings.

* * *

George Chapman

Inspector Abberline appears to have reached a conclusion about the Ripper's identity only in retirement, when he said that George Chapman was the Ripper. The facts of Chapman's murderous career do not support this notion. Although violent and possibly sadistic towards women, Chapman was a poisoner. It is highly unlikely that he would have used two methods of dispatch and kept those methods separate for different killings.

Chapman was born Severin Antoniovich Klosowski on 14 December 1865 in the Polish village of Nargornak. After a brief and somewhat unsatisfactory career as a surgeon, he is thought to have arrived in London in February 1887. He married Lucy Baderski in October 1889, five weeks after meeting her, his first bigamous marriage since he was still legally married to a woman in Poland.

The last mention of the name Klosowski in any official records appears in the national census of 1891. Lucy and Klosowski emigrated to

America, returning separately in 1892. Later Lucy would say that while they were in the States George had threatened her with a knife and as a result of this she had left him.

In late 1893 Klosowski met Annie Chapman (not the Ripper victim of the same name). He offered no support to her during her pregnancy but took her name, presumably to escape the consequences of previous affairs. A further bogus marriage took place, this time to an alcoholic called Mary Spink. The couple became well-known for their 'musical shaves', so-called because Mary would provide piano accompaniment as George shaved his customers. Less happily, Mary became the subject of many brutal beatings.

On 3 April 1897, Chapman purchased one ounce of tartar-emetic from the chemists William Davidson. The effects of this colourless, odourless and almost tasteless poison were little known then. Administered in small doses it causes slow, painful death. It also preserves the body of the deceased.

When the barber shop failed, Chapman moved on to manage the Prince of Wales public house. It was here that Spink started suffering from severe stomach pains and nausea. She died on Christmas Day 1897, the cause of her death given as phthisis, or consumption.

Two more women were to fall victim to Chapman: Bessie Taylor and Maud Marsh. Chapman showed a degree of heartlessness and dispassion to the third 'Mrs Chapman' that was remarked upon by many. Concerned for her daughter's well-being, Maud's mother brought in an independent doctor to examine her. This scared Chapman into administering a massive dose of tartar-emetic. The post-mortem carried out after her death on 22 October 1902 revealed the poison.

Chapman's former 'wives' were exhumed in November and December of 1902. Bessie's body was found to be extremely well preserved as was Mary's. Chapman was convicted of Maud's death on 20 March 1903 and hanged on 7 April 1903 at Wandsworth Prison.

Thomas Neill Cream

Cream was a poisoner who allegedly told his hangman, a man named Billington, that he was Jack the Ripper. Although his handwriting appears to match that in two of the 'Jack the Ripper' letters, Cream was a poisoner not a mutilator. Furthermore, he could not possibly have committed the murders because he was in prison in America at the time.

Born in Scotland in May 1850, Thomas Cream was the eldest of nine children. He emigrated with his family to Canada, where he graduated from McGill University. He then studied obstetrics at St

Thomas's Hospital in London and also obtained a qualification from the Royal College of Physicians and Surgeons in Edinburgh. At some point he performed an abortion on a rich girlfriend, whose family pursued him. Cream fled back to Canada, where he became an abortionist. Some time later the dead body of a young chambermaid was discovered by a child in the back yard at Cream's office with a bottle of chloroform lying beside her. Despite the damning evidence against him, Cream was not charged with murder.

In August 1880, a Julia Faulkener died in mysterious circumstances. Cream, who had moved to Chicago at the time of her death, was arrested. Again he escaped conviction. In 1881 he was imprisoned for the murder of Daniel Stott, who had sent his wife to Cream for pills which were said to be able to cure his epilepsy. Cream had seduced her and poisoned Stott. He had then telegraphed the coroner, claiming that the druggist who had made up the prescription had put in too much strychnine. He had also begun to seek damages from the drug company. Cream was charged with the murder when Stott's wife turned State's evidence.

Cream served ten years for Stott's murder and was released - as a fit and proper subject for clemency - on 31 July 1891. It would seem that Cream's brother succeeded in securing his release by using an inheritance from his father, who had died in 1887. We can be certain that Cream was not Jack the Ripper because he was imprisoned in Illinois State Penitentiary at Joliet during the four months in which the murders were committed.

Thomas Hayne Cutbush

Cutbush came under suspicion some years after the murders, initially through the press, when it was discovered that in 1888 he had been working in the Minories, a thoroughfare close to Whitechapel, and had subsequently left his job. He is thought to have contracted syphilis around 1888 and as a result of this began to suffer delusions, believing that people were trying to poison him.

Cutbush was detained as a lunatic at Lambeth Infirmary on 5 March 1891, escaped and was re-arrested on 9 March 1891. According to Macnaghten, during his few days at liberty Cutbush stabbed - or attempted to stab - women in the bottom with a penknife, apparently in imitation of a man called Colicott, who police believed was responsible for several cases of 'jobbing', or stabbing, women from behind earlier that year in Kennington.

In his now famous memorandum Melville Macnaghten dismissed

the idea of Cutbush being Jack the Ripper. It was absurd, he suggested, to suppose that the disemboweller would 'rest' for two years and then resume his attacks by stabbing women in the bottom.

There was no firm evidence at the time to link Cutbush to the Whitechapel murders. The only conceivable one is the possibility that Martha Tabram was stabbed with a penknife, the instrument used by Cutbush.

Frederick Deeming

Frederick Bailey Deeming did not come under suspicion until he claimed to be Jack the Ripper while in prison awaiting execution in 1892 for the murder of his second wife in Melbourne, Australia. A plumber and fitter by trade, he had already dispatched his first wife together with their four children in Rainhill, Liverpool, in 1891, hiding their bodies under the floorboards in the kitchen of the family home. For some time the myth of Deeming being the Ripper was perpetuated by the presentation of his death mask by New Scotland Yard as being that of Jack the Ripper. This rather ghoulish practice was used by the police principally to prove that miscreants were dead and so the public could rest easy in their beds. In fact, at the time of the Ripper murders Deeming was in prison, possibly in South Africa.

Aaron Kosminski

Both Swanson and Macnaghten named a man called Aaron Kosminski as the killer, Swanson famously in the handwritten notes (now known as the Swanson marginalia) he made in his personal copy of Sir Robert Anderson's memoirs *The Lighter Side of My Official Life*.

Nowadays Kosminksi would be classified as schizophrenic. Macnaghten claimed that this man became insane owing to many years' indulgence in 'solitary vices' (presumably a reference to masturbation), that he had a great hatred of prostitutes, and that he was removed to a lunatic asylum about March 1889. Kosminski is said to have refused to eat food unless it had been picked up from the streets, and spent much of his time in an unwashed state. He believed that everyone in the world viewed him negatively and for this reason he could not permit himself to accept food in the normal way. This behaviour is a particularly negative manifestation of a state which can occasionally occur through the development of mediumship, when there can be a complete mistrust of the real world and a preference for living within the shadows of the mind. Successfully navigated and unclouded by disease, possibly syphilis in Kosminski's case, the perception of the world in which the subject lives is much enhanced. Kosminski, however, increasingly became incoherent and withdrawn. He was transferred to Leavesdon, another asylum, in 1894 and died in 1919.

Among Swanson's notes is the following statement: 'After the suspect had been identified at the Seaside Home where he had been sent by us with difficulty in order to subject him to identification and he knew he was identified. On suspect's return to his brother's house in Whitechapel he was watched by police (City CID) by day and night. In a very short time the suspect with his hands tied behind his back he was sent to Stepney Workhouse and then to Colney Hatch and died there shortly afterwards - Kosminski was the suspect - D.S.S.'

Aaron Kosminski did not die for another thirty years, so one way or another Swanson's information was wrong. Swanson's notes also make reference to an Aaron Davis Cohen (sometimes known as David Cohen), another inmate of Colney Hatch asylum at the relevant time, so perhaps he was confusing the two men. The possible confusion over identities and the absence of any further information about either of these men have led me to exclude them as suspects for the purposes of this book.

We have seen in the previous section how anyone thought to be acting suspiciously came under police scrutiny. The mentally ill naturally fell into the category of 'acting suspiciously'. If the murders could not be pinned on a foreigner, then the guilty Englishman must be insane. Given that there seemed to be an inordinate number of people shut up in asylums such as Colney Hatch, there were a lot of suspects to choose from. In addition to Kosminski, three insane medical students were implicated. Two of them were traced and then exonerated, but the third, one John Sanders, appears to have gone abroad. Inspector Abberline informed Sir Charles Warren that attempts had been made to trace this individual without success.

Michael Ostrog

Ostrog was one of Macnaghten's three principal suspects; Druitt and Kosminski were the other two. Little is known about Ostrog, and without his date of birth we were unable to find out more astrologically. However, what is known about him does not point to him being a likely candidate. Ostrog was essentially a petty criminal, a career con man of 30 years' standing who was much pursued and watched by the police, appearing in the *Police Gazette* on more than one occasion. One suspects that he was put in the frame for the murders simply because he was a foreigner. He was later incarcerated in a lunatic asylum.

Dr Alexander Pedachenko

There seems to have been a preponderance of doctors connected with the case of Jack the Ripper. Obviously this is partly because doctors became natural suspects due to the so-called surgical nature of the mutilations.

The poor often doctored themselves by using patent medicines, herbalists and chemists. In more serious cases they came to rely on different types of medical care-givers. Many doctors employed unqualified assistants, but more dangerous were the 'irregulars' who were able to set up business with very few, if any, qualifications. These practices were often a cover for nefarious deeds, such as black market operations or back street abortions. One such dubious medic is Dr Alexander Pedachenko, who is said by some sources to have set himself up as a barber-surgeon in South London.

Pedachenko was the alias of Vasilly Konovalov. Born in 1857 at Torshok, Tver in Russia, he was of medium height, broad shouldered but slightly built. His eyes were dark blue with heavy dark eyebrows and he usually wore a black moustache curled and waxed at the ends. His profession was that of a junior surgeon. On occasion he was known to disguise himself as a woman.

A great deal of confusion surrounds Pedachenko. In some sources his activities are merged or linked with those of Ostrog. In others he is said to have been a Russian secret agent, or agent provocateur, sent to Britain to discredit the police force and/or the government and eventually smuggled back to his homeland by the Moscow Ochrana (the secret police). Proof of this is said to be contained in the Rasputin papers, found after the death of the so-called 'Mad Monk' in 1916. These papers are almost certainly a forgery because they are in French and could not possibly have been written by the semi-illiterate holy man.

At one time Pedachenko and Klosowski/George Chapman (see page 69) - another Russian barber-surgeon - were thought to have been one and the same. I cast charts for both Chapman and Pedachenko and my assessment is that they were two distinct personalities and that Pedachenko did not have the ability to be a murderer.

James Kenneth Stephen

Stephen only became a suspect in 1972 when it was suggested that from 1887 he had become a patient of Sir William Gull (see page 81) and a possible accomplice in the murders.

J. K. Stephen was a tutor to the Duke of Clarence at Cambridge, where the two men are said to have had a particularly close, possibly homosexual, relationship. In 1887 Stephen suffered a serious brain injury, caused - depending on the source one believes - either by an object thrown from a moving train or by the moving vane of a windmill which struck his head when the horse he was riding shied. In February 1892, having become a barrister and a fellow of his college, Stephen died of his injury.

Some modern psychologists suggest that two preconditions are necessary to create a murderer: one is ill-treatment during childhood, the other is trauma to the brain. In Stephen's case the injury certainly caused erratic and irrational behaviour, ranging from the often-quoted incident of him stabbing a loaf of bread with a sword (interpreted as revealing a hatred of women) to the decision to run his own weekly journal, *The Reflector*, which quickly ran into financial trouble. Stephen's family found his behaviour difficult to tolerate.

However, the idea that someone as unstable as Stephen could have been used by Gull to commit the murders is implausible, for surely the risk of discovery would have been too great. Equally implausible is the notion that Stephen would have been capable of committing the murders on his own.

An interesting twist to the Stephen story is that Stephen's father (Sir James Fitzjames Stephen) was the judge who mishandled the Maybrick poisoning case in Liverpool in 1889 (see page 84). Judge Stephen was forced to retire in 1891 because he was patently unable to make rational decisions and was suffering from 'brain disease', possibly Alzheimer's disease.

PRIME SUSPECTS

Having dispensed with the minor suspects, most of whom were put in the frame at or around the time of the murders, we turn our attention now to those we regard as the prime suspects. Some of these individuals have come under close scrutiny only recently, after years of rumour and conflicting evidence. We have included only those candidates who, we believe, have a case to answer, thereby excluding some of the wilder speculative theories that seem to have abounded since the 1970s.

The suspects we have selected are Joe Barnett, Montague Druitt, Sir William Gull, James Maybrick, Robert D'Onston Stephenson and Francis Tumblety. In this section we present the known facts about each of them.

JOE BARNETT

Some researchers suspect Mary Kelly's lover, Joe Barnett, of committing at least her murder. When we came to research him, we uncovered a mini-mystery all of its own. Other investigators had already discovered that there are two possible candidates for the character of Joe Barnett, one whose birth date is given as 25 May 1858, and another whose birth date is given as 23 December 1860. In the process of trying to discover which of these two was most likely to be the 'real' Joe Barnett, we uncovered a third candidate, a Joseph Charles Barnett. We cast charts for all three and on the basis of the information these gave us - and the fact that no other research has shown Barnett to have had a middle name - decided that the man we have called Joseph Barnett 1 (born 25 May 1858) was Mary Kelly's lover and thus the Joe Barnett of the Ripper story. For the sake of interest and to enable readers to make their own assessment, we have included astrological charts for Joe Barnett 1 and 2 (see pages 167-169); there seemed little point in including the chart for Joseph Charles Barnett because he so obviously was not the Joe Barnett we were looking for.

Putting aside what had been discovered about this Joe (Joseph Barnett) through later research, we started off with what was known about him at the time of the murders - which was remarkably little. He is known to have been questioned for four hours after Mary's death, and to have told the police what little he knew about Mary's life. At the inquest he gave the impression of a man who paid attention to detail and to his own appearance. He was of nervous disposition and suffered from a speech impediment called echolalia - the repeating of the last few words of what he had just heard. Until a few months before the murder he had been employed as a fish porter, and seems to have tried to keep Mary Kelly happy with, in his own words, 'little gifts of meat and such'.

The two had been living together for about eighteen months, having taken up with one another after only their second meeting. They were living in what for the time was expensive accommodation (4/6d a week) and the rent only seems to have fallen into arrears after he lost his job (rumour has it, for stealing). Even taking into account that Joe had a relatively well paid job, one cannot help wondering how they were able to afford such accommodation. Approximately six weeks' rent was owed at the time of Mary's death; it was Thomas Bowyer, the landlord's assistant, who found her body when he went there to collect the arrears.

Joe disliked Mary working as a prostitute and also disliked her consorting with other prostitutes. The final straw for him was when Mary allowed her friends to use their room. He seems to have watched Mary very carefully and they apparently had a very volatile relationship, Mary often being the aggressor.

Modern researchers have discovered that Joe's father died when he was six and his mother deserted the family shortly afterwards. His older brothers and sisters did a passable job of raising the family and ensuring that he had a decent education. He kept out of trouble and maintained a good lifestyle until he met Mary Kelly.

On the face of it there was no reason to suspect such a quiet, unassuming man of murder, and the police at the time did not. Joe Barnett regained his Billingsgate fish porter's licence in 1906. He died in 1926.

MONTAGUE JOHN DRUITT: THE THIRD MAN

Druitt is one of the three men most likely to have been Jack the Ripper, according to Melville Macnaghten (Kosminski and Ostrog were the others).

In exonerating Thomas Cutbush, Macnaghten's exact words are: 'I may mention the cases of 3 men, any one of whom would have been more likely than Cutbush to have committed this series of murders:-
1) A Mr M. J. Druitt, said to be a doctor and of good family, who disappeared at the time of the Millers Court murder, and whose body (which was said to have been upwards of a month in the water) was

found in the Thames on 31st Dec. - or about 7 weeks after that murder. He was sexually insane and from private info I have little doubt but that his own family believed him to have been the murderer.'

There are several difficulties in addition to the inaccuracies contained in Macnaghten's statement: Druitt was not a doctor; he did not disappear until a further three weeks after the final murder. The term 'sexually insane' is not explained, nor is evidence given to support this assertion. The 'private info' is suspect. According to Sir Melville Macnaghten, it was the family who suspected Montague of being the Ripper, and researchers have since discovered a connection between the Druitt and Macnaghten families. Another reason for disregarding Macnaghten as a sound source when it comes to putting a name to the Ripper is the fact that he came to the case 'cold' and did not take up his post until six months after the last of the Whitechapel murders.

It is almost as though Montague has been damned for lack of evidence. Let us look at the hard facts first.

* * *

Montague John Druitt was born on 15 August 1857 in Wimborne, Dorset, to a medical practitioner and his wife. He attended Winchester School, where his reputation as a good scholar and pillar of the debating society still survives; today pupils at the school are aware of the bed space that was his. Druitt enjoyed sport and excelled at both cricket and fives. Cricket remained part of his regular routine after he left school, an activity that would have ensured he developed above-average strength in his arms and wrists. While many Ripper theorists feel that his sporting commitments would have prevented his involvement in the killings, others believe that he could have successfully juggled the two.

Druitt graduated with a somewhat mediocre degree in 1880, and thereafter was employed as a schoolmaster at a school in Blackheath run by a Mr Valentine. In May 1882 he was admitted to the Inner Temple and in April 1885 he was called to the bar. Throughout this period it would appear that he continued to teach at Mr Valentine's school.

In order to set himself up in Chambers, Druitt borrowed £500 (which amounts to about £15,000 in today's money) from his father against a future legacy. Some modern Ripperologists have assumed that he must have had financial worries. Montague saw none of the £16,579 left by his father in 1885 because it would not stretch to cover all the bequests in his will. One assumes Montague must have been disappointed by such a betrayal, yet as a 'special pleader' for the Western

Circuit and Hampshire, Portsmouth and Southampton Assizes he seems to have been working successfully shortly before his own death. He left considerably more than he could have earned simply as a teacher or a failed barrister.

Probably as a result of her husband's death, Montague's mother, Mrs Ann Druitt, was suffering very badly from depression and paranoid delusions. In July 1888 she tried to commit suicide, one of her delusions being that she was being electrocuted. She was sent to the Brooke Asylum in Clapton, where she was certified insane. One can only assume that by September she was marginally better, because at this time she was transferred to an establishment in Brighton where she remained until she was moved to the Manor House Asylum in Chiswick in 1890. One might conjecture that Montague may well have been researching possible placements for his mother at the time of his death, a possible reason for his being in the Chiswick area.

Mrs Druitt suffered from diabetes. It is now known that diabetes and mediumship can be closely linked, as can epilepsy and mediumship. Nowadays it is accepted by many researchers that diabetic coma and epilepsy show changes in alpha rhythms in the brain akin to those seen in mediumship. Both cause a change in consciousness. In Montague's time such conditions would be seen to induce suicidal tendencies and 'melancholia' and therefore insanity. Montague's family seem to have been particularly afflicted with these tendencies: his maternal grandmother committed suicide and his aunt attempted to do so. Small wonder that when Montague was dismissed from his post at Valentine's school - for reasons which have never been quite understood but are revealed more fully in our contact session on page 131-, he should write 'Since Friday [the date of his dismissal] I felt that I was going to be like mother, and it would be best for all concerned if I were to die.' This suggests that he was seriously disturbed.

On 11 December 1888 William Harvey Druitt, Montague's elder brother, was informed that he had not been seen for a week. On 31 December Montague's body was found floating in the Thames at Chiswick. In his pockets, among the stones which weighted down the body, were found two cheques, his season ticket, the return half of a ticket from Charing Cross to Hammersmith dated 1 December and a few other personal articles. This is odd since, if he were planning to commit suicide, there is no reason for him to have bought a return ticket, nor, unless he was meeting someone, to particularly have chosen Chiswick as his place of death. Our feeling is that Montague may have entered the water at Teddington.

The manner of his death is peculiar. It is surely strange that someone as physically fit and sporty as Montague Druitt would have chosen drowning as his method of suicide. The stones in his pockets were obviously used to ensure that he drowned and that his body remained submerged for some time. But the human body has an instinct for survival and one wonders whether an auxiliary method, such as a drug of some sort, self-administered or otherwise, might have been used. There is no way of ascertaining with any accuracy through conventional means if this was so, since in common with much of the official documentation relevant to the Ripper case the coroner's papers have gone missing.

Druitt's brother, William, is said to have described himself and his mother as Montague's only relatives, though it is known that his sisters were still alive. He could have done this to save them the embarrassment or social stigma that a verdict of suicide would bring. The verdict at the inquest was that Druitt had killed himself 'while of unsound mind'. Up until comparatively recently this form of verdict was used to allow the body to be buried in consecrated ground, and so it was with Montague. He was buried in Wimborne, Dorset, his death being reported in the local paper.

Closing the Case

One of the most influential proponents of the theory that Druitt and Jack the Ripper were one and the same was the journalist and historian G. R. Sims. He took a peculiar delight in having once been suspected of being the Ripper; a street vendor, identifying him as such after seeing a photograph on the jacket of one of his books, informed the police. Sims was certain that the killings stopped because the murderer had committed suicide. Druitt fitted the bill and thus he had to be the killer. Sims pushed this theory at every opportunity, and it seems that the police also went along with it, despite the obvious counter-argument that there are many reasons other than suicide as to why the killings should stop: for example, fear of discovery, illness, moving away. In early March 1889 a member of the vigilante committee was informed - and sworn to secrecy - that the police considered the case closed with the drowning in the Thames of one of their suspects.

If the police had already decided on Druitt as the Ripper it seems strange that in 1892 they should have changed horses to the even less likely Deeming (see page 72), whose death mask was often exhibited as being that of Jack the Ripper. Could this perhaps have been part of an elaborate cover-up or a convenient escape route to dispose of a case which could not be solved?

SIR WILLIAM WITHEY GULL

Both at the time of the murders and subsequently there seems to have been a need to fit a medical figure into the frame, and who better than Sir William Withey Gull? Gull was first associated with the Ripper case in 1895 when the Chicago *Sunday-Times Herald* newspaper stated that he was believed to be 'the perpetrator of the crimes'. Some modern theorists have cast Gull in the role of mastermind behind the killings, with J. K. Stephen (see page 74) as the instrument. However, one of Gull's specialisms was the treatment of insanity (the other was kidney disease), and it is not surprising that when Stephen - having sustained head injuries in an accident - began to show signs of odd behaviour, Gull should have been consulted by the Stephen family. The idea that these two acting together were 'Jack' seems far fetched.

Another theory involving Gull surfaced when in an article published in 1970 a Dr Thomas Stowell made public information he is said to have learnt from Gull's daughter, Mrs Theodore Dyke Acland, in the 1930s. Papers she inherited from her father are said to have revealed that Prince Albert Victor, Duke of Clarence and Avondale, died in January 1892 not from influenza, as had always been thought, but from 'softening of the brain' caused by syphilis. Prior to this revelation there had been no breath of a suspicion that he had been insane. Stowell further implicated Gull by claiming that the man Robert Lees sighted when he was on the omnibus was, in fact, Gull. Stowell also claimed that Sir William Gull was in the East End for the purpose of certifying the murderer to be insane. Such rumours were unheard of prior to Stowell's article, except in the East End.

On the face of it Sir William Withey Gull seems to have led an exemplary life, and his story is a fascinating one of 'local boy makes good'. Success, though, did not mean that Gull turned his back on his origins. Indeed, he maintained an association with the county in which he was raised throughout his life. Gull was born to a bargemaster and his wife near Hythe in Essex on 31 December 1816. Gull's father died when he was ten, and it was reputedly quite difficult for his mother to maintain the lifestyle to which the family was accustomed.

Estates around the village of Thorpe le Soken, to which the family had moved, were owned by Guy's Hospital. It was through the good offices of the local vicar that William came to the notice of the treasurer of that establishment. William is said to have shown an early interest in botany and natural studies. He first began work at the hospital as a clerk, having previously acted as a pupil assistant at the school he attended, where he had been enabled to continue his own studies there by teaching younger boys. It is a feature of William's life that he consistently showed a tremendous capacity for hard work. He was also an exceptionally good teacher. Later in his capacity as tutor at the Hospital he would introduce the idea of giving students 'hands-on' experience.

When Gull gained his degree in medicine in 1841, a lectureship in Natural Philosophy was almost immediately found for him at Guy's, a measure perhaps of the high regard in which he was held by his mentors. In 1843 he was given an additional position by the board of Guy's, when he was appointed Resident Superintendent of their asylum in Fulham for twenty insane women. This appointment would seem to have been a way of providing accommodation for him, and perhaps also of ensuring his continuing loyalty to the hospital.

William seems to have had the happy knack of being in the right place at the right time. By 1861 he had a practice in Mayfair and was highly regarded by colleagues and patients alike. He came to the notice of Queen Victoria in that year when Prince Albert was mortally sick with typhoid, an illness he had caught while pursuing his errant son, the Prince of Wales, Prince Albert Edward, to Ireland. Gull was called in during the illness, together with Sir William Jenner. A year later Gull was made a baronet and appointed Physician Extraordinary to Queen Victoria and Physician in Ordinary to the Prince of Wales.

In 1887, the same year in which he was made Governor of Guy's Hospital, he is known to have had a mild stroke followed by epileptiform attacks. These do not seem to have incapacitated him, although he could be abrupt almost to the point of rudeness. However, given his age (72) and condition at this time, it is unlikely that he would have been capable of masterminding the Ripper murders, let alone carrying them out.

Gull died in January 1890 after a further severe stroke; some researchers believe that he had suffered another stroke earlier. His death certificate was signed by his son-in-law, Dr Theodore Dyke Acland, a somewhat unusual occurrence. There is a belief in the community of Thorpe-le-Soken that the impressive funeral was a sham, that his coffin contained merely stones, and that he did not, in fact, die until some time later. This would tie in with the story in the Chicago newspaper which stated that the doctor trailed by psychic Robert Lees (see page 66) - and now widely assumed to be Sir William Gull - was incarcerated in an insane asylum in Islington as Thomas Mason, Inmate 124. This patient died in 1896 and is buried in Kensal Green cemetery. Interestingly, too, it would also explain how the papers bequeathed to Mrs Dyke Acland by her father could reveal the true circumstances in which Albert Victor died in 1892, because if Gull had indeed died in 1890 these could not have been known by him.

There is a strange anomaly insofar as Gull's will is concerned. It seems that double probate was granted - the second time in 1897. This would lead one to believe that there was some irregularity in the first application in 1890. Perhaps not enough time had elapsed since the death in 1890 to allow for proving of the will, or the settling of debts owed to the estate. His estate is said to have been in excess of £300,000, considerably more than would have been expected.

Sir William was reputed to have been a highly principled and moral man; this is supported by his astrological chart (see page 177). He is said to have been exceptionally honest with patients nearing the point of death and would not offer the solace of hope where there was none. He would challenge authority if he thought his actions were valid, and frequently did so. One outstanding example of this occurred when he defended nursing staff against accusations of negligence in a case of meningitis when he could prove that they could not have known the prognosis. On the debit side, legend has it that he appropriated the heart of a dead patient prior to full permission for a post-mortem being given. If he were insane, as some modern theorists contend, then one supposes that he could have stolen human organs without guilt; organs were missing from several of the Ripper's victims. His mental health is a moot point, however. The real mystery surrounds his death, burial and private life and whether, as seems likely, he was protecting someone or something.

One might be forgiven for assuming that, having dedicated himself to saving the lives of others, William Gull would have been an unlikely party to murder. Our astrological and psychic research suggests that he was probably too complex an individual for such an assumption to be made.

JAMES MAYBRICK

Born in Liverpool on 24 October 1838, James Maybrick was a gentleman cotton merchant who achieved notoriety when his American-born wife, Florence, with whom he had had two children, was accused of his murder and subsequently convicted in a thoroughly unsatisfactory trial. Maybrick was a drug user, particularly ingesting arsenic as a stimulant and aphrodisiac, and an adulterer; his justification for being the latter was his wife's adultery with another cotton merchant. His house in Liverpool was known as Battlecrease and his family motto was, interestingly, 'Time will reveal all'.

The presiding judge at Florence's trial was, coincidentally, Sir James Fitzjames Stephen, who was the father of J. K. Stephen, a suspect in the Ripper case. Sir James patently failed to grasp the full significance of much of the evidence and sentenced Florence to death, which was later reduced to life imprisonment. She served fifteen years of this sentence.

James Maybrick only became a suspect in the Ripper case with the emergence of the so-called Maybrick diary in May 1991. The diary was apparently given to a Mr Mike Barrett by a friend of his - Tony Devereux, a retired print worker, whom he met in the Saddle Inn, Liverpool. It later emerged that Barrett's estranged wife had been given the diary by her father which had been left to him by his grandmother shortly before the Second World War. It was she who had given the diary to Tony Devereux.

The diary consists of 63 hand-written pages in an old scrapbook. The first 48 pages which had been removed had supposedly held pictures or photographs. It is claimed to be a record of Jack the Ripper's activities, written by James Maybrick.

The diary begins in March 1887. It reveals that the author, who signs himself Jack the Ripper, was driven by a pathological hatred of someone he calls 'Bunny' or 'Florry'; the latter is, of course, a diminutive of Florence. He also talks about two children, Bobo and Gladys. The diary reveals a neurotic personality that fed off the extremes of love and hate, life and death. It intimates that he was both thrilled and tortured by the fact that his wife was sleeping with 'the whoremaster'.

There is much argument over whether the diary was actually written by James Maybrick. What is evident is that certain information which one suspects could only have been known by the killer is talked of in the journal. For instance, it is not widely known that Elizabeth Stride had red hair, or that there is a possibility that she was killed with her own knife. The diary also reveals that Emma Smith and Martha Tabram were victims of his, thus going against popular theory. If the diary was a hoax, it is to be presumed that the writer would have gone with popular theory.

If the diary is a transcript of Maybrick's thoughts, then it would appear to confirm the type of personality that we have uncovered. In the diary the writer plays games. He writes, 'If they want me to be a Jew, then so I shall be'. He also talks of the frying and eating of Annie Chapman's uterus, something which would be virtually impossible, given its muscular nature. There are references in the diary to rings and farthings associated with this murder, which highlight one of the mysteries which have never been successfully explained. Annie was in the habit of wearing two brass rings on her fingers, which were missing when the body was found. Press reports also suggested that two brightly polished farthings were laid out near the body as though in a pattern, and it was this which gave rise to the theory of Masonic involvement. It is worth noting that the use of drugs links the persona to an area of symbolism within the mind of the user and might lead to some kind of ritualization which is not necessarily available to other people. It has been suggested that the red leather cigarette case found near Catharine Eddowes' body and possibly the tin matchbox were not hers and had been dropped by her murderer.

None of Maybrick's known movements conflict with the murder dates; he appears to have been ill during October when there were no known murders. He seems to claim that he has left many clues for those who have eyes to see. Maybrick talks of 'cutting the horse's head off and shoving it down the throat of the whore'. This may refer to the pony which shied at Elizabeth Stride's body. The diary refers to the 'Dear Boss' letter (one of a series of letters purporting to be from Jack the Ripper which were sent to a news agency) as being written by Maybrick - again contradicting popular belief about the writer of this letter. Some of the mutilations are said to form the letter 'M' when put together, and in the case of Mary Kelly the bloodstains appeared to form the letters 'FM' on the wall in her room.

Maybrick cannot be dismissed as a suspect. What was surprising, perhaps, was the contact session, which revealed his need to lead a double life (see page 139).

ROBERT D'ONSTON STEPHENSON

Stephenson has come to prominence in the Jack the Ripper story through stories told about him by others. The most potent of these is that he possessed a box of blood-stained ties belonging to the murderer. The organs removed from the victims were, it is claimed, concealed beneath these ties when the killer made his escape from the scenes of his crimes. Why Stephenson should keep the ties for so long, except as a source of secret pleasure if he were the Ripper, is a mystery. The background to the story is as follows.

The most prominent peddler of stories about Stephenson was Baroness Vittoria Cremers. She was business editor of the Theosophical Society's magazine *Lucifer*, and while she was there she became friendly with Mabel Collins (the two are believed to have been lovers), the magazine's associate editor, who had written an impressive spiritual book called *Light on the Path*. Mabel told the baroness that she was associated with a Dr Stephenson who possessed wonderful magical secrets. Vittoria seems to have been unimpressed by the man with whom Mabel was so infatuated, describing him as a 'tall fair-haired man of unassuming appearance at whom one would not look twice'.

When Mabel and Stephenson met, he had just come out of hospital. He told her many stories, claiming variously that he had taken part in the Gold Rush in California, had travelled widely, had fought under Garibaldi when he was a military surgeon and had done many wonderful things. He is said to have revealed that he had been married. For some reason, the baroness seems to have been under the impression that he had murdered his wife.

D'Onston, as he liked to be known, revealed something to Mabel about which she could not speak, and because of this she seems to have suspected him of being Jack the Ripper. Baroness Cremers carried out her own investigations when given the chance. During the course of these she unearthed some old-fashioned black ties which were stained with something that made them stiff. Of his own volition Stephenson told her that he had met Jack the Ripper while in hospital where he had described his way of working. (This story is suspiciously close to a theory put forward by author Leonard Matters that a Dr Stanley had been guilty of the crimes.) It was at this point that Stephenson hinted at occult reasons for the murder. In later years the baroness apparently related this story to Aleister Crowley.

The real story of Robert Donston (without the apostrophe) Stephenson is very different from the one he claimed for himself. The son of a seedcrusher, he was born on 20 April 1841 in Sculcoates, Yorkshire, a far cry from the landed gentry background he seems to have hinted at later in his career. One story he told was of an affair with a prostitute which had resulted in his father cutting off his allowance, and that he had kept a ghostly assignation with this woman, who had committed suicide. It is surely unlikely that a seed crusher would have sufficient wherewithal to make his son an allowance, and Stephenson was perpetually short of money. He claimed to have studied chemistry in Germany, to have studied the Doppelgänger effect, which today is also known as astral projection, and to have been initiated into the Hermetic Lodge of Alexandria by Bulwer Lytton, a famous occultist. His knowledge of magic seems to have impressed many people, though there is little evidence of conventional study. Given his background, it is unlikely that he would have been a commissioned officer, and if he served in the forces at all he would have progressed through the ranks. Much of his travel may therefore have been done while in Her Majesty's service.

Stephenson seems to have been something of a misfit in terms of how he functioned in the real world. The degree to which he immersed himself in magic (see page 67) probably strained his relationships with the everyday and made him seem a remote, other-worldly individual. Much has been made of the fact that in later years he wrote a highly spiritual book, *The Patristic Gospels*, through which it has been suggested he may have tried to expiate the sin of murder. If Stephenson had indeed been guilty of murder it is unlikely that he would have thought this action could remove the burden of such a deed. Death and all that entails was no mystery to him, and his belief in the concept of Karmic debt (in which our actions in this life are either paid for or rewarded in subsequent incarnations) would, I feel, make him an unlikely murderer.

Stephenson is shown by his astrological chart to have been a man of great complexity. He was, without doubt, capable of making people believe what he wanted them to. The mystery is perhaps whether he wished people to believe he was Jack the Ripper, or whether by clouding the issue he wished to make them believe he was not.

Stephenson died, according to Crowley, in 1912.

FRANCIS TUMBLETY

Francis Tumblety surfaced as a suspect in the minds of researchers with the finding of the Littlechild Letter in 1993. This was a three-page document dated 23 September 1913 written by Chief Inspector John Littlechild in response to a question about a Doctor D. put by the journalist G. R. Sims. It is possible that Sims was trying to get Littlechild to identify his own pet-suspect Montague John Druitt (see page 77). In his reply, Littlechild denies knowledge of a Dr D. but writes of a Doctor T., whom he describes as 'a very likely suspect', and identifies Tumblety.

Francis J. Tumblety was born in Canada (or possibly in Ireland) in 1833, the youngest of eleven children. His father, Frank, was Irish, his mother, Margaret, was American. The family moved to Rochester, in New York state, and settled on Sophia Street, about a mile from the city centre. The Tumbletys had no close neighbours. Francis was a solitary type with few friends. Edward Hayward, a boyhood acquaintance, remembered him as dirty, awkward and ignorant, with irresponsible parents. At the age of fifteen Tumblety was selling pornographic material, which he passed off to the uninitiated as literature from the Society for the Prevention of Vice in New York. Tumblety left the family home when he was sixteen and moved in with his elder brother, Frank, who was employed as a steward by Dr Fitzhugh, a prominent physician. Francis worked with a Dr Lispenard in a disreputable drug store; Tumblety's interest in herbal and alternative medicines probably dates from this experience.

Around 1850 Francis left the area. He seems to have travelled widely, and to have been intent on becoming successful. In 1857 he placed an advertisement in a Montreal newspaper to announce his decision not to stand as an Irish nationalist in a local election despite many requests for him to do so. He was in no doubt that should he choose to stand at a future date he would be successful. In 1858 his activities as a physician in St John, New Brunswick, led to suspicions of charlatanism and he quickly left for Boston. Here, a coroner's jury blamed the death of one of his patients, a Mr Podmore, on gross malpractice.

In 1860 Tumblety returned home, from Detroit, to cut a dash as a prosperous physician. By now the dandy, he wore a full-length light fur overcoat with dark collar and cuffs, and was accompanied by a large greyhound, which would become something of a trademark. This liking for public display is also evident in the way he drew attention to himself by distributing food to the poor in some cities. On the other hand, his tendency was to ignore the people who had once known him.

During the American Civil War (1861-65) Tumblety moved to Washington where he professed to being on familiar terms with Abraham Lincoln and other prominent figures. He took to wearing military uniform - a habit for which he was arrested more than once - and claimed that he had been a surgeon with the Union armies. One of the aliases he used was Blackburn; this was also the name of a Confederate doctor who had deliberately tried to start an epidemic of yellow fever. While he was in Washington, Tumblety developed a patent medicine known as the Tumblety Pimple Destroyer.

Legend has it that he told a Colonel Dunham, a military acquaintance, and others of a collection of anatomical specimens. This collection 'contained the wombs of every class of women'. When asked why he disliked women so much, he is said to have revealed that he had 'fallen in love with a cruel taunting woman, only to find out that she was a prostitute who visited brothels when she needed extra money'. From the moment of this discovery, it is alleged, Tumblety renounced women.

After the war, Tumblety travelled widely and is known to have visited, among other places, Liverpool and London. Tumblety was in London at the time of the Ripper murders. He was arrested there on 7 November 1888 and charged just over a week later with eight counts of gross indecency and indecent assault against four men. The dates of the assaults were 27 July, 31 August, 14 October and 2 November.

Tumblety was bailed on 16 November by two people he had only recently met. On 20 November, at a hearing at the Old Bailey, his trial was postponed until 10 December. Within four days of the date being set Tumblety had fled, first to France and then back to America. Enquiries in New York uncovered the fact that Tumblety had a habit of simply disappearing when in trouble, sometimes leaving debts behind him, sometimes large sums of money.

The rumour that he was suspected of being Jack the Ripper gained momentum when he was pursued by a colleague of Inspector Abberline, Inspector Andrews, who seems to have been directed to follow Tumblety after completing other police business in Canada. Tumblety fled from lodgings in New York which he had used for many years and did not surface again until 1893 in Rochester, New York, where he was known to be living with a female relative. One must assume that by this point the Metropolitan Police had dismissed him as a suspect, because they did not attempt to question him. After his death in 1903, a collection of preserved uteri was found among his possessions.

FITTING THE PROFILE

The plain facts about our six prime suspects provide nothing telling as far as the murders are concerned. At this point they are all equal in their presumed innocence for lack of hard evidence against them. We need to use tools that will get behind their masks and at the truth.

There are those who believe that it is impossible to predict who will murder and who will not. Certainly, no-one can say 'this man [or woman] *will* murder'. However, it *is* possible to identify violent tendencies in an individual and therefore to assess accurately whether someone would be capable of committing murder. Just as a competent psychologist can draw up the profile of a serial killer, so should an astrologer be able to outline the astrological profile of a typical killer. Obviously it helps if one has some kind of template. Choosing someone who is known to have murdered several times is a good starting point.

We chose as our template American mass murderer Jeffrey Dahmer, a modern-day example of what is now known as a serial killer, and as a kind of check we also cast a chart for Ian Brady, the infamous Moors Murderer. Dahmer's chart shows some interesting aspects. (It is the aspects or angles between the planets which highlight our individuality, and how we handle stress.) Dahmer mutilated his victims and then appears to have kept them with him for company. At the same time he also ate their flesh. His Pluto (transformation) is opposite Chiron - the planet of healing - with Neptune, which can represent personal gain, standing in the Third House. Thus, in some perverted way, he had perhaps reverted to an ancient belief that in eating this flesh he would internalize some of the qualities of his victims. Equally, one would suppose that he felt he was benefiting his victims in allowing their bodies to be transformed through him. Although his activities were private, there is also in his chart an aspect which seeks acknowledgement as a performer. With Moon and Mars conjunct in Aries, and Moon square Saturn, there is evidence here of a temper of considerable force, controlled because of some attitude towards his relationship with his parents. He could also have felt that he was liberating his victims in some way. Remembering that his victims were young and male, he may well have felt that he was freeing them from their frustrations.

The chart of Ian Brady also shows a need for freedom, but for himself. Jupiter, which represents expansion, is opposed to Pluto. In this case it would seem that he was fully aware of the gremlins held within his subconscious, and wished to escape from them, or to set them free.

Neptune in opposition to Saturn indicates that these gremlins arose from his perception of the way his father treated him as a child. It can be assumed that one of his motives for murder was the power it gave him over young people. An opposition to Chiron - this time to Venus - is also evident in his chart. This might suggest a recognition of the need to heal some injury to the feminine; perversely, this healing is through hurting and cruelty. (In astrological terms Brady's chart is quite 'feminine' and passive, so the murders may well have been an attempt to make better the damaged part of himself.) The pornographic element in the Moors case seems to arise from his association with his partner, Myra Hindley, rather than directly from him or her.

Now let us turn to each of our six prime suspects.

Joe Barnett

The man we have called Joe Barnett 1 has a strong opposition of Moon to Pluto. His chart shows an exceptionally intense nature - indicated by five planets within thirty degrees of one another. The Pluto/Moon opposition would, therefore, indicate that his relationship with his mother was a difficult one and would mean that relationships with women would be fraught with danger. His mother is known to have disappeared by the time he was thirteen and there could here be a perception that he had killed her. Whether this was an actuality or not does not matter - in his eyes she was lost to him and he had done it. Without getting too deeply involved in 'pop' psychology, more relevant to today's understanding than Victorian times, it does appear that a Mars / Uranus opposition could give rise to sexual inadequacy and possibly impotence. This may well have manifested as premature ejaculation. Coincidentally there is a Venus/Neptune square that indicates the creation of a fair degree of fantasy so far as women are concerned. Thus he would be more likely to have viewed them as 'goddesses' and to have put them on a pedestal. It would be quite likely that he would find Mary Kelly's sexuality - both as a former lover of Joe Flemming, who she continued to see while with Joe, and as a working prostitute - difficult to handle. Again, she would be 'lost' to him. A Moon/Mercury opposition would make it difficult for him to communicate his feelings, and perhaps would lead to the echolalia already mentioned. Planets in Scorpio often indicate a familiarity with knives and machinery, and Joe Barnett has two, Moon and Mars, though they are not conjunct.

The Joe Barnett we have called Joe Barnett 2 has a conjunction of Pluto and the Moon, which, in addition, is what astrologers call combust. This means that they are actually within one degree of one another, giving a life of tremendous emotional upheaval and difficulty. It would be more than likely that his mother died in childbirth, again giving a strong sense of abandonment, but for a different reason. This man's Mars - the planet of masculinity and sexual expression - was in Pisces, which makes it particularly weak, and was also conjunct Neptune, which would give a dreamy unpractical side to his nature. Venus was in Scorpio but had a very easy aspect to Mars, so it could not be expected that his relationships with women were particularly difficult. His Uranus/Mercury opposition was likely to make it difficult for him to express himself. He was by nature artistic, and may well have worked in a healing environment. So far as we can see, if he did choose to murder it would be to put his victims out of their misery - it would be against his character to mutilate.

Montague John Druitt

Druitt does not have any oppositions to Pluto, but does have a square to Mars in Leo. This shows stress in the way he expressed himself sexually and also indicates - because of the Mars placing - that his need to escape might lead to suicide. There is evidence in his horoscope (see page 172) that the decision to end his life was a sudden one. There would not seem to be any evidence of the potential to mutilate, though his chart does indicate that his attitude to women would have been ambivalent.

Our astrological assessment of Druitt's state of mind around the times of the murders revealed that, during August, he was under considerable pressure. On several occasions there would appear to have been the potential for family arguments and/or problems with authority. There also seem to have been occasions when his energy was very low, and there was a fair amount of suspect, devious behaviour around him. At this time he would have been going through a number of enforced changes and would not have felt that he was in any way in control.

I had wondered if Druitt was responsible for killing Elizabeth Stride. However, although he was having a great deal of personal difficulty throughout the period of the murders, there is no astrological evidence of the ability to murder. Druitt's only likeness to the Ripper is in physical appearance, which fits the descriptions given in some witness accounts. The contact session with Druitt (see page 131) confirmed this view of him.

Sir William Withey Gull

The only opposition in Gull's chart is a strong one from the Moon to Jupiter. This could well mean that he perceived women as capable of standing in his way, but would also give him the ability to use them for his own advancement. Pluto, however, is conjunct Chiron (the healing planet) in Pisces, which would suggest a man geared towards healing spiritually as well as physically. The square to Neptune from Pluto might feasibly have given some form of megalomania, and the square from Chiron to Uranus could result in sudden flare-ups of healing energy. On balance, it is unlikely that he would have killed for his own ends. The chart indicates that the death of his father when he was young helped him to come to terms with the concept of death, and therefore of spiritual advancement. His chart shows a great deal of intensity, and a Mars/Uranus conjunction which would give quite a temper, or possibly outbursts of emotion.

James Maybrick

James Maybrick has Pluto opposed Venus. In its positive form this suggests an awareness of the transformative power of the feminine, and in its negative the need to destroy anything that is beautiful and also to disturb the feminine. This placing means that relationships with women are always painful. It is, perhaps, this aspect which gives the cynicism noted in our contact session with him (see page 139), in which I was aware of having been 'played with'. He also has an opposition from Pluto to Mercury, giving an obsessive personality and the need continually to probe what he is feeling and experiencing. He also has an opposition to the Moon (this was from Chiron), suggesting a highly emotional approach to the healer within himself, and possibly an inability to express himself properly with tenderness and sensitivity. This would spark off the need for an escape from the intensity of feeling, and would explain his use of drugs. (Additionally, Neptune, the planet of illusion, acts rather coldly and in a dissociated fashion in Aquarius.)

Robert D'Onston Stephenson

Robert D'Onston Stephenson also has an opposition to Pluto, that from Mars. This can give a deep-seated anger, particularly against injustice, and also the ability to manipulate other people. It suggests the propensity for applying controlling forces upon other people, and this ability would have been heightened by his taciturn behaviour. By and large, because of a more favourable aspect between Pluto and Jupiter, he would use charm to do this. Pluto conjunct the Moon suggests the need to understand and come to terms with feminine energy at its most destructive. Possibly there was some form of loss of the nurturing female at around the age of three. It is, one supposes, feasible that his quest for nurturing may have led to the perversion of searching for that symbol of femininity, the uterus, thus freeing his victims from their earthly toils. The motive here would not necessarily be sexual in origin, but, to him, an appropriate use of his masculine energy. That same energy used magically or even hypnotically might have accounted for the silence and the speed with which the Ripper overcame his victims. However, it is difficult to see how D'Onston Stephenson would have been able to continue with his own life in peace after committing such acts. The only way would presumably have been to live his life as spiritually as possible to atone for past misdeeds.

Francis Tumblety

We have been unable to discover Tumblety's birthdate, which makes it impossible to assess his character astrologically. The available evidence suggests that he fits the conventional picture of the murderer - in his flamboyance, ability to disappear and hatred of women. The dates of Tumblety's alleged involvement in the acts of gross indecency show that he was in London at the time of the murders. It is possible that these were holding charges until the police were able to uncover more evidence. At some point Scotland Yard sent for samples of Tumblety's handwriting to see if it matched that displayed in the 'Jack the Ripper letters' they had received.

Assuming that he was on bail from the 'indecency' charges, it is possible that he could have been involved in the earlier murders. However, if indeed the police did suspect Tumblety of being Jack, one assumes they would have watched his movements while he was out on bail and this would have made it almost impossible for him to murder at this time without being caught. It would appear that he was in custody at the time of the Kelly murder, and unless - as seems unlikely - he had been released on police bail and that fact went unrecorded, he could not have been responsible for her death.

Most of the prime suspects display the characteristics of self-interest and arrogance. When these are coupled with sheer deviousness, as in Francis Tumblety's case, a murderous intent may become manifest. When I attempted to contact Francis Tumblety, I had no sense of being able to get hold of anything approaching the reality of him, and can only assume that his various roles and disguises were getting in the way of communication. A strong sense of nastiness - it could not be called evil - also made me reluctant to delve any further. That said, his vibration was not recognizable in any of the other sessions.

* * *

To summarize, astrologically three people show the potential to murder. They are James Maybrick, D'Onston Stephenson and Joe Barnett 1. However, only one of them shows the potential for mutilation - Joe Barnett 1. At this stage, the finger of suspicion is pointing firmly in his direction.

THE RIPPER'S PROFILE

One of the ways of building a profile of the Ripper would be to look at the moment of death for each of the victims. Somewhat unsurprisingly, since Neptune and Pluto are very slow moving, in all of them the two planets sit together in the first degrees of Gemini. This would create an influence which is both divisive and fantastical. It touches the deep, dark and hidden places within the souls of the victims. At the time of all of the murders, except of Mary Kelly's, Jupiter and Mars conjunct (which usually represents some kind of excessive reaction) are opposed to the two former planets. This would suggest that the murderer or murderers were trying to escape from their own sexual constraints. Only in Mary Kelly's case is Jupiter conjunct Venus, leading us to suppose that this act of murder was a perverted way of attempting to free her from her beauty and femininity. This could be considered a negative application of her own need for freedom and a new life.

The charts cast for the supposed moments of death allow the assumption that the murderer was attempting to rid himself of extreme anger. This seems to be anger against women, but not necessarily with a sexual motive. He would have wanted to place some constraints on the women around him, but he would also have wished to be recognized in a very specific way for what he was doing. This might suggest a difficult placing for Saturn in his own chart and therefore a man who had difficulty in expressing himself properly. Mercury might therefore be in a weak sign. Jack the Ripper's argument seems to have been as much with the society in which he lived, which would mean that there was possibly a square to Neptune (which can represent idealism).

Since all the women except Mary Kelly (who was 25) were older, he might well have problems in relating to, or coming to terms with, 'the mother', so the Moon may well be in a difficult position. His motive could well have been to rid the world of mothers rather than prostitutes. It could be suggested that in killing Mary Kelly he had destroyed in her the potential to be a mother - and therefore 'saucy Jack' need kill no more. Both Barnett - with his sense of loss at the disappearance of his mother - and Maybrick - with his relationship difficulties - fit this category.

As a risk-taker Uranus might reveal the ability to show a new or innovative approach to a situation, while a Jupiter/Pluto aspect might indicate an ability to 'sail close to the wind' in terms of what is legal.

PSYCHOLOGICAL PROFILING

One tool of criminal investigative work that was not available to the police in the 1880s is psychological profiling.

Five key characteristics are identified by modern psychologists in profiling serial killers:

1. Most serial killers are white males in their 20s or 30s;
2. They tend to come from dysfunctional families with absentee fathers and/or mothers or mothers who are unloving; the loneliness that such a man experiences comes to the fore initially between the ages of 8 and 10;
3. Many serial killers can only find employment far below their intellectual capabilities;
4. Serial killers often have some sort of disability or physical ailment;
5. Pre-crime stress can sometimes spark off the desire to kill; this stress may be caused by problems with money or relationships, or by some sort of physical trauma.

It has long been supposed that Jack the Ripper was a serial killer who was also a sexual sadist. However, examination of the facts shows that his killings do not totally fit this category. According to criminal psychologists Hazelwood, Dietz and Warren, 'Sexual sadism is a persistent pattern of becoming sexually excited in response to another's suffering ... Sexually sadistic offenders commit well-planned and carefully concealed crimes. Their crimes are repetitive, serious and shocking, and they take special steps to avoid detection. The harm that these men wreak is so devastating and their techniques so sophisticated that those who attempt to apprehend and convict them must be armed with uncommon insight, extensive knowledge and sophisticated investigative resources'.

Few sexual sadists mutilate after death, and it is not normal to retain a trophy of a body part, although it is usual for them to keep something belonging to the victim. Pain is used to bring out the response of obedience, humiliation and submission.

In Jack the Ripper's case we must consider that his true motive was not necessarily sexual gratification. Whatever the nature of his need, it was satiated by the act of mutilation rather than the killing. The injuries of the victims attest to the notion that the need for gratification escalated with each killing, culminating in the final horrific bloodbath. In the end his need was to mutilate not just women but that symbol of womanhood, the uterus, and finally, in Mary Kelly's case, even those symbols of motherhood, the breasts. I believe the motive for the killing had nothing to do with femininity and everything to do with motherhood. One presumes there was also the need to silence these perverted symbols of motherhood, given that the throat was attacked (in strangulation to keep them quiet and also in cutting to kill).

All of our suspects with heavy Plutonian influence can be seen to have some or all of the characteristics of serial killers and/or sexual sadists. James Maybrick does not fit the pattern quite so closely. He was over forty, we do not know whether he had an absentee father, he was not working below his capacity. He used drugs to a considerable extent, which it could be suggested is a physical ailment, and he is known to have been under considerable stress due to difficulties in his relationships.

Not enough is known about Stephenson at the time of the murders to make an accurate assessment, though it is known that he had a difficult relationship with his father. He is also known to have been intellectually very able.

Joe Barnett most closely fits the serial killer profile, since he is known to have lost both his father and his mother, to have done a menial job (fish-portering) which he had just lost, and on top of that he was known to be experiencing difficulties in his relationship with Mary Kelly. Coincidentally, his speech impediment worsened under stress.

SILENT WITNESSES

I knew that any attempt to read the Akashic records concerning the deaths of the victims of Jack the Ripper would be harrowing. I had no wish to experience the ferocity of the murders and yet with this type of contact the medium must sometimes take on the physical feelings and emotions of the individual with whom contact is being made while preserving a degree of objectivity so that the circumstances can be accurately assessed. I had to trust that my communicators - in all dimensions - would at times of deep distress bring me away from particularly disturbing situations or enable me to take the position of observer. The feelings and impressions experienced by the others present also had their own validity; these ranged from anger through extreme fatigue to nausea.

The sessions were not held in the same sequence as the murders were committed, and thus the natural assumptions one would expect to have - i.e. that the killer was the same person each time - did not arise. By doing it in this way we came afresh to the enquiry each time and were able to pick up in later discussions both the similarities and the differences in our perception of each subject. Much research had been undertaken by the time the contact sessions took place, but not by me. It was hoped that by deliberately limiting my exposure to the circumstances surrounding each victim's death the sessions would be uncontaminated by any preconceptions formed through prior knowledge. However, I was interested to see if a piece of information I received during our first psychic experiment on 8 July would find its echo in this phase of the investigation. My feeling then was that two men were associated with the victims of the Ripper, and that one of them seemed to have had an ear infection.

Catharine Eddowes was our first contact. She made herself known to us and set the pattern for the rest of the sessions. Thus, contact seemed random but was appropriate to the particular conditions. At the beginning of each session I would relax into a comfortable position and by using deep breathing would bring about a change of consciousness which would allow contact between the dimensions. This contact was experienced by me almost as a conversation in my head; this is known as clairaudience. When the communicating spirit felt that enough information had been given, or I began to tire, the link would weaken, with contact eventually being lost; from the receiver's perspective this is similar to the distortion and 'break up' that can occur during a call to or from a mobile phone.

The contacts deepened as the investigation progressed and making the necessary links became easier. This deepening may be seen as the difference between the session dealing with Elizabeth Stride and the one dealing with Polly Ann Nichols, the latter being more emotional and less objective. Also I began to gain a greater sense of the murderer's personality or personalities. My awareness, particularly of the women, heightened and at times it seemed as though they were becoming almost my constant companions. Catharine Eddowes, for example, made her presence felt many times outside the sessions.

At times I was frustrated by my desire to find out more - there were many ancillary questions it would have been fascinating to explore on a psychic level, such as whether the women knew one another (something which we came to believe) or the murder suspects knew the victims. However, because the effects of each session lasted approximately 48 hours, during which I was incapable of giving my full attention to other aspects of my work, it would not have been feasible to have extended the time given over to the sessions. I must confess to a part of me being extremely glad of this excuse.

CATHARINE EDDOWES - 22 JULY 1997

Present: Pam, Fiona, James

I suppose if I were to admit to having a favourite among the Ripper's victims, it would be Catharine Eddowes. This may be partly because she was born at the same time of year as myself (April) or it may be because she came across as the most sympathetic and interesting of the women. It is significant that she was the first of the victims to come forward, and with her the feeling was strongest that she needed to make her story known. The feeling was that she knew she had been misjudged and that there were things she wanted to put right.

I had a sense of someone who was unconventional even by the 'easy come, easy go' standards of the environment in which she lived, and who cared about other people. She seemed a feisty woman who had done her best to make life work for her. Perhaps more than the others she recognized that her security lay in the people around her. There is a sense that she could survive anything if she kept faith with them while simultaneously maintaining the small kingdom of belongings that, snail-like, she took with her wherever she went.

* * *

P: There is the sensation of something pressing on my heart. No, a constriction in my heart. I have a strong sense of knowing her, which I surmise is because of the similarities in our character *(Pause)* There is a strong sense of ... her ... what's coming across is a sense of urgency. Is she the one with the problems with the eyes because my eyes are in fact very sore?

J: Not especially, I don't think.

P: It doesn't seem to be in the sense of ... sense of fear ... as far as I can see, it's just simply a sense of urgency ... *(pause)* this is something she was aware of. *(pause)* She wasn't very tall, either was she? The shadow is at the back of her. There is this feeling of being pulled down and to the left, but I don't think she was found lying on her left hand-side, it's being pulled down. It doesn't necessarily feel ... *(pause)*. It's an energy that she knows. *(Pause, cough)*

F: Any idea why she was murdered?

P: I think she knew something.

F: Any idea what she knew?

P: She seems to be one of those people who knew everything, if you know what I mean. She kept her ear to the ground.

F: Was she a gossip?

P: Not as such. I don't feel that she was terribly - she was good fun - and because she was good fun people told her things, but I don't necessarily think she was a gossip.

F: What's the story behind her shawl? *(A shawl is said to have been found by Catharine's body - see page 146.)*

P: She says it had been given to her.

F: Who by?

P: It had been given to her previously.

F: Did it have any special significance for her, or was it just a nice thing to have?

P: It was hers.

F: Was it new when it came to her?

P: I don't think so, doesn't feel new as 'new', it wasn't well worn. I'm not having much success with her ... it's very closed now ... but my jaw hurts ... my jaw here ... he stands over her.

F: Is she lying on the ground or standing?

P: She's on the ground. Don't know how he does this but it's to do with the left side. Was she found lying on her back, or was she turned round?

F: Not sure.

P: He seems to come ... he goes off ...

F: Behind her ...

P: Behind her ....

J: She was seriously mutilated, more than the others.

F: Not as much as Mary Kelly.

P: It was her kidney that was taken, so he would have had to have had her on her stomach to begin with, presumably...

F: Sorry?

P: On her left-hand side.

F: She was the one who had been arrested and then been released.

P: That's right, she was released, and she was in a hurry to go somewhere ... I think she was going to meet him ... whoever he was.

F: She was the one who carried a lot of stuff with her.

P: She carried all her little bags and things like that, didn't she?

F: Is there any significance to the cigarette case? *(Fiona was referring to the possibility that the case may have belonged to the murderer.)*

P: I have to be careful of what I've thought ... what has been thought ... what I've thought and what isn't ... if I'm looking at it from her point of view there doesn't seem to be any particular significance in it.

F: So it was actually her cigarette case?

P: Part of the things she carried ...

F: Right, there wasn't any ... it wasn't something she'd picked up recently, she'd had it for some time?

P: The thing was with quite a lot of her stuff, it would come and go.

F: Right.

P: I still have a problem with her prostitution ...

J: What kind of a problem?

P: ... because I don't think she was.

F: There isn't any direct evidence that she prostituted herself.

P: I still have problems with it: she doesn't feel as though she particularly uses prostitution.

F: Neither her sister nor the chap at the lodging house nor John Kelly, her partner, say that they knew she prostituted herself, though they could have been denying that for their own reasons. There's no proof anywhere that she was a prostitute. She'd only ever been arrested for drunk and disorderly, she'd not been arrested for soliciting.

P: Prostitution ... and this is very much the way that I feel with her, which would mean she wasn't meeting a client, she has to have been meeting somebody.

F: The person that she was meeting - did she think they were the murderer - and was she attempting to blackmail them in some way, because she was the one who claimed she'd come back from 'hopping' in Kent to get the reward?

P: But she'd also come back from Kent absolutely destitute.

F: The chap that you say she was going to meet, was he that person?

P: I can't say that he was, quote, 'the murderer'.

F: Was he something to do with it?

P: He ... it's this information thing again.

F: Who do you think she was going to meet?

P: Stop whispering and say out loud ... because yes, I think it is now ... I think it's ... whoever he was.

F: So she was going to meet somebody. Was this person going to give her information, or was she going to give him information?

P: It wasn't just information - she knew that it was dangerous.

F: Was it the danger that she found attractive?

P: Yes.

F: Did the chap she meet - was he the one who killed her?

P: I would have thought so ... I can't get a fix on it. I don't know whether it's because I'm blocking. ... I can't get a feeling of her murderer. Except as a rather stocky individual. I don't even recognize it as a vibration ... which is confusing. I can't get a sense of this at all, it's like working through treacle. She's standing there, and then she isn't.

F: Standing where?

P: She's standing watching, and then she isn't, she's on the ground, she's been pulled down onto the ground. The mutilations weren't sexual. The reason she had everything with her was because she never knew where she was going to land up. She didn't know where she was going to land up because of the 'hopping' and what have you.

F: Was she happy with that, or did she actually want a settled environment in which to live?

P: She had the ability to do whatever was necessary. She settled to whatever went on, she got on with it, she made the best of it, she did what was there ...

F: How did she end up in the East End?

P: That was through drink. She sort of 'gravitated' there. *(Pause)* That was what she did after ... being found ... found space where you could.

F: Where you could live?

P: Yes. You do get the sense with her that she actually knew something.

F: What sense do you get of her murderer? What was he like?

P: *(Pause)* It's a strong dark energy. *(Pause)* Can't get much sense of him at all ... he's speeded up ...

F: Who speeded up?

P: The murderer *(Pam discomforted)*

F: What do you mean 'speeded up'?

P: He doesn't work at normal speed. I think I'm going to have to come out of this because I'm not getting anything. I'm just playing around on the periphery.

(There was a strong sensation as though the 'records' themselves were being speeded up almost too fast to be able to get hold of what was going on. Pam felt she had not properly locked onto either Catharine, her attacker or the situation itself.)

P: I can't get hold of either of them. I can't actually get into it. Let me try coming out and going back in again.

(Conditions became very uncomfortable for Pam and contact was not re-established.)

ELIZABETH STRIDE - 29 JULY 1997

Present: Pam, Fiona, James

This session gives a clear indication of Elizabeth's feelings around the time of her murder. She seems to have experienced extreme emotions which possibly made her careless in what she was doing. This is the first session in which the mystery figure identified as 'The Catcher' makes an appearance. The feeling was that this person was known and tolerated in the East End.

There was throughout a sense of this session being different from the others in some way, and it was difficult to decide whether it was Elizabeth who was different from the other girls, or whether it was simply because the circumstances were different. In some ways Elizabeth seemed to be much more her own person than the other women, and, I felt, well able to protect herself under normal circumstances.

The session left me with a sense of inevitability, of having taken a risk, and it not working out properly. After the session I found myself feeling very let down, and could not decide whether the feeling belonged to Elizabeth or to me. I finally decided that it was more her feeling than mine, and felt that we really ought to spend more time with her. At the same time there was a strong sense of what can best be described as surprise that this was all that life contained. It was a very strange feeling.

* * *

P: Don't get any sense of her at the moment; seem to be within the district, within the area. That's interesting, whereas I felt sick last time, this time I'm angry. I think her over-riding feeling must have been one of anger. *(Long pause)*

I don't like the feeling I've got. I'm much more in touch with her now, there's actually a sense of desperation in her. *(Pause)* I'm picking her up earlier than the actual time of the ... *(Long pause - a plane flies over)*

F: Maybe that's to bring you back to the 20th century! It doesn't appear to be working, does it?

P: Yes, it does. I'm just watching at the moment. The feeling is she was going to meet someone special. She wasn't just trawling, if you know what I mean, not initially. She was actually going to meet somebody special. She was very angry. The feeling is that she was careless. I do not get the feeling that she knew who her murderer was, and what's more it doesn't feel the same sort of feeling as with Catharine Eddowes.

F: A different person?

P: Yes, I think it was. You'd have to compare the heights of the women, but the one who has come up behind her is taller and she was quite tall. He feels taller than her. She looked up at him that way, from the left, which is odd because that would make it quite difficult to get in there, and yet he tended to pull her round, round and down. It's that that has been making my neck and leg hurt. I don't know whether it's her, but it's certainly the feeling of being pulled. *(Pause)* She had a curiosity the others didn't have.

(Elizabeth's chart confirms this curiosity, see page 188. When using this kind of contact the medium will often pick up apparently inconsequential information. This type of statement is fairly typical of such information and has been included for the purposes of later cross-referencing.)

F: What for?

P: Everything in general.

F: Why was she doing what she was doing?

P: Because she'd always done it ... but *she* only did it when she got drunk.

F: Even though she'd always done it?

P: Yes. She'd always done it, it didn't bother her to do it, she didn't need to do it.

F: She did it for extras, as opposed to necessities?

P: Yes, and she only did it when she got drunk anyway. *(Long pause)* The bloke who stands behind her has a hat on.

F: What type of hat?

P: More a hat than a cap.

F: What's it made out of? Felt?

P: It's not a felt cap.

F: Has it got a wide rim?

P: The daft thing is that I would have said it was more of a top hat; this is crazy.

F: Don't dismiss things, just say whatever's there.

P: He seems taller because of his hat; it makes him more imposing. It's not a tall top hat - were they called stove-pipes? Not a bowler. It doesn't have a particularly wide brim but it does make him imposing; he seems to be thinner, he seems to be thinner than the other.

F: Does he have a moustache?

P: Yes, but it's a cultivated one, rather than a grown one.

F: Is it one that's curly at the end?

P: It's much trimmer than the archetypal Victorian moustache.

F: Much more looked after as opposed to just not shaving? What colour is it?

P: There's a feeling that it's dark. Let's see if we can get hold of him.

J: Does he have eyelashes?

P: Eyelashes or eyebrows?

J: Eyelashes.

P: His eyes are very funny, very weird.

F: Are they very light?

P: That's probably what it is: his eyes are not very good.

F: You mean he had poor eyesight? Was that because of his occupation or just bad eyesight?

P: Bad eyesight. I think he'd had an accident with his eyes. They sting. If this truly is Jack the Ripper, he doesn't feel terribly evil.

F: Is he not a different man to the one who did the others? Is the one who did Elizabeth Stride the Ripper, or is the one who did Catharine Eddowes the Ripper, if they are different men?

P: They feel very different, in height, in appearance, one's slimmer, the other's stocky.

F: What sort of age?

P: Catharine Eddowes' was younger, bit difficult to tell, early thirties. The other one feels older, early forties I would say.

F: Is it the same man that killed Mary Kelly?

P: No *(emphatically. Pam simply accepted this information at the time).*

F: Did they operate together or were they completely separate?

P: No, they were separate. Stride's is much more troubled, but even then I don't know whether he knows what he's doing. The fellow I can see behind her is much more troubled. I've got the feeling that would be too convenient. What I don't understand with this is that Elizabeth Stride seems to be leading him on. If I go back, she actually seems to be leading him on.

F: Is that why he did what he did?

P: No, it's because she got angry.

F: What was so different about him that made her angry?

P: Because he wouldn't co-operate

F: Wouldn't co-operate in what respect?

P: She wanted money, she wanted money for sex.

F: Well, she was a prostitute.

P: Yes, but he didn't, this one didn't, he wasn't interested in sex.

F: Did they know each other?

P: I can't clarify that. When I first felt it, it felt as if she knew him, but now I'm not sure. He was looking for something.

F: Something or somebody?

P: Something. *(Long pause)* Why did she take him there?

F: Where did she take him?

P: She took him in where it was dark.

F: That was quite common practice.

P: She knew that was dangerous, she knew that was ... I don't know, this is very jumbled. It feels as though she would have felt safe with him, which would lead one to suppose that she knew him, but she wouldn't have known him like this.

F: Like what?

J: It could be a policeman.

P: I don't understand; she's acting in a way she wouldn't normally do.

F: Was she acting as a decoy?

P: She knew she was taking a risk.

F: Was this man a policeman?

P: Doesn't feel like it. He has authority but he's not a policeman.

F: Did he have authority over her or over society in general?

P: He had status. He had status among the women.

F: Was he the one known as 'Leather Apron'?

P: No. He's too well dressed for that.

F: Was he their pimp?

P: Not a pimp. I think he's a minder.

F: Was he a religious figure?

P: Catcher.

F: A what?

P: Catcher.

F: Catcher of what?

P: I asked for what he was called and they said 'The Catcher'.

F: Was that just what they called him or what he was?

P: That's what he did, 'The Catcher'. I'm not sure whether he's a ... I don't think he's a policeman.

F: Was he from the vigilante groups?

P: She tends to work alone anyway.

(Pam was showing some discomfort on the left side of her neck. Remembering that Elizabeth's scarf had been

pulled tight, she was attempting to sort out her impressions.)

F: What's wrong with your neck?

P: I don't know whether it's the way I'm lying or what I am feeling. *(Long pause)*

F: Did 'The Catcher' feel it was his duty to rid the streets of prostitutes?

P: I suppose you could call it an early pimp.

F: Call it a what?

P: An early pimp, because she wasn't working for him, she wasn't working with him.

F: He wanted money from her and wasn't overly bothered how he got it?

P: No, it wasn't money. The clearest I can get is that he was known.

F: By whom?

P: He was known by anyone.

F: Is it the same man you referred to in a previous session?

P: I don't remember. I only know he is different. ... this feels much like a set-up. He's not the East End type. I find this very difficult because her impressions are very jumbled. If I shift to him, he's just cold, do you know what I mean? ... I can't get hold of him. Try and sort out these impressions. She doesn't seem to be particularly concerned - she knows it's dangerous. She's out for a good time. She doesn't care, she doesn't much care how she gets it. I get this feeling of anger with her. I can't make up my mind whether at herself or with him. *(Long pause)* He pulled her round from the back, from the left side. She was waiting for someone, she was either waiting for him or for someone. She looks up at him.

F: Are you sure it was Elizabeth Stride?

P: Yes. Then he actually slashes at her. He doesn't cut her, he slashes. Then I can't hold it together.

F: Maybe that's enough for today.

(Long pause)

(Pam experiences a shift of consciousness, normally an indication that she is losing contact. However, because she is still receiving impressions from the murder she decides to continue with the session.)

P: He pulled her round and then he stood over her. He pulled her round to the left and then stood over her, and as he's standing he's standing on the right.

F: So he pulled her round to the left and is standing on her right?

P: And that's the last thing that she's conscious of. But she's also aware of what was going on after she died.

J: Was she aware of being interrupted - of any thing, any sound that would interrupt and him going away?

P: That's the feeling that I get, that's why I'm confused. Because he seems to be standing on the left, then he's standing on the right, he's standing over her. He seems to go off in a backwards direction, but I'm conscious of people to the right, down at the bottom.

F: He was disturbed by other people, he was interrupted?

P: But it's a crowd, a number of people, about four or five. I'm going to have to come back and try again to differentiate between her as she was standing there, and her as having actually been murdered. It's a very weird feeling ... I think the slashing wasn't to any particular design.

F: It was random and haphazard?

P: It feels so.

J: He would have had to have been behind her because of the blood.

P: *(With much armwaving, probably more consciously than previously)* Presumably pulling her down that way *(to the left)*, blood would have gone that way *(forward)*, then he pulls her this way *(downwards)* . He then almost rips her that way. But I don't understand how she's aware, unless she's still in her body, unless spirit-wise she was still within her body because she is aware of people over there *(to the right)*, which I wasn't first of all. It's only when I shift and he's here - when he's standing over her then she seems to be conscious of something else over here *(to the front right-hand side)* and he goes off that way *(behind her)* ... I've got a nasty feeling he was still around. ... I think again I'm going to have to leave that and pick this up and continue to do this.

(Long pause)

Very definitely going to have to continue to do this because I have three very different viewpoints. For what it's worth, if I'm up here *(overlooking on the right)* I'm watching what's going on, I can see her, I can feel him - but I can't see him, and I can also sense people over here *(to the right)*. But it's not going to do me any good anyway. Once again I get this feeling in my shoulder *[left]* That is something that has come up with each of them. There's something about the way he treats this shoulder *[left]*. Something to do with that. He must spin them by the left shoulder or something.

* * *

A malfunction with the tape machine occurred at this point and interference was too great to be able to decipher the rest of the question and answer session. We agreed to abandon the session.

The link with Elizabeth had felt very tenuous. I was amazed that she was still consciously aware of sounds and people. I had not realized that it has always been thought that the killer was disturbed in his grisly deed and that Elizabeth may well have still been alive when Diemschutz entered Dutfield's Yard. I felt that the murderer was still in the yard at the time Elizabeth was aware of the other people there. This would have meant that he was risking detection, but presumably would have left the yard when Diemschutz went for help. If the same man did murder Catharine Eddowes, he would have had to move very quickly to be in Mitre Square in time to commit the murder there.

ANNIE CHAPMAN - 5 AUGUST 1997

Present: Pam, Fiona, James

In this session there is a sense initially of being in touch with the real personality of Annie Chapman - a gentle person, light at heart and with a sense of humour, then running the gamut of the various emotions experienced by her as her life fell apart, and finally the resignation as her life drew to a close. It was a very uncomfortable session and in the aftermath - or de-briefing - period I did wonder if we had the right to read the 'records' to the extent we were doing.

I found myself also pondering on the link between Annie and her attacker, and trying to imagine what would have happened if Annie had not simply stood there accepting her fate. Had she fought back, would Jack perhaps have run off? What did he really want? Glimpses of the motivation behind the attacks on the women are discernible. This man was clearly motivated not just by a grudge against women, but also by a grudge against mothers. This line of reasoning had been suggested to me by my own son in jest, and I found myself wondering what sort of a mother Jack's would have been. As happened so often in our investigation, this question had to be shelved till a later date when the danger of our becoming sidetracked from the main purpose would be less of a problem.

Sometimes when working psychically, physical symptoms can manifest in the sitters, and this type of phenomenon was experienced at various times by both Fiona and James. At the beginning of this session James complained of having earache.

* * *

P: I think 'Dark Annie' must have had, at some point or another, quite a sense of humour because this one is a lot lighter than all the others. It's not so dark and gloomy.
J: She was on her way out *[dying]*, by the way.
P: She was?
F: Who, Dark Annie?
J: Lungs.
P: It was lungs. I thought so.
J: And her brain as well.
P: It was tubercular, I think, tubercular encephala ... something or other.
F: Probably syphilis as well.
P: *(Coughs loudly and exhales)* Oh ... You know you said about your ear, James; she also had something wrong with her ears. *(Having difficulty in breathing)* There is such a thing as dying of shortness of breath ... It all feels far too much like hard work.
(Long pause) Can we check what sort of conditions she lived in? - they feel very damp. There is also a big clock that she works not far from. That might be Spitalfields, but I don't know. Correction, I think she did work somewhere near Spitalfields. *(Exhales loudly)* She drank to relieve the pain.
F: Physical pain or mental pain?
P: Physical ... both. Physical partially. You know, one of the things is that all of these women are branded as prostitutes.
F: You don't think they were?
P: She doesn't feel *(coughs)*, she doesn't feel like a prostitute at all ... She did drink, and she was unhappy ... she was very unhappy most of the time.
F: What about?
P: It's an underlying unhappiness the whole time.
J: She wasn't a huge drinker, though, was she?
P: I don't think so, but, as I say, I get the feeling that she drank when it got too much for her. Is she known to have worked the streets?
J: Yes, I think so, but not really full time.
P: Not on a full-time basis, but just as a supplement. Is she the one that used her hands, because my hands are going ... , are tingling.
(It is worth noting that Martha Tabram also had problems with her hands. This session was done several weeks before Martha's.)
F: I don't know. She is the one who had all the problems with her children, things started off very well, but then ...
P: She is the one who ...
F: A couple of her children died and one went to France with a circus.
P: And she lost it, she lost it after that, after her elder daughter died ... I think that was when she started drinking.

F: Yes, that's what they actually thought.

J: She used to do some crocheting.

P: Yes, with her hands. See if you can find out if hatmaking is mentioned, because I've got those hats again. *(Images of hats and bonnets had repeatedly been coming into Pam's mind, even outside the sessions.)*

F: It's just said that she did crocheting, made antimaccasars and sold flowers.

(Pam's feeling is that Annie probably decorated hats.)

P: This is another one I can't get into very well, I'm sort of skating along the top. *(Coughs)* I'm not sure that I particularly want to.

F: She did have tuberculosis and was malnourished.

P: *(Long pause)* I don't think she was particularly drunk when she was attacked. She doesn't give the same feeling, that light-headed feeling ... It's that same feeling on the shoulders, it's made worse by the fact that she can't breathe.

F: She was slightly drunk when she died, not overly drunk?

P: Yes. You know the thing that strikes me about this?

F: What?

P: It's the whole sense of surprise.

F: So far as she was concerned?

P: Yes. I don't even think she saw him. *(Long pause)* You know ... I still think it's very much to do with this man's mother. We need to find out if any of the suspects' mothers were likely to have been prostitutes. *(Coughs)* The only thing I've got on this is that again it's the same feeling as the other two.

F: What's that?

P: That the man feels ... stocky, he's not overly tall. *(Coughs, long pause)* There are two impressions here, first of all there is this sadness I'm talking about but there is also this ... this sense of humour. The best thing ... it's a sort of ... there's a 'Cockney' sense of humour about her.

F: What do you mean?

P: Even though she had problems, there was still the ability to see the funny side of things. Her speech is impaired in some way, it doesn't feel just like drunk slurring: it's something else. It's not putting words together properly. I think that's one of the things that is the element of surprise. *(Long pause. A change of awareness occurs, and a shift of 'levels' in Pam's consciousness.)* Looking at it from their perspective at the moment of murder, the thing that strikes me is that they are all aware of their helplessness. They are aware of what is happening to their bodies. *(Pam at this point is aware of what is happening to Annie and at the same time seems to be assessing the murderer's motives.)* This was almost a sort of ... quick ... quick slash throat all around and disappear. This man has to have known all the back alleys, he has to have known how to disappear ... because he is literally so light-footed. This one almost feels as though it's been done ... for fun is the wrong word, it's just been done to satisfy an urge. If we are looking for motive, then there almost doesn't seem to be one. It's just sort of literally cut them all - cut and run. This is the one that ... this is the one that started it all off in some way. This one was too easy. It was so easy to do. Let's concentrate on Annie's left lung. We also need to look at his ... *(long pause).*

F: We need to look at his what?

P: His lungs and at his brain.

F: His what?

P: His brain ... I don't understand, I don't understand this and I'm not at this point prepared to go deeper. Can you look at whether any of the suspects had any contact with tropical diseases. It feels as though there's something ... this ... you get this dissociation, but it feels as though there's something in my head. This is him, this isn't her. *(Annie was already affected by the disease which would have eventually killed her, but Pam was quite clear that it was the murderer who had something wrong with him.)(Pause)* Was she stabbed in the genitals?

F: She was the one where they thought he had some anatomical knowledge. She was mutilated after she'd been ...

P: After she'd been killed. That's what I meant when I said it was frightening to think that they were all aware of what was being done. The feeling of the cut seems to have gone round there. It feels like one long slash round there. *(Pointing to the abdomen)*

F: Apparently, he extracted her pelvic organs; he extracted her uterus.

P: That's what makes me think of this mother/baby thing. Somebody is trying to take away the ... trying to take away the ability to be a mother.

P: Was she the one whose throat was mutilated, too?

F: Yes.

P: Was actually mutilated?

F: Yes.

P: Cut that way *(from left to right)* and cut that way. It's the shoulder, cut there.

F: Where? On your right-hand side?

P: Yes. One of the problems I have is that there tend to be numbers of impressions coming in. It's very difficult to sort out all of the impressions ... She didn't care ... There's a pain in the jaw. *(Long pause)* I'm going to have to come out of this, I keep stopping breathing. *(Prolonged coughing)* Was she stabbed in the lungs? *(More coughing)*

F: It doesn't say so.

J: I don't think so.

F: She was suffocated ... She was partially suffocated and what actually killed her was loss of blood to the brain when her throat was cut.

P: Something with her left jaw as well.

J: They thought that she might have been held by the jaw when having her throat cut.

P: That's exactly what it feels like. That's what I was trying to get, but when I do that I stop breathing, so I think I'm going to come back out of it. I'll try again if we can. I can't get past the stopping breathing.

F: That's probably no bad thing really *(humorously)*.

P: I'd like to get through that. *(Coughing)* I still think it's the same man.

F: But you thought one of them was by a different man.

P: No, that's Stride. Stride was done differently. *(Coughing)*

F: Her throat had been cut but while she was lying on her back. They think that he grabbed her by the chin.

(Pam is obviously experiencing considerable discomfort.)

P: I still can't properly get hold of him. He doesn't seem as fierce as he did last time. It makes me wonder why we didn't do it chronologically.

F: Because you didn't want to.

P: There is hate.

F: On her part or his part?

P: His.

J: Hate of what?

P: Women, prostitutes, mothers, *(pause)* people, not achieving. Not being able to ... *(surprised)*

F: Not being able to what?

P: Not being able to have sex, not being able to successfully have sex.

F: So he was impotent?

P: He was impotent, blaming his mother ... that's what his motive was.

F: What? What was his motive?

P: Having sex with his mother and not being able to.

F: He'd had sex with his mother or wanted to have sex with his mother?

P: No, he wanted to have sex with his mother - hence the older prostitutes. Then, murdering them so easily ... That's too clever, that's too subtle.

F: Don't dismiss it.

P: He definitely had problems with his mother ... He chose older women because they would have had children ... and then he could make it that they could no longer be mothers.

109

F: But he killed them then mutilated them, not the other way round.

P: Yes, precisely. He killed them because it was like killing his own mother, but then he mutilated them because that finished them off as women.

F: Did he kill his own mother?

P: I don't think so. His mother ... no, no, he didn't kill his own mother.

F: Did he want to?

P: Yes.

F: What stopped him?

P: She wasn't there.

F: Had she left him?

P: *(Pause)* He won't let me see that. Yes, she left him, but he won't see what it did. He won't let me see what it did. Literally, it left him impotent.

F: Did his mother die or did she just leave him?

P: No, she just left.

F: Abandoned him?

P: Well, there's a sense of abandonment ... There's a strong control element in him too.

F: In him?

P: Yes.

F: He needed to control or be controlled?

P: He needed to control ... he needed to control what was happening to him. He needed set routines, he needed to know what he was doing. Hence the dissociation. What a mess ... She made it easy for him.

F: Who, his mother?

P: No.

F: Annie?

P: Yes.

F: That's why he went and did more, because she was so easy?

P: She just sort of ... stood there.

F: She let him kill her?

P: Absolutely.

(Pam becomes very upset and very emotional)

F: I think we'd better come out of this now.

MARY ANN (POLLY) NICHOLS - 19 AUGUST 1997

Present: Pam, Fiona, James

During a conversation prior to the session, I had already begun to experience a shift of consciousness without deliberately making a link with Polly Ann. Although we had intended to link with her there was no positive identification until later. In some conditions this can sometimes happen and the medium can take on the physical feeling of the person with whom she is making contact in order to facilitate identification. This seems to be what happened in this case.

This session revealed a good deal about the personality of the murderer. In many ways it was strange to feel somewhat removed from the whole situation, and during the period immediately after this session, there was quite a high degree of disorientation. It was not dissociation, but a sense of dislocation, of not being in the right place. In this state there is a need to be very peaceful, and all of the senses are heightened considerably. The strongest feeling - which I continued to experience even when fully conscious - was the sense of pressure on the neck. This again would lead me to believe that perhaps the murderer had some knowledge of neural pathways or perhaps of ways to paralyse by using the pressure points in the body.

* * *

P: My immediate impression is of low energy. I can't get any sort of feeling of energy with her. *(Pause)* The second thing I get is the most excruciating backache ... The whole of one side again has gone numb.

F: The left or the right side?

P: Left side. *(Pause)* A heavy weight on the left shoulder, feels as though I'm being pulled down that way *[to the left]* .. Can't breathe properly ... I think this one was strangled. *(Long pause)* It feels again as though my head is actually being pushed round that way, again to the left. My head's actually being pushed round.

F: Is it like your neck is being broken?

P: The first thing was it felt like strangulation. It felt as though I was being strangled and I couldn't breathe. Then it feels as though the head's literally being forced apart, forced down and that way.

F: Down and to the left?

P: Yes. But I don't know whether I'm with her. I don't get any sense of her.

F: Who do you think you might be with? *(Such a question can often help to stabilize the energies and make a more successful contact possible.)*

P: I don't know, that's what's bothering me because I asked for her ... She was very drunk whoever this one was. It's the weirdest feeling. I can't keep my head on my body ... Ugh ... The person that's standing there *(pointing)*.

F: In front of you, to the right?

P: Yes, I don't understand the feeling that I'm getting, because it feels as though I'm being pushed down to the left, but he is standing there *(pointing)*.

F: In front of you?

P: And he feels very much the same as it felt with Catharine Eddowes, but not the same as Elizabeth Stride. It just isn't.

F: Is it a different man with Elizabeth Stride?

P: It's a different man altogether than Elizabeth Stride. Let me stick with this one ... Why does he mutilate after death? What the hell is he after? ... There's anger.

F: From him?

P: Yeah.

F: Do we know who he's with at the moment?

P: Well, with this one it's just a body.

F: Do you have any idea who this one is?

P: *(Pause)* No, because I'm not with her.

F: Are you with him?

P: Yeah.

F: Do you know who he is?

P: I don't know who he is but he's totally clinical. I don't mean by that he's medical.

F: He's dissociated from what he's doing?

P: Totally, totally dissociated. I don't even know if he knows what he's doing ... Oh shit *(Pam's*

111

neck giving her pain) ... Although it was taken as being a certain modus operandi, each one is in actual fact different. The original act is different. Must look at the strangulation, the bruising and so on. I think this is duality, because I've got her on my neck.

F: Who are you with?

P: I think it is Polly Ann ... This fellow doesn't feel very tall, whereas Elizabeth Stride's was sort of thin and gaunt.

F: And the one who did her was taller than she was?

P: Yes.

F: So this is a different man?

P: This is a different man. This still feels much more like the Catharine Eddowes one.

F: Were they working in conjunction, or were they two completely separate people who didn't have anything to do with one another?

P: No, they were the same person.

F: It was the same person who did it to all of them, or they knew each other?

P: I don't know. The same person who did it to Polly Ann as did it to Catharine.

F: But a different one to Elizabeth?

P: A different one to Elizabeth.

F: Did the person who attacked Elizabeth know the one who attacked Polly Ann?

P: Don't know.

F: Did Polly know 'The Catcher'?

P: I don't know. It's a known feeling but I don't know whether it's just a type. I'm going to try and get hold of *him* ... Education is the wrong word for it, but this man knows what he's doing. I would have thought there was a degree of schizophrenia in this because he's not even 'in' his surroundings.

F: Do you think it's purely that he's been drinking or ...?

P: It's not drink, I would recognize that vibration. It's closer to mania.

F: Does he know how to handle a knife properly?

P: Well, this is almost where the dissociation comes in. Because if he's got a knife in his hand, he dissociates.

F: It's just a job?

P: Yes.

(At this point Pam shows some discomfort, and begins scratching her arm.)

F: What's wrong with your skin?

P: It's crawling. *(Pause)* I can't get beyond this, his ... out of it thing, his dissociation. I can't get a feeling of him.

F: Does he put himself into trance in order to do it?

P: I think trance is the wrong word, but it's an altered state of consciousness.

F: Do you think it's the psychic man, Robert Lees?

P: No. *(Long pause)* This man puts himself ... 'out of it' when he can't handle his own anger. When he gets so angry that he can't handle himself.

F: What makes him angry?

P: Fear.

F: Is he afraid of him, or is he afraid of others?

P: He's afraid of people.

F: Why is he afraid of them?

P: *(Pause)* He's afraid of what ... they can do to him, but he's also afraid of what he can do to them.

F: Why is he afraid of what they can do to him? Has he been in hospital?

P: They take away his control.

F: Control over himself?

P: Yes ... You know the phrase 'being beside yourself'? That is the closest I can come to.

F: So is it almost like an out-of-body experience with him, watching this other person doing these deeds?

P: Yes. It's totally distinct ... It's so cold, it's not even cruel.

F: He's gone past that point?

P: Yes.

F: Does he know who he is?

P: I almost don't get that. What I'm seeing is a record, I'm not actually even linking with him. I'm not linking with her - I'm linking with them as they were. *(Long pause)* Let's check. Were there potentially people around? *(Pam seems to be asking herself the question.)*

F: Around where?

P: Where she was murdered.

F: Who, Polly Ann?

P: Yes. I get the sound of an engine in the environment. *(Pause)* I'm going to have to come back.

(At this point the feeling of there being two very distinct aspects to the possible murderer was very strong. From Pam's point of view the lack of mental connection in him was worrying enough to make her want to break the link.)

P: Something to do with being a mother. It's something to do with his mother, but also being a mother. *(Long pause)* He worked so quickly. *(Pause)* He doesn't feel old.

F: How old do you think he is?

P: I would have thought early thirties. I think we can discount Gull, at least on this one. He's too young for that.

F: Do you think it's Barnett?

P: I don't know.

F: Do you think it's Druitt?

P: No, it's not Druitt, I think Stride is much more likely to be Druitt ... This man feels much more chunky, solid. This one feels much more pre-meditated than the Eddowes one. *(Pam's awareness of Druitt was as a result of having made links with him through his astrological chart.)*

F: In that having done it once, it was easier to do it again?

P: It's almost as though with Eddowes he just did it, but this one he actually went out to do it.

F: He actually planned to do it?

P: *(Pause)* There is a very weird sound ... it's a very, very weird high-pitched whine. *(Pause)* Ow!

F: What?

P: Is she the one whose vertebrae were severed because my neck has just gone very peculiar again ... It's the twisting of the head that does it ... forcing down, forcing to the left, then it's almost a snapping of the neck.

F: Like you would with a chicken?

P: I was just going to say - almost like killing a chicken. It's cut, slash and jerk back. Again, it's just simply so clinical.

(Pam's perception obviously changes at this point and she re-links with Polly. This was a feature of this particular session, since it seemed as though there was little control over who she was linking with at any one time.)

J: Do you know if Polly is the first victim of this man?

P: I don't think so ... I don't think so because, as I say, it feels so clinical. I think if it had been the first there would have been fear. It's almost as though he knows he can do it. Again, I get that weird thing that he is here *(pointing)*.

F: Behind you?

P: Not so much behind me, but standing to my right. Let me see if I can get ... pushes down to the left, catches on the right, snaps and then moves down there *(pointing)*.

F: He moves down where, to the right in front?

P: Yes, but this is just it, it's such a quick movement ... I don't know where the blood went with Polly Ann, I can't find it. If she had still been alive, would she have bled?

F: Yes. Once you are dead, the heart stops beating, so it's not pumping the blood round. You would bleed much more if still alive.

P: That's what I mean. I am not overly conscious of blood. Again, it's the mutilation after. I wonder was she pregnant? She certainly had back-ache ... I think I'm going to have to come out of this.

F: Right.

P: There is a question that needs to be asked. I don't know what it is because I can't hold her vibration. A question I need answering is - Had she had lots of children? *(Long pause)* She is still trying to tell me something about her neck. This is different to the feeling with Stride. It's something to do with her neck - the way he dealt with her neck. *(Pause)* She was very drunk.

F: Was she aware of what was going on?

P: Woozy - I don't think particularly so.

* * *

Pam takes some time to reorientate herself after this session, and there is a good deal of external noise. What follows is part of a discussion that took place once the contact session had ended.

P: What do we know about her?

J: The most important thing is that she's supposed to be the first victim of the Ripper. But if you're saying you felt that this guy had killed before?

F: Or you said you thought he'd done Catharine Eddowes.

J: We need to think about that.

P: If he had done Martha Tabram?

J: She had had a number of children. Five, I think.

P: Had she?

F: Martha Tabram? Had she had children?

J: I don't know about her *(Polly)*.

P: What about the blood? What were her mutilations? *(Referring to Polly.)*

J: Disembowelled.

P: Was her uterus cut out?

J: No, I don't think so. I think her spinal cord was cut.

P: So her spinal cord was cut? ... No wonder, no wonder the lack of sensation down one side.

J: She did drink much more than the others.

P: She was completely drunk. What about this ... how was she found?

F: Dead!

P: Was there a lot of blood around when she was found?

J: No, because the people who found her, I think, had said 'There's a girl here who's either asleep or dead'. So presumably if they thought her asleep there wasn't much blood.

P: Because there is not the feeling of there being a whole lot of blood.

J: I don't think there was.

P: Was she strangled?

J: No, she had her throat cut. I don't think she was strangled. They said that her dress was all pushed up, and then this guy tried to make it look decent.

P: That's exactly the feeling that you get. Wasn't it her that they didn't realize until they got to the mortuary that she had been disembowelled?

J: That's right.

P: Well, certainly ... I mean, the feeling is of actually having your neck snapped. Were there signs of strangulation because it's here ... that would identify for me more than anything that it's the same person, because it's pressing down on here, on that ... that presumably is the carotid artery. I think there is actually pressing into the collar bone. It's almost pulling her down and round and then it's just totally clinical. That feeling is really weird, it doesn't feel as though it's particularly a surgeon, but he does have ... he is skilled with the knife, because he's totally clinical when he's doing it. No, clinical is the wrong word - cold.

MARTHA TABRAM - 30 SEPTEMBER 1997

Present: Pam, Fiona, James, Andrew

What we were inclined to call the 'group of three' (Pamela, Fiona and James) had intended to meet several times previously in order to contact Martha Tabram, and for various reasons had been unable to do so. Many readers will consider this to be sheer coincidence, while others will recognize the principle of synchronicity - something needs to happen in the right place at the right time for the right reasons. On the day that the session finally took place, a fourth person, Pamela's son, Andrew, was present, purely coincidentally in that he just 'happened to be there'. The technique used when a medium makes a contact with a different dimension simply takes account of the different energies present, and accommodates them.

This session was both the most surprising and the most worrying to date, because it totally cut across the knowledge we were building up.

* * *

P: This woman seems to be fairly within her own skin. She ... she's another one who does what she has to do, so to speak. Was she known to be a prostitute or was she an occasional prostitute?

F: She wasn't known to be, she wasn't registered or anything like that.

P: Because I don't get the feeling that there was the same need with her, the same drive.

A: Did she have money?

P: No, she didn't have money, but she had enough.

A: Did she like sex then?

P: No, it wasn't that.

A: Why was she a prostitute?

P: *(Pause)* I don't know that she was, I can't get that feeling ... of actually going out for men.

A: Not going for men, or not going out for men for money?

P: Both, she feels more stable than the others. Have I got the right person?

F: Did she actually drink?

P: I don't get the same sense of inebriation either.

(It is perhaps worth recording here that at this point Pam felt that Martha's reasons for drinking were different from those of the other victims, and that she 'held' her drink in a different way. In fact, Martha was a hardened drinker, and would probably not have reacted to drink in the same way as the others.)

A: Is she married, did she have any children?

P: Wait a minute, wait a minute. *(Pause)* I get this same feeling that she did what she had to do. She liked a drink, but I don't think she was an alcoholic in the same way.

A: Was her partner violent or an alcoholic? ... Is that why she needed the money?

P: Can't feel, can't get behind her ... She had children.

A: How many?

P: I can feel three, but I think there was a miscarriage or termination, or something.

A: Did she ever have any long-term partners in her life at all?

P: Yes.

A: Did she love them or just use them, or did they use her? What was her background, was she an orphan or from a poor background?

P: She was an East End girl. I can't move her at this stage away from the East End. It's almost as though she doesn't want to come away from the East End.

A: Is she still there now?

P: No. Where was she born? She was born in the East End, wasn't she?

F: She was born in London Road, Southwark.

P: Was she a widow?

F: No.

P: I can't seem to find her.

F: She split from her husband about six years after they were married. He gave her money until she took up with another man.

A: Were they divorced?

P: No, they didn't divorce in that time anyway.

F: Did she go with soldiers?

P: She had a good time.

F: She was a good time girl?

P: She ... enjoyed good company. She was fairly commercial in that she expected to pay for it.

F: She expected to pay?

P: She expected to pay for it. That's an interesting twist.

A: Was she a sadist?

P: No.

F: She expected to pay for what?

P: She had a good time and then she paid for it as it were. Paid for it with sex.

A: So she'd get drunk, have a good time and then ...

P: I don't think we need to make assumptions. She used alcohol more than alcohol used her.

J: Maybe you've got Emma Smith [*thought at one time to be a victim of the Ripper*] coming over.

P: This is what I'm wondering, because I'm getting two reference points.

F: What points are you getting?

P: It doesn't feel like Martha Tabram felt the first time around, the first session we did *(referring to the session held on 8 July)*. It doesn't feel like her. Let me see if I can clear that. It doesn't feel like Martha Tabram because she's not big.

F: Who do you think it is?

P: She's slim, she's dark-haired.

F: How old is she?

P: I would have thought she was early thirties.

F: Do you think you have got Mary Kelly again?

P: No, it doesn't feel like her. Let me try and clarify what we are getting because ...

(Long pause. At this point Pam is made aware of something happening within a different time frame to the one she is in. Experience teaches the necessity of going with such a change, although as can be seen it does not prevent her from questioning the information she is getting. This stage of awareness is one she calls light control, which is where she observes what is going on, but does not take on the personality of the communicating spirit.)

P: I've gone right back.

F: Where to?

P: Feels like the 1860s *(questioningly)*.

A: Was she abused as a child?

P: This one that I've got wasn't. Wait a minute... Oh, this is great. *(Disbelief)* ... It feels as though I'm in a hospital. I'm not a patient.

A: Are you a visitor?

P: No, I'm working there.

F: What are you working there as?

P: Skivvy ... What have I got hold of?

F: Have you got hold of a woman or a man.

P: It's a woman.

A: Is she giving birth?

116

P: No, she's working at the hospital.

F: Is it one of the victims?

P: No. You know what I'm doing? I know what's happened. I haven't got Martha Tabram at all.

F: Who have you got?

(At this point Pam rubs her hands, scratching them vigorously.) Have you got itchy hands?

F: Who've we got?

P: I think ... I think we've got Guy's *[hospital]*.

F: Do you think we've got Gull?

P: No, we haven't got him yet. We're just around him.

F: OK. Why have we gone back that far?

P: Just being difficult. *(Laughter)*

A: Does Martha know who the killer is?

P: No, because it's not Martha. I'll need to clear what I'm doing, why I'm in the hospital. Who is the woman?

J: It's not Joseph Barnett's mother, is it, working in the hospital?

P: I can't be sure. Let's see if we can get hold of ... I don't like not being able to identify.

F: Do you think that you've been brought to the hospital ... whoever you are with is just an entry into the hospital. They are not particularly relevant?

P: No, that's what I asked, and they seem to be relevant to this.

A: Is it a male or female? Could it be a doctor?

P: Female.

A: Is it a midwife? ... *(Pam rubs her hands again.)* Are you washing your hands now?

P: No, my hands hurt.

F: Do they hurt or are they itchy?

P: Both. *(Pam holds her ribcage.)*

F: Do your ribs hurt as well?

P: What am I doing in the 1860s?

F: Just go with it, don't try and analyse it

P: *(Pause)* It's got something to do with childbirth, but I'm not pregnant.

F: Is it anyone we've come across before?

(Long pause. Pam begins to experience considerable physical and mental discomfort. This is not uncommon; when a proper link is established the information being given is experienced by the medium. She sees and feels things through the personality of her communicator, which enables her to give an accurate picture of what happened to that entity.)

F: Why is your breathing changing?

P: I can see all sorts of weird and wonderful things.

F: What can you see? Describe what you can see.

P: No, this is in whoever the woman's head is.

F: Is it one of the victims?

P: No.

A: Is she taking laudanum?

P: This is a hospital for the insane.

F: Are you with Druitt's mother?

P: No, I don't think it is Druitt's mother, because I've already asked her that. As I say, it's too far back. *(Pause)* I know what this is, it's post-natal depression.

F: Who are you with?

P: *(Pause)* I think I am with Martha Tabram, but Martha Tabram as she was.

F: Is that how she came to be living in the East End in the state she was?

P: No, that's how she came to keep herself to herself. Because she ... I'm very confused on this one.

J: Do you think that you are being led somewhere in order ... so we would have to try and discover something for ourselves - something that may not be in any book?

P: Yes I do: that's what's bothering me. I can't get through this post-natal stuff.

F: Are you sure it is post-natal, or is it somebody who has lost a child, a miscarriage?

P: All I can say is that it's post-natal. It's bordering on insanity.

A: Is the person actually insane or is it temporary?

P: It's temporary, but bordering on insanity.

F: Did they come out of it?

P: Bloody well hope so!

A: Did she give birth to the child or not?

P: Yes, she did, because I said I'm not pregnant.

A: What happened to the child?

P: It was taken away.

F: Are you with Martha's mother?

P: No.

A: Can you be specific on the year?

F: Is it before her father died, or is that what's hit her there. Is that when her father died?

P: 1863.

F: Before her father died.

J: Do you think there is a link between the events in the early 1860s and the murders in the late 1880s?

P: Yes *(emphatically)*.

F: Are you sure you're still with Martha? Are you sure that's the link?

P: Yes. I'm not sure what happened to her in 1863 ... Did she have a child or not?

F: No. According to the records she had a child in 1871 and then another one in 1872. She did drink fairly heavily.

A: Did she know her killer?

P: Stay with the time.

A: Did she know her killer from the 1860s?

P: I want to work with this because she's working in the hospital, then she's in the hospital for the insane. I can't be sure that it's Martha Tabram but it's a certain vibration. I can't imagine that she would be let out.

A: Could it be perhaps her sister?

P: No. *(Pam clutches the side of her head and is obviously in some distress.)*

F: What's wrong with your head?

P: If I hold it, it will stay together.

(Long pause)

F: Should we come out of this?

(Long pause)

P: I want to come out of this. *(Long pause)* Martha Tabram did not know her killer. No, I'll put that a different way, she didn't ... I can't get close to her so far as that's concerned, but she knew something that she wasn't supposed to know.

A: Do you think it could have been her child?

P: *(Long pause)* If there was a baby born in 1863, then in 1888 it would have been 25, 26.

F: Was it her baby?

P: Looking at it from here, it doesn't feel like her baby. But whoever that was, it felt more as though Martha Tabram was the hospital worker.

F: Was it anything to do ... with the Prince's illegitimate child? *[Prince Albert Victor - see page 149]*

P: No, it's too far back.

A: Did perhaps she steal a baby?

P: No.

A: So, what's the connection between her and the murderer? You say she didn't know him, but there was a connection. What was that connection?

P: We need to find out when Martha started drinking because she didn't consider herself to be a drinker. So she didn't look at drink as a party-time thing. She would look on drink as blotting something out.

F: By the time she was 26, her marriage had ended, or foundered, because of her heavy drinking. She got married when she was 20, by the time she was 26 that was the end of her marriage - finished.

P: She would have been 26 when?

F: In 1875.

P: That's not fitting.

A: Nor does it fit with being in hospital in 1863 ... It may have with her being a skivvy actually.

F: In 1863 she would have been 14, so she could have had a child or she could have been a skivvy.

A: Did her father give her her child?

P: No.

F: Are you sure it was her child?

P: No, this is just it, I'm not. I can't sort it out.

F: Do you think it might have been a sister?

P: Right from the start I have had at least two things coming in, and it's not schizophrenic ... Have to check whether she worked at Guy's or not. Do you remember you kept saying ... kept 'picking something up'. *(To Fiona)* Who looked after her children?

F: Doesn't say. The only mention of them apart from the fact that they were born, is the years in which they were born.

P: I'm certain I'm back in the hospital ... the skivvy is her.

F: But not the person who has got the depression?

P: I don't know. *(Pause)* I think what I'm going to have to do is come out and get hold of the depression again.

F: OK.

* * *

In the discussion that took place after the session I was fairly certain that the time-frame had been March 1863. We concluded that we were being directed to another avenue of enquiry, and that in order to find answers to the many questions raised we would have to hold another contact session. This we did a few days later.

My main aim before the session was that we should find out what had happened to the baby. There are several instances where happenings came across faster than I could interpret them. Often the sense of the information was difficult to explain because it dealt more with feeling than understanding.

For reasons that will quickly become apparent, we decided to call this session 'Mountford'.

'MOUNTFORD' - 3 OCTOBER 1997

Present: Pam, Fiona, James

P: My stomach is churning like nobody's business. *(Long pause)* First thing I'm conscious of is I am back with my hands again. My hands feel strange. They feel bigger than they should do, and this would lead me to suppose that it was the stuff that she used to clean with which would make her hands feel like this. *(Pause)* My hands are actually burning, they are sore, whereas before they were itchy. They are more sore now ... I seem to be back in the same condition as I was and still the feeling of it being a hospital. Let's see if I can find out where. *(A disturbance outside seems to bring Pam 'back in'.)*

F: Shall we start again?

P: No ... This is somewhere in South London, it's not North London.

F: Do you mean very south, or somewhere just around the middle?

P: I'm not certain - but I think it's in Tooting, that's what's come up. Let's see if I can go along with it. *(Pause)* I keep getting this split location again. *(This is something that happens quite often when working in this way.)* I'm on two edges or with two people I think, this time it's a split location.

F: Do you know the name of the hospital?

P: *(Long pause)* I'm not sure if it's St James or St Johns, or St James and St Johns.

F: You definitely feel that it's Tooting?

P: *(Pause)* If I took a map, an old-style map, I think I would be able to indicate where it was. If you take Guy's as being there, it's sort of down here. *(Pam gesticulates, as though she were looking at a wall map)* We'll do that, try and get hold of what's going on. *(Pause)* This is quite a small establishment but it's got two separate parts. It's got one which is a hospital for the poor and one which is for the insane.

F: Which part are you in?

P: I wasn't; I was over the top of the hospital ... If I bring myself down into it then I'm in the part for the insane.

F: Are you with the same person as before?

P: I've got the same feeling as before, which is very frightened - I'm very frightened because I don't know what's going on. I'm with ... I assume it must be Martha because it's the one with the hands.

F: Do you have any information on the baby?

P: *(Pause)* It's not a baby girl, it's a boy.

F: Do you know who the mother is?

P: *(Long pause)* No, but she shouldn't be here.

F: Because she's not actually insane; it is depression?

P: Yes, but she's also not poor.

F: Was she being hidden away? Were people ashamed of her?

P: We're not supposed to go into her room.

F: Do you mean the hospital staff?

P: Mmm.

F: Do you know why not?

P: She's funny, she's dangerous. *(Pause)* But I don't know why I'm here anyway.

F: Are you there as you or as Martha?

P: No, as Martha. *(Pause)* I don't like it because it smells.

F: What does it smell of?

P: Hospitals! *(Long pause)* She just seemed to be there.

F: Who did?

P: Martha. Let's see if I can cut to the baby. *(Exhales deeply - long pause)* I think there was something wrong with the baby. It's not breathing properly.

F: How old is the baby?

P: It's only just been born ... March the 28th.

F: That's the date the baby was born? ... 1863.

P: Mmm.

F: Have they given him a name?

P: No ... I don't know what the connection is, though.

F: Was the woman hospitalized before or after the birth of the baby?

P: That's what I'm trying to sort out, I think it was after ... I'm not sure about this but I think the baby was premature. It's still not breathing properly. *(Pause)* I don't understand the difference I am getting between the feeling of the mother, where she feels to be quite educated, but I don't know whether she is.

F: Do you know if she was married?

P: I think so.

F: Was the baby her husband's?

P: I don't think so. Her name's Jenny.

F: Jenny?

P: Mmm.

F: Do you know her surname?

P: *(Pause)* The name that comes to mind is 'Mountford'.

F: Mountford? Do you know how old she is?

P: I think about 31, 32. She shouldn't have had a baby anyway.

F: Why shouldn't she have had a baby?

P: Because she wasn't strong enough.

F: Physically or mentally?

P: Both.

F: Why did she go ahead with the baby?

P: She hid it. *(Pam becomes quite distressed.)*

F: She hid the pregnancy?

P: Yes ... I don't know where the baby went, though ... she hid it till it was too late. I think she had a heart condition - but I don't know if that was caused by the baby. Where does Martha come into this and why is it important later? I don't want to follow this up for the minute, I'm going to try and move forward and see if I can come up to 1888. *(Very long pause)* I think the baby was a cretin - what today would be called a thyroid deficiency. My throat has got a huge ... something in it. *[In the 1880s cretinism would have been seen as idiocy. It was not until the mid 20th century that synthetic hormones brought the condition under control, and it is now rarely seen.]*

F: What happened to the baby?

P: It was taken to the other part, but I don't know what happened to it afterwards.

F: Do you know what they called him?

P: *(Pause)* That would be too much of a coincidence.

F: What?

P: I'll have to come back and check that. I think his name was Joe.

F: Joe?

P: Yes ... It was Joseph.

F: What surname did he take, or was he given?

P: I've got 'me' cutting across here ... I don't know, I'll need to come back to that.

F: OK, move on.

P: *(Pause)* I think the connection is that Martha knew something, that in fact drink wouldn't allow her to put them, the facts, together.

F: When did she start drinking?

P: She was about 18.

F: What made her start?

P: She couldn't handle the images.

F: The images from when she was in the hospital?

P: No, just the images that she got.

F: What do you mean by that?

P: In my terms, I'm having to come out of this because I can see her as she is. It's the psychic energies.

F: Is that what she couldn't cope with?

P: But they wouldn't have known what that was.

F: Is that what she had problems with?

P: That's what they thought ... that's what they ... that's the epilepsy bit.

F: That's what they thought was wrong with the other woman?

P: That's what they thought was ... she started ... her hysterical fits.

F: Martha's?

P: Yes. They were actually 'psychic blasts'. They were images breaking through. What I call her 'door' opening - and she started drinking to try and control that ... That's a fairly consistent story, because, of course, she ... when she had the children, she would be even more sensitive. *[It seems as though Martha was not stable enough to cope with what went on in her own head. Pam's own distinct impression is that she was an untrained psychic. If she was in the habit of receiving negative images, and had not been trained to cope with them, she may well have been only able to rationalize them as, in Mary Kelly's words, 'the horrors of drink'. When under the influence of alcohol it would not have been easy for her to differentiate between the various states of awareness that are natural to a psychic.]*

F: When she had her own children?

P: Yes. When she had her own children she would ... of course she would be more sensitive anyway. And then the memories would come back. *(Pause)* She started 'shooting her mouth off'.

F: When she was drunk?

P: Yeah.

F: Is that why she was killed?

P: *(Pause)* There is a link between all of them. They all had certain bits of knowledge, apart from ... apart from Elizabeth Stride.

F: What did they have knowledge about?

P: *(Pause)* See what the connection is between Guy's and Lambeth Workhouse *(Pam appears to be musing to herself). (Pause)* I can't hold with her and an image of her murderer.

F: Where do you want to go? What do you want to look at?

P: Well, I don't get any particular feeling. There's no particular feeling of recognition.

F: Were they all murdered because of something going back to when Martha was in the hospital, when she worked in the hospital?

P: It wasn't just that, it was the whole period.

F: When she was in the hospital, or later ... 1888?

P: It's because the pattern was coming out.

F: What pattern?

P: What happened ... what happened to women. *(Again, Pam felt as though she were viewing two events simultaneously: the earlier period and the bad treatment of women and also the period of the murders when, in theory, the treatment should have been different.)*

F: When? Do you mean the pattern of what happened to women?

P: The pattern of what happened to 'unfortunates'.

F: You mean how they got to be in the situation?

P: No. How they were got rid of anyway. How they were going to be 'cleared'.

J: Why would they need to be cleared? Who would care what these women knew, even if they knew 'things'. Who would care that much?

P: It was something to do with the ... 'clearing' of the East End. *(Pause)* Attention had been brought to the East End by all of the clearance ... the clearance programmes ... the need to do something ... and there were so many secrets hidden in all sorts of places. *(This was difficult to explain, because it felt so intrinsically dark and devious. The closest image to express it is like a mud-spring which brings all sorts of hidden matter to the surface.)*

F: Were the people put in the East End so they would be hidden?

P: No, you just landed up in the East End, but because you landed up in the East End it was ... there were secrets, there were lies.

F: Do you know what it was that all the girls knew?

P: It was to do with the sexual immorality.

F: Of the men or the women?

P: Men.

F: Had they all had the same ... client?

P: No, it was to do with the whole exposure of prostitution.

F: It was a group of people who were concerned as opposed to an individual?

P: Well, the reforms, the need for reform was pushing to ... you could hide and be hidden in the East End and nobody could find you.

F: But with the attention that was being brought on it, the danger was that these people would be found?

P: No, it wasn't the people, it was the secrets.

F: Was it secrets that the people who were killed knew?

P: I think the secrets were obvious, they were obvious ... in the East End.

F: Would they be secret in the East End? Is it something that would shock people nowadays?

P: Not particularly.

J: Have you got any idea what these secrets might be pertaining to?

P: *(Long pause)* It was power, it was money, it was what was being taken away. It was the malpractice. It was the ... malpractice on all levels.

F: Were people being used for some sort of experiment?

P: No. But it was the criminal ... it was criminals ... it was the criminal element in the East End, that in actual fact, it would be exposure of criminal practices ... it was the political stuff ... the 'not doing anything' the ... money that had been ... it was an overall thing much as it was an individual thing.

F: What do you mean an overall thing?

P: The programmes for improvement, the neglect that had actually been going on for years. The building, the rebuilding, the *(pause)* Jack The Ripper gave a focus to the East End which allowed it to be cleaned up - and cleaned up without exposing the secrets that it hid.

J: Surely the Jack the Ripper murders put more focus on the East End than ever?

P: Precisely, it gave it a legitimate excuse to, to ... I've never thought of it in this way. Who was Shaftesbury's opponent? Who opposed Shaftesbury's reforms? What was the ... I don't want to get too far out on this but it was the ... it focused attention on the East End which meant that it had to be cleaned up. *(The sensation of fear was quite strong here, as though nobody - neither the denizens of the East End nor the political leaders - knew exactly what would be revealed and when.)*

F: Was Jack the Ripper working alone, or of his own decision, or had somebody instructed him to do it?

P: No, ultimately he was working alone, it started off ... I don't understand, it seems that each of the women had part of the 'puzzle'.

F: What was the 'puzzle'?

P: The treatment of women.

F: Why was it particularly them that were killed as opposed to five other prostitutes in the East End?

P: *(Pause)* I think it was the arrival of Mary Kelly.

F: Was she the last piece in the jigsaw, did she know something that could have been harmful?

P: I think somehow she fitted it into place.

F: Can you be more specific than just the general problems of the East End? What was hidden, what was being hidden?

P: *(Pause)* The prostitution - it was known.

F: Was something known about the prostitution?

P: It was how women became prostitutes.

F: Were they forced into it?

P: They weren't forced into it. They were forced to do it.

F: What's the difference?

P: It wasn't a case of 'you will be a prostitute'.

F: What was it a case of?

P: It was almost a ghetto thing. It was taking women ... it was taking intelligent women, pushing them as far as they can go. It was manipulation.

J: By?

P: Those in authority.

J: Political authority or 'street' authority.

P: It was more political authority. *(Pause)* The original thing was taking away the femininity.

F: Why should that be taken away?

P: Because they were less than feminine.

F: Was this specifically the victims or were women in general?

P: It became the victims ... Oh, this is too ridiculous *(irritated)*.

F: What is?

P: The women ... they were all strong women, they were all women who ... for want of a better word, needed something else. There is a sense in which they were going to become ring leaders. I don't know that they necessarily knew one another at that stage.

F: What were they going to be the ring leaders of?

P: The movement out of the East End.

F: What relevance does that have to the events in 1863?

P: That was one end of the scale.

F: What was the other end?

P: The degradation. *(Pause)* The boy was deformed and had to be got rid of and I want to follow that up.

F: Do you want to do that today?

P: No. Because I'm getting irritated.

F: OK. Do you want to come out?

P: Yes.

* * *

I spent several sleepless nights trying to sort out my impressions. Again, the questions seemed to be multiplying. If, as is suggested, the woman by the name of Jenny was being concealed in some way, was she being concealed because of her own unstable condition, or because she was pregnant? The baby's name (Joseph) does not necessarily tie him in with any person known to us in this investigation. We have extensively researched the births and deaths registers for evidence of the existence of the baby and the mother - looking under the name Mountford and every variation on it we could think of - but have found no trace of them. We have researched possible establishments for the insane in the Tooting area, and looked at the records at St Thomas' Hospital. After 1861 Guy's Hospital stopped admitting the insane to any of their establishments, though Dr William Gull had had in his charge an establishment in Fulham for twenty insane women.

I was left with the feeling that there was much more behind the story than royal/political involvement or even social cleansing. I became increasingly convinced that we were not looking at an either/or situation, but possibly something which included all of these things. But how did they fit with the Ripper murders?

If it had not been for the support of the team, and for the fact that I had made a commitment, I would have given up at this point. It was just too much to try to find out psychically what went on one hundred and ten years ago, take in the information which so many people had collated over the years, write about what was going on, and try to live a normal life into the bargain. The cumulative effects of the contact sessions were taking their toll. If we continued we would have to be prepared to push the investigation beyond our brief and in order to do that I would have to have sufficient reserves of mental and physical energy.

We decided to let the information that came out of the Tabram and Mountford sessions settle in our consciousness, and to continue with the rest of the investigation.

MARY JANE KELLY - 14 OCTOBER 1997

Present: Pam, Fiona, James

This session was initially intended to make contact with Mary Jane Kelly. However, preparatory research had established that there were three different people known as Joe Barnett, all born around the same time. Before attempting to contact Kelly, we tried to clarify, by dowsing, which of the three Joe Barnetts was Mary Kelly's lover. This turned out to be something of a training session for Fiona and James. Fiona had previous experience of dowsing, James had not. The response of the pendulum is specific to each dowser: in my case, for example, the pendulum will circle clockwise for Yes and swing for No. Both 'students' had to establish what was a negative or a positive response for them.

It is important to note that we first asked for identification of Mary Kelly's Joe Barnett and not whether he murdered her. Only later is the question changed to 'Did Joe Barnett murder Mary Kelly?'

I found this session particularly disturbing because by this time it was becoming increasingly difficult to preserve an open mind and almost inevitably ideas and theories were beginning to present themselves. It also seemed that we were becoming both obsessive and subjective, states of mind which, I feared, might bias the investigation and affect the results.

* * *

P: Having been introduced to the idea that the body in Millers Court might not have been Mary Kelly, we decided to check by dowsing.
F: Yes.
P: OK. By me dowsing: was the body found in Mary Kelly's room actually Mary Kelly? ... The

125

pendulum indicates Yes.

F: Very strongly.

P: Therefore, was the woman seen on the morning after the murder ... was that sighting genuine? Somebody was seen on the morning after the murder, Richardson or whatever her name was ... Was the person who saw Mary Kelly mistaken? ...*(Here, Pam becomes aware of the presence of other entities)* Oh, my God, we've got ghosts! ... No *(in answer to dowsing question)* Was the time given for Mary Kelly's murder accurate?

J: As far as I know.

P: That comes out as Yes, too *(using the pendulum)*. But I do get a No *(intuitively)*.

(This was confusing in that we seemed to be getting two different answers which should have been clarified by supplementary questions.)

J: Wasn't she discovered late in the day?

P: Yes.

J: Well, early in the morning.

P: She wasn't found till after 10 o'clock.

(Mary Kelly was found much later in the day than the other victims, possibly because hers was the only murder committed indoors.)

F: It's gone all cold in here. *(This can be a sign of spirit presence.)*

P: Has it?

F: Yes.

P: What are you picking up?

F: Don't know, ugh.

P: *(Using pendulum)* Was her murderer Joe Barnett? ... That says Yes. I want you to try it, too.

F: James? *(hopefully)*.

P: Both of you.

J: What do you want me to do?

(A somewhat reluctant/ 'blocked'. James tries to establish the way the pendulum is running for him, i.e., the swing for Yes or No. Initially, it fails to do anything.)

P: OK. You may be our control. Let's see if it works with Fiona.

F: Shall I turn the computer off? *(The computer seemed to be making more noise than usual - it is not unusual for electric equipment to be affected when working psychically. Fiona now takes the pendulum and has more success. The pendulum swing is established - backwards and forwards for Yes, and clockwise for No.)*

P: OK, so now you ask the same questions as I did. Was it Mary Kelly's body? *(To Fiona)* Bring your arms down, you're holding it at tension.

F: Was it the woman known as Mary Kelly? ... Yes.

P: Did the woman who thought she saw Mary Kelly really see Mary Kelly?

F: ... No.

P: Is the time ...

F: Hang on ... Hang on ... got to let it stop.

P: Sorry ... is the time ...

F: Hang on ... slow down.

P: Is the time of Mary Kelly's death accurate?

F: ... Yes. It's weird because it goes backward and forwards and then it starts going round - goes from left to right. Right, what was the other one...

P: Did Joe Barnett kill Mary Kelly? Try and blank your mind on this one ...

F: Did Joe Barnett kill Mary Kelly?

P: Does that say No?

F: It's sort of circling ... which is....Yes.

P: Circling is No. Backwards and forwards is Yes, because you're the opposite to me.

F: Well let's ask this question again.

P: Did Joe Barnett kill Mary Kelly?

F: It's going backwards and forwards.

P: Yes.

F: OK, that was it then, wasn't it?

P: Yes, that was all we asked. We have designated the three Joe Barnetts we have found as Joe Barnett 1, Joe Barnett 2 and Joe Barnett 3: Which one is Mary Kelly's Joe Barnett? Is that fair enough?

F: Yes.

P: So, is Mary Kelly's Joe Barnett, Joe 1, Joe 2, or Joe 3?... Joe Barnett 1, which is the one we did last week, which I said to you ...

F: Was the 25th of May *(birthdate)* wasn't it? ...

P: ... We ought to check ... and James can also try on this one, see if it works for him ... if he wants to.

J: Alright, don't mind.

F: Alright, so, I can't remember who is who...

P: ... So the ones we've called Joe 1, 2 and 3...

F: What was the question?

P: Is Mary Kelly's Joe Barnett, Joe 1?

(Fiona repeats the question; pause)

P: All of this is valid, all of this can go in the book.

F: Yes, right, *(repeats question)* ... .it comes up as Yes.

(The same question of Joe 2, and Joe 3 is asked: the answer is No on both counts: James then tries: the pendulum swing is established - different again from that for Fiona and Pam. James has much more success than on his previous attempt - he is 'unblocked' as it were.)

J: Did Joe Barnett 1 murder Mary Kelly? ... It would appear to be Yes.

F: That was very much like mine, a bit uncertain to start with, and then a definite.

(The result, after querying Joe 1, Joe 2, and Joe 3, is that Joe Barnett 1 is the culprit.)

P: So it all comes out as Yes for Joe Barnett 1. Alright, switch off the tape.

The Session Begins:

P: The first thing that immediately happens is that Mary Kelly was seen going into her room: but if people knew Joe Barnett they would have been able to identify him - so, in fact, Joe Barnett wasn't seen entering the establishment. *(Long pause)* I'm in the same situation as I was before but I'm, at this stage, more with Mary Kelly. She doesn't appear to be, at this point, dead. She's much more sleeping. Feels much more of a sleep. Again I get that same feeling of nausea as I got when we went to Millers Court *(on the Whitechapel Walk)*. *(Long pause)* I can't get a proper fix on this. I think I've oriented myself through Mary Kelly's room, but I'm not actually there.

F: Do you know where you are?

P: No, but I do know I've got a disgusting headache.

J: Hangover or headache?

P: Feels more like a hangover ... That's the first time I've had that same feeling. I think I'm with him.

(Often in these contact sessions there was a feeling of being in contact with two of the people concerned. Occasionally, Pam had the sense of being in a situation which she had experienced from someone else's perspective.)

J: Joe Barnett?

P: Yes, I think I'm with him because I've got the same sense of 'splittedness' if I can put it that way. It's a dissociation, it's got something different in it ... He has to get angry to get into that state.

F: What state?

P: This state of being 'out of it'. Let's see if I can find out what happens. What I think happens is, is that he gets depressed, then he gets angry. *(Pam has the sense that he became so angry, he was incapable of speech.)* He gets depressed, he gets angry, and then he flips out: he becomes ... he feels like something else ... He's done that since he was a youngster - very young.

F: What, 'flipping out'?

P: Yes.

F: Why does he do it?

P: I'm not sure he actually 'does it', it just happens. He has to get into a certain ... most of the time he's OK ... he doesn't get into that state. When he does ... I've touched in on this one before. I've touched in on that feeling before.

(At this point, Pam begins rubbing and holding her stomach.)

F: Why are you feeling your stomach?

P: Because I'm trying to stay with Joe Barnett and I'm not 'with him'.

F: Right.

P: I think that's where the frenzy comes in, because he flips out, he's totally cold, and then the frenzy. The mania - it's not strictly mania - it's more correctly a frenzy, then occurs as he's coming back in.

F: Back in ...?

P: I can only describe it as 'back into himself'.

F: Is he schizophrenic?

P: It doesn't feel like what I would call schizophrenia.

F: Is it conventional schizophrenia?

P: No, it's two - maybe three - very distinct states, but it doesn't feel like schizophrenia. He hasn't got any voices telling him what to do *(pause)*. He doesn't see things that aren't there. He's not hallucinating. Doesn't smell things that aren't there. It's just dissociation. The closest I can get is that it's just a copping out. It's not being where you are. I'm trying to get back to before this state of dissociation. *(Long pause)* Mary Kelly was going away.

F: Where was she going?

P: I don't get any particular feeling. She was just going away.

F: Was she going away from him?

P: Yes, she was going to disappear again. That's what she did ... that's what she did when she was ... whatever it was ... 20 or 21.

F: What did she do?

P: She just disappeared. Sort of left.

F: Was she going with anyone or by herself, this time?

P: This time she was going by herself.

F: Did anyone else know she was going, apart from Joe Barnett?

P: I think people thought she would.

F: What was she running away from?

P: She was frightened ... she was frightened of him, but she was also frightened of other things around her.

F: What other things was she frightened of?

P: It wasn't working for her.

F: What wasn't?

P: Her life.

F: She was going to go away and reinvent herself?

P: She had that ability.

F: Does it have anything to do with when she disappeared before?

P: She does this to get out of situations - situations she can't handle.

F: What situation was she in that she couldn't handle?

P: This time ...?

F: This time, and is it connected to the last time?

P: This time she thought it was going to be easy to get rid of Joe Barnett, but he wouldn't go away ... there's more behind it as well. *(Pause)* You know the sheet?

F: That was covering her?

P: ... Yes ... the sheet that was covering her face ...

F: What about it?

P: It was the only way he could do it.

128

F: So that he couldn't see her face, so that he wasn't doing her? ... If he couldn't see her face, he didn't think he was doing her?

P: Yes, it's back to it just being a job.

F: Had he done anything similar before?

P: That's what I mean when I say it's the same feeling ... I've had this feeling of dissociation ... of breaking out of it ... He's aware of what he's doing up to the point where he cuts their throat ... her throat.

F: Do you mean 'her', or, like you say, do you mean 'their'?

P: Let's stick with this one. He was aware of what he was doing up until the time he cut her throat - then he isn't.

F: Is he aware that he's doing anything?

P: No.

F: Does he go into some sort of trance?

P: Yes.

F: Was this the first time he'd ever done it?

P: I want to say Yes, but I'm also getting No ... Does anybody know what happened to his mother? Did they ever trace his mother?

F: No, it's thought that she left - after the father died. Why do you ask?

P: Because he knows he's capable of murder.

F: Did he murder his mother?

(This was an unintentionally leading question. Pam did not wish to answer this, fearing that it might take her away from the matter in hand.)

P: That was an intrusion rather than an actuality. That was a flip back to the younger him.

F: So we don't want to stay with that?

P: No thank you.

F: Right.

P: My abdomen is getting very cold. I don't know about being schizophrenic but it feels as though one half is with her, and one half is with him. *(Here Pam felt that she was aware of both Mary Jane and Joe Barnett. The coldness seemed to belong to Mary Jane.)*

F: Probably was at some point!

P: The wounds to the face were after death. *(Pause)* You know, this mutilation is the first one that's done while she's dying ... that's what makes it different.

F: So were the others dead?

P: Mmm ... Do you know what's odd is this thing with the left arm again.

F: What's wrong with the left arm?

P: It's as though it's been immobilized. Was she bruised, were there bruises?

F: I don't think they could tell.

P: It's something to do with ... the way that the cut goes. It somehow immobilizes the left arm. There must be a nerve or something. But hers was different anyway. I'll have to describe what I'm feeling. The whole of the left side of my face has gone numb.

F: You're not having a stroke, are you?

P: No ... this is not me, if you see what I mean. I'm just reproducing the feeling. The pain is there *(pointing to collar-bone)* and it goes down into my heart.

F: Is it just below your collar-bone?

P: The bruise seems as though it's there *(pointing to heart)* but the pain is there *(pointing to collar-bone)*.

F: So is the bruise just below your collar-bone?

P: No. The pain is there. The bruise isn't.

F: Right ... that's very unclear.

P: The pain is inside, the bruise is outside. That feels bruised - above my collar-bone - but the pain is inside.

F: Right.

P: I can't feel anything else. *(Long pause)* Then he starts slashing her. *(Pause)* I wouldn't like to put this in film. When her face is slashed it's so there are no traces left.

F: Of her?

P: Yes. He's completely obliterating her. He's completely ... when he cuts all the bits off ... it's so she can't be put back together again. It's total and absolute destruction. Now, why did he do that? Yes, he was looking for something.

F: What was he looking for?

P: If she was pregnant, it couldn't have been his.

F: Why not?

P: Because I don't think he could ... he was impotent ... correction - he was impotent with her, so even if she was pregnant it couldn't have been his ... he knew this and so did she. That's a question to ask the pendulum.

F: She told him she was pregnant, when in actual fact she wasn't?

P: I don't get that feeling. I get the feeling that he was told.

F: Who told him?

P: He was told or he assumed. I think he assumed - it was all part of the madness.

F: Was she actually pregnant?

P: I don't get that at all. I don't get that she was pregnant. No, I can't get that she was pregnant.. I don't even know if she thought that she was pregnant. *(Long pause)* The slashing and the maiming was part of it.

F: Part of what?

P: Part of ... the brewing - there's an escalation ... and then, as I say, there's just the sitting there. I can't get away from the fact that he wanted them to catch him.

F: Why did he want them to catch them?

P: Because it meant that he was something, he was somebody.

F: He was recognized? If that was the case why didn't he do something similar again?

P: Because I think that he'd actually got the recognition that he needed. *(Pause)* I get this sense of ... this is almost ... start again. I thought it was me first of all flipping from one to the other, from Mary to him, but in actual fact that's part of the madness, that's part of the ... whatever this was ... the ability to be the victim at the same time as you're doing it ... that's horrible. *(Pam felt it was as though he would blame Mary for the fact of killing her.)* That's horrible and I'm going to come away from that. I'm coming out.

* * *

The following is part of the discussion that took place immediately after the session.

P: We need to find out more about this because he over-identified with his mother as the victim. I don't think he murdered his mother, but he over-identified with her as a victim, and women always went away from him: and he had an ability to identify with victims, it wasn't just his own victims. There's a new twist to it ... get rid of the victims of society ... I think we'll consider that later.

F: What's wrong with your tummy, are you feeling that it's there?

P: It's absolutely freezing. Oh, I don't like this, it tends to get terribly muddly. What a very odd man. Do you know if the sheet was cut? Did he cut her face through the sheet or did he take the sheet off her face?

J: Wasn't it covered?... I don't think he did do that. Are you saying that he covered her and then did the business?

P: He covered her face.

F: It's said that she was mutilated beyond recognition, but it's not known if it was covering her face when he did it.

P: No, I think he covered her face and cut her throat. Was it over ... Did they have to lift it off to discover the mutilations?

F: Well, no ... it doesn't say ...

J: You want to know if the sheet was cut through.

P: He covered her face with the sheet, he cut her throat and then he mutilated, and I want to know if the sheet was cut because it doesn't feel as though it is. Because he wouldn't have been able to mutilate her, until after he'd got into a frenzy. She was no longer Mary Kelly by that time. Do you see what I mean? She was just something to be slashed at, something to ... that was when the frenzy took over. Was her uterus taken out as well? I know everything was taken out. Was her uterus moved, was it still there or had it been taken away?

* * *

Subsequently we established that the uterus had been removed from the body but that it had been left close to it. The heart had been taken away. This could explain why the police revisited the scene of the crime - to establish whether the heart had been burnt in the fireplace or removed by the murderer. Even psychically, we cannot establish beyond reasonable doubt what happened to Mary's heart.

MONTAGUE JOHN DRUITT - 21 OCTOBER 1997

Present: Pam, Fiona, James

In this session I was surprised to find myself going back with Druitt to a younger age, to a time of indecision, so that I could sense the processes of his mind. It seemed important that certain things about him should be understood. I discovered quite quickly that his vibration - or energy - was not right for the crime of murder, thus confirming the astrological evidence we had. To an extent this meant having to suspend my own beliefs and accept a different viewpoint. I was left with the strong feeling that, although Druitt was not capable of murder, he was certainly very troubled.

On the morning after the session I woke up with the definite feeling that an account had been cleared and that at least so far as he was concerned matters could rest. It was as though Montague Druitt had, at last, been able to tell his side of the story.

* * *

P: I've almost gone back to the very first session, you know when I was sort of over the area. I am sort of scanning things, being aware ... of pockets of energy, pockets of problems, for want of a better word.

I'm asking for contact with or knowledge of Montague Druitt.

(Pause) What I'm actually linking in with immediately is an energy which is very sensitive, very

finely drawn and very creative. *(Pause)* It feels younger than I would have thought to link with him at the time of his death, so I'm assuming I've actually got hold of him as he would want to be remembered. At this stage he is, I would think, probably 22, 23, but also quite immature. He doesn't seem to have a proper hold on life. *(Pause)* He doesn't seem to ... He seems to wander through life trying to please people. He doesn't seem to know which direction to go in, in particular, in any way whatsoever. It's almost ... it's something that's peculiar to him - if you put him at a cross-roads - physically - he'd probably spend time trying to decide what it was he should be doing. I think the purpose of this is to give some feeling of where he's coming from. *(Long pause)* He doesn't feel to be interested in women. Now, what do I mean by that?

At a time when you would think at 22, 23, something like that, when you would have expected him to be going out and having a good time, in one way or another, he doesn't actually feel like that sort of a person - he's almost too serious. He's busy ... let's see if we can bring him up to date. Just as a matter of interest we need to look at what year it was when he was 22.

F: 1879.

P: Because it feels as though that's a decisive time for him.

F: He went to the school in Blackheath in 1880, and left Oxford University in 1880 as well.

P: So he'd just be coming down from university.

F: Yes.

P: Very much the feeling with him that he would take on, and cope with, what life threw him, and I think that's the important point - would cope with. Let's see whether we can move him forward. So he would have been nearly ten years at the school?

F: Yes. He was employed in 1880, and then was dismissed at the end of November 1888.

P: So when did he study the law?

F: He was educated at Winchester and Oxford, got a B.A. - a third - in Lit. Hum., which I presume is Literary Humanities. Was admitted to the Inner Temple in 1882 and called to the bar in 1885. He joined chambers in 1884.

P: But was he at the school at Blackheath part-time?

F: Doesn't say.

P: OK, let's see if I can get hold of him. Certainly that would tie in with very much the feeling that he doesn't know what he wants to be doing. *(Long pause)* I get a strong feeling of extreme loneliness all the way through. I wouldn't like to think that I was making assumptions because I don't like the feeling I'm getting. It's almost the feeling of not being able to get anything right. I think this man was a dreamer. He was a dreamer with too much expected of him.

F: Is that why he studied law?

P: Mmm.

F: When he'd rather be in teaching?

P: No, I think it was the need to prove something ... to prove something to himself ... that he could actually do it. I would certainly feel that he had a temper, but it's a temper that's very firmly under control. He's quite secretive, too.

F: What's he secretive about?

P: Doesn't want anybody to know what he's doing anyway ... living a half life. I wouldn't have thought he had it in him to murder.

F: Is that your thought or is that his?

P: That feels like him. It's not just that I would want to think well of him. I think he's aware of his own instability. I think there's the potential for rage. There is a love-hate relationship with his mother, there's also a love-hate relationship with his father. Where does he come in the family?

F: Doesn't much say. He had an older sister, but it's not said where he was.

P: About four years older than him?

F: Don't know.

J: He was born three years into the marriage.

P: *(indecipherable)* ... He suffered from headaches.

F: Were they bad headaches?

P: Yes, proper full-blown migraines. Migraines with the flashing lights.

F: Is that why he thought he was going mad?

P: I think he'd always suffered with them, because I can also see the child ... I think perhaps they increased.

J: He wouldn't have understood it as migraine in the way that we do.

P: No, not as we do, because it's the flashing lights, it's the altered state of consciousness ... the sheer absolute pain, and ... not being in control.

F: It says he had six siblings. It doesn't say if they were brothers or sisters.

P: *(Long pause)* I think we've got hold of something ... I think we've got the reason he was dismissed.

F: What was the reason?

P: He broke down in front of the children.

F: So he didn't actually attack the children. Did he lose his temper, or did he get emotional?

P: No, he broke down, he broke down completely.

F: Like a nervous breakdown?

P: Yes ... It's sheer emotional overload ... he's absolutely appalled.

F: About what?

P: His own behaviour.

F: Was he dismissed, or did he resign or was it a joint decision?

P: It was a joint decision. *(Pause)* He was given to going off on his own, which is why his family thought he was the murderer.

F: So you're saying that he wasn't?

P: I can't connect Elizabeth Stride with him at this point ... but it feels like I'm not in the right time.

F: Is he responsible for any of the others?

P: Let me stay with what I'm getting because I think it explains him. He was angry, but he was angry at his own mis-treatment and when that happened he used to go ... I suppose we would call it 'walk-about'. *(Pause)* I find it very difficult to connect him with the East End.

F: Did he ever go there?

P: Yes.

F: For what reason?

(At this point, Pam seemed to become disconcerted.)

P: I think I'm going to come out of this. I'm not sure whether what I'm getting is genuine.

F: What are you getting?

P: All sorts of impressions.

F: Could that be his state of mind?

P: Yes, it could be, but that's one of the reasons I want to come out.

F: OK.

P: Let's switch the tape off.

* * *

It was important at this stage to be able to report accurately what I was observing, but not to get sucked into the emotional content of what had been going on in Druitt's mind. He seemed to be very distressed over what had happened. His state of mind was certainly not rational. There was a sense that, in losing control in front of the boys, he had let himself down as well as them. What seems to have been happening during the contact session was that the privacy barrier that operates with my clients in the present day was also working on this occasion, coupled with Druitt's own need to keep his sexual orientation a secret. It did not feel as though he had ever revealed his homosexuality, but relationships were certainly uppermost in his mind. I was very aware that it was not his influence over the boys that was a problem - in other words, there was no hint of paedophilia - but his mishandling of what was happening to him. There also seemed to be a need to clarify certain details regarding the letter he left for his brother. I wondered whether the Friday mentioned in the letter addressed to his brother was, in fact, referring to 30 November - an oddity yet to be resolved. Certainly I experienced numerous confused emotions and states of mind connected with that weekend.

Partway through the discussion, my perception seemed to deepen. The decision was made to continue recording. A transcript of the rest of the session follows.

* * *

P: Doesn't fit.

F: What doesn't?

P: Can't get him there. Can't get him the way he feels ... the way he felt at 22, and the way he felt at the end, I can't get him to ... to Stride. *(Pause)* Because although he was depressed, he was perfectly lucid. He was perfectly lucid. There wasn't the same flipping out ... you know the dissociation? I don't think Druitt could do that. What he was experiencing was everything inside. It wasn't flipping out and ... flipping out and away from it. There wasn't the cold dissociation. It's a *totally* different feeling. This is all inside ... this is all tied up inside, it's all tied up in knots ... and ... horribleness.

F: What do you mean, horribleness?

P: It's total self-involvement, totally self involved ... his madness, for want of a better word. It was a mixture of all sorts of states of mind which were seeping into one another. He wasn't capable of that emotional coldness. He wasn't capable of the disassociation [*sic*], that being something and doing something and not knowing what you were doing. Not even at that stage.

F: What stage?

P: Not even given his state of mind during that last weekend. *(Pause)* He wouldn't have been able to murder and then live with it. If he'd murdered and then gone off and done his suicide, so to speak, he would not have been able to have lived with having murdered somebody ... Apart from which his fear of exposure was too great anyway. That's what broke him up, the sheer fact that he was now exposed. He was open to everything. Literally, the whole of his life, that carefully constructed life, that successful ... successful façade - he didn't have that anymore. He would have used the periphery of the East End. There is no way he would have 'known' the East End. He wouldn't have known the highways and the byways. *(Pause)* No, I can't get him as being *(pause)* he doesn't have the temperament for murder. Again, the only thing that I can say is that he was afraid of women.

POLICE NOTICE.

TO THE OCCUPIER.

On the mornings of Friday, 31st August, Saturday 8th, and Sunday, 30th September, 1888, Women were murdered in or near Whitechapel, supposed by some one residing in the immediate neighbourhood. Should you know of any person to whom suspicion is attached, you are earnestly requested to communicate at once with the nearest Police Station.

Metropolitan Police Office,
  30th September, 1888.

Printed by McCorquodale & Co. Limited, " The Armoury," Southwark.

Above left: The notice issued by the police after the double murder of Elizabeth Stride and Catharine Eddowes on 30 September 1888. It reveals the assumption by the authorities that the culprit was local.

Above right: Sir Melville Macnaghten, who was brought in by James Monro, Warren's successor as Commissioner, several months after the last murder was committed. He identified three people as possible suspects.

Left: The death mask of Fredrick Deeming was presented as being that of the Ripper by Scotland Yard despite the fact that Deeming could not have been responsible for Jack's crimes.

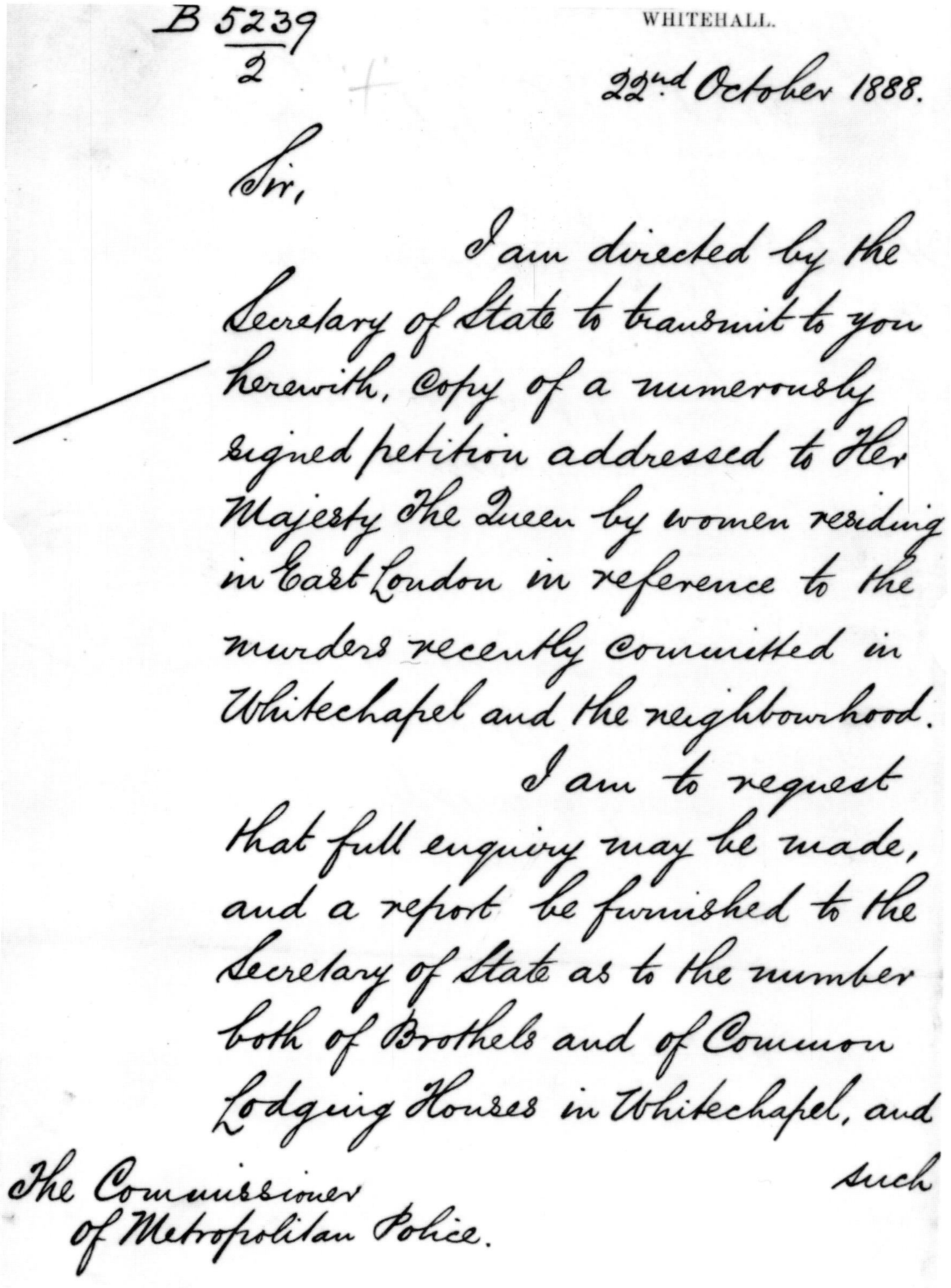

B 5239
2

22nd October 1888.

Sir,

I am directed by the Secretary of State to transmit to you herewith, copy of a numerously signed petition addressed to Her Majesty The Queen by women residing in East London in reference to the murders recently committed in Whitechapel and the neighbourhood.

I am to request that full enquiry may be made, and a report be furnished to the Secretary of State as to the number both of Brothels and of Common Lodging Houses in Whitechapel, and such

The Commissioner
of Metropolitan Police.

Above: The petition sent by East-End women to Queen Victoria had a galvanizing effect on the authorities, if only short term. As this extract from Sir Geoffrey Lushington's memo of 22 October 1888 shows the Home Secretary was moved - one suspects because of Victoria's concern - to request a report into living conditions in Whitechapel.

Right: Punch *magazine's satirical view of progress in the police investigation.*

BLIND-MAN'S BUFF.

(*As played by the Police.*)

"TURN ROUND THREE TIMES,
AND CATCH WHOM YOU MAY!"

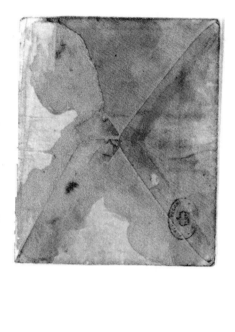

Opposite page: The 'Dear Boss' letter, purportedly written by the killer, in which the pseudonym Jack the Ripper was used for the first time.

Left: The role of the clairvoyant and psychic James Lees has never been fully explained. In the contact session with him it emerged that he was not prepared to break the vow of silence he had maintained up until his death.

Below: One of the most significant of the psychic trails Lees was said to have picked up in connection with the Ripper murders occurred while he was travelling on a bus, probably a 'knifeboard' type such as this. A psychic vision of the culprit had become a reality when from the bus he saw the man.

London W.

METROPOLITAN POLICE
RECEIVED
25 JUL. 89
CRIMINAL INVESTIGATION DEPT

Dear Boss

You have not caught me yet you see, with all your cunning, with all your "Lecs" with all your blue bottles.

I have made two narrow squeaks this week, but still though disturbed I got clear before I could get to work — I will give the foreigners a turn now I think — for a change — Germans especially if I can — I was conversing with two or three of your men last night — their eyes of course were shut & thus they

Opposite page: The so-called 'Lees letter' of July 1889 shows that some people were aware of Lees' involvement in the case, although this was not common knowledge until 1895.

Above: Sir William Withey Gull - thought by many to be a major suspect. Our investigations revealed the complex nature of his possible involvement in the killings.

Left: Montague John Druitt, one of Macnaghten's three suspects. The contact session revealed a troubled, sensitive man. His astrological profile showed an inability to murder.

James Maybrick - The Catcher?

Above: One of the 'Dear Boss' letters sent to a news agency during the Ripper's 'autumn of terror'. Was the specific taunt linked with the individual identified by us as 'The Catcher'?

Dear Boss

Catch me I you can, you will soon hear of me again. Yours Respectfully "Jack the Ripper"

Far left: J.K. Stephen- implicated by some but from an examination of the facts alone a most unlikely candidate.

Left: R.D. Stephenson - a magician and meddler but not a murderer.

Artist impressions of Joe Barnett - a quiet man with a care for his appearance. Psychic investigation revealed him to be not at all what he seemed.

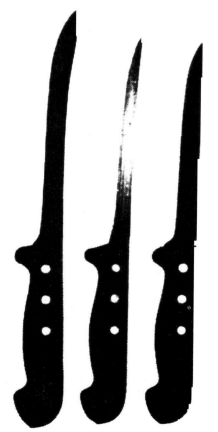

Left: These knives most closely resemble my perception of the murder weapon. They are the type of knife that a fish porter like Joe Barnett would have used routinely in his work.

Opposite page, top: Many letters from the public contained grains of truth. This one makes unflattering references to the 'pot-bellied prince' (Prince Albert Edward).

Opposite page, bottom: Anonymous letters sent to the police undoubtedly contained a large element of fantasy projection, as in this example in which the writer alludes to 'mother murder'.

Say now boss no "narrow escape"
your officers are lying free I
heaps of time . guess I am
coming west now for I am a
moral man and am determined
to put down wholesale whoredom
I am going for "lady prostitutes"
now and there are millions
then too some well known card shar
pers and other sports will be attended
to I have located one a scorcher
not far from portman square who
will be found properly carved and
his tool ears tongue and ears I shall
cut off and send you leaving his
guts on the side walk this wont be
mean anyway I am a new god
to reform abuses and advantage players
must be stopped going around _ no more
crimping at poker, and the sucker shall
have a look in no more ringing in a
cold deck no more reflectors for that boss I
guess he may chuck his bugs and

...lds out for I am ___ to his vila
right away , he euchred a mate of
mine and so I am going to stick
him and others pig sticking I call
it shall be around Scotland
yard soon I am "a foreign butcher" am
I you cannot locate me I guess
but you see I am an instrument of
god for good and when I divide
neatly some titled bosses wife a lady
lord guess you will be mad and
feel a bit mean and there is no one
to squeal for I do it all myself
. . . .

a word of warning beware and
protect your low immoral potbellied prince
god has marked him for destruction and
"mutilation" , keep your men about
pimlico and belgravia _ soon there will
be two more stiff on the side walks and
ladies now ⟵ ___ ⟶ his tool.
106 " Jack the ripper " N.b. other letters not gen . . .

12 Whitechapel Road
E.

Dear Boss
I hope when you get home
You will find your Mother Murdered
for that is what you deserve
Yours truly
Jack the ripper

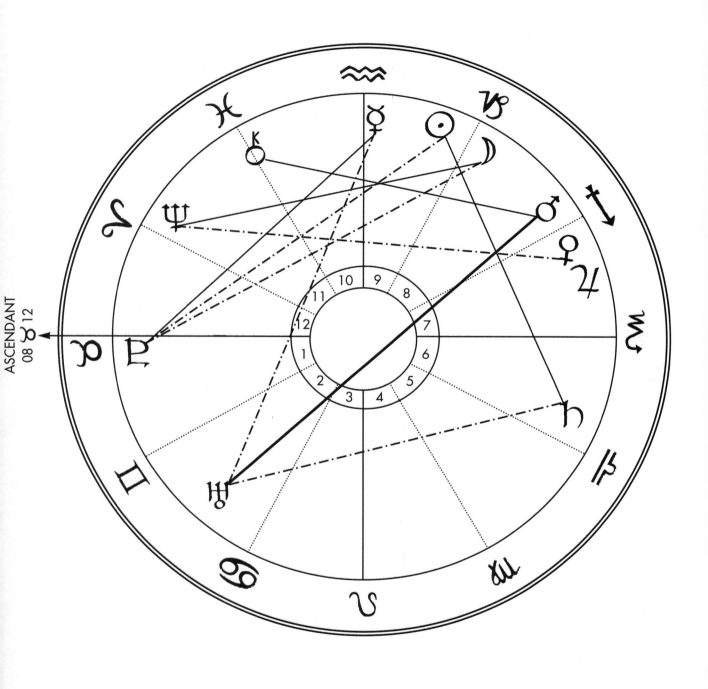

ASCENDANT
08 ♉ 12

Left: Prince Albert Victor, the brother of the Prince of Wales, who on very little evidence has been implicated in the murders.

Above: A simplified astrological chart for Albert Victor; see page 149 for interpretation.

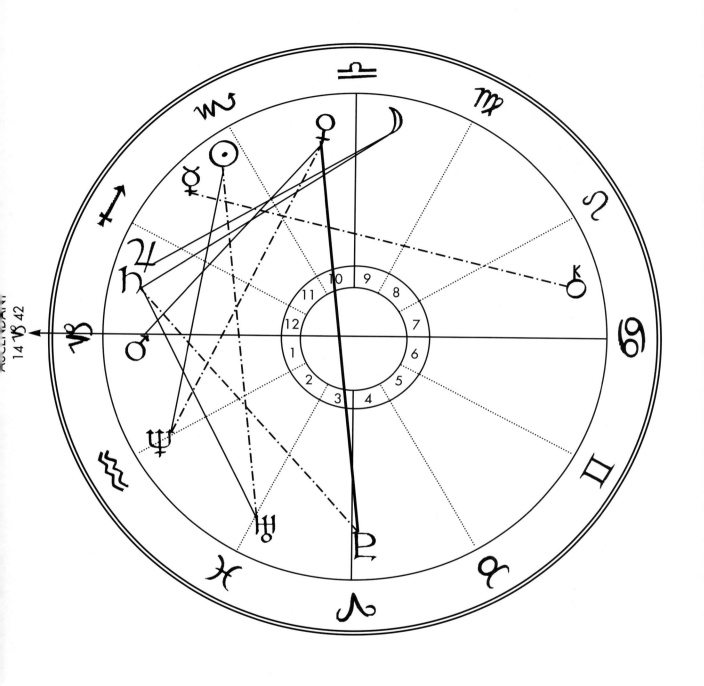

ASCENDANT
14 ♑ 42

ft: 'Bertie', the future King Edward VII. Should a country have been entrusted to a man like that?

bove: A simplified astrological chart for Albert Edward; see pages 149-50 for interpretation.

The shawl thought to have belonged to Catharine Eddowes (a belief supported by the author), with Ripp *investigators Andy and Sue Parlour and the shawl's present owner.*

The infamous Maybrick Diary. Psychometry revealed that it appears to have been transcribed by someo *other than James Maybrick.*

ROBERT LEES - 4 NOVEMBER 1997

Present: Pam, James, Fiona

This session was set up in order to ascertain the truth about Robert Lees' involvement in the Jack The Ripper case. We hoped also to be made aware of his perception of the identity of the murderer. Contact with Lees was somewhat easier than with the other subjects, presumably because he was and is a trained 'communicator'.

* * *

P: What I want to do first of all is slightly different. I want to 'scan' his records, if you like, almost starting off going back, rather than linking with the 'histrionic' side of him. *(Long pause)* There would appear to be something which did occur ... at around the age of 12. There's a shock to the system - I think that's something to do with his mother - correction, probably to do with his grandmother, ... and it was that, that actually opened up the clairvoyant faculty. *(Pam felt that Mr Lees possibly had a very strong connection in some way with his grandmother, who seemed to be quite a formidable lady.)* His years as a young man are quite dark and quite ... I was going to say clouded, but in actual fact it's coming out 'crowded'. There's a lot of darkness around, a lot of difficulty. *(This is possibly to do with his connection with the Salvation Army, something we did not know at the time.)* *(Long pause)* We should be able to verify this, but something very odd happened. There's a complete change of direction when he was 27. We would need to find out if he actually had a patron at that time. Books talk about Keir Hardie; I don't know if it's Keir Hardie or not, but there's an older man in the background with him. There's definitely an older man guiding him in some way, and that's 27, 28. *(Long pause)* I would have thought that there was some truth ... the question I'm asking is, What is the truth of the connection with Victoria? *(Long pause)* From where I'm seeing it the connection seems much more tenuous than in actual fact him having 'read' for her. I would suggest that the connection is more through the people that he consorts with.
F: What sort of people does he consort with?
P: He seems to have had a lot to do with social reformers. I can only assume I'm right when I say he would have had a connection with Dr Barnardo's ... Dr Barnardo *(the connection was with the man not the organization).*
J: Personal or general?
P: It feels fairly personal; it feels as though they thought and talked in the same way. Whatever the establishment was ... again it's been called variously a school ... it's been called all sorts of things ... it feels very much to me like the sort of spiritualist church type thing.
J: Which?
P: His establishment that he ran in Peckham. *(This appears to refer to the beginning of the initial lectures which eventually led to the People's League.)*
F: Lees?
P: Yes. It's ... it's almost a ... it has the same feeling as the spiritualist type thing.... you know the 'run on a shoe-string' thing. He's called a philanthropist. I don't necessarily think he's a philanthropist in that sense. I think he just managed money well.
F: Who do you mean Barnardo or Lees?
P: Lees. He's simply a social reformer. He's doing what he can within the framework of what he's got. He uses his talents.
F: Why did he become involved in the Jack the Ripper saga?
P: I would suggest in the same way that any clairvoyant would become involved in that.
F: Which is...

JACK THE RIPPER

P: The atrocities were around him and because he was clairvoyant, because he was open, he was therefore affected by it. *(It is possible that Lees may have had some connection with the East End prostitutes, particularly with Elizabeth Stride, through their mutual appreciation of Dr Barnardo's work.)*
F: Was he doing it from the sense of recognition, or purely and simply because he wanted to help to resolve the situation?
P: Purely and simply to resolve the situation.
F: Even though he knew it would hold him up to ridicule?
P: I think that's partly why I have such sympathy for him. Because he's actually taking a risk, and taking a risk that could go wrong ... In actual fact, it did go wrong for him.
F: In what way?
P: Because it stopped him doing what he did well. It lost him quite a lot of credibility, even though he knew he was right. *(Lees appears to have changed direction personally after his involvement in the Jack the Ripper case.)*
F: Did he think that he knew who the person he saw from the bus was, the one who he followed home?
P: You mean, did he identify him?
F: Yes.
P: I don't get that he was identified as a public figure.
F: He was just a ...
P: He went on the feeling ...
F: Right.
P: He went on the feeling ... and I actually ... do you know, I'm not even certain that the bus thing is right.
F: If it isn't, then where did the story come from?
P: In essence it's correct, he did get this sense of evil ... no wait a minute that's daft.
F: Remember you're saying what he felt, not what you think he felt.
P: No, I was just thinking ... because ... that's my fault, I was trying to connect it with a bus ... *(Pam in raptures, Fiona and James bemused)* ... and, of course, it wouldn't be a bus, would it?... it wouldn't be a petrol bus.
(Here there was some confusion because Pam's image of a bus was the now well known one of a big red London bus which, of course, would not be genuine. It actually presented to her as a horse-drawn hansom cab, and not even as a horse-drawn bus.)
F: No.
P: OK, this man has a sense of humour. *(More fits of laughter from Pam, more bemusement from Fiona and James)* ... it wasn't a bus, it was a carriage.
F: Right. So he was in a carriage, as in the equivalent of a taxi cab?
P: I would have thought so.
F: Right.
P: I suppose you had horse-drawn buses. I'd need to see a picture of one to be able to identify which it was. It looks more like ... the person getting off is much more the sort of person who would ride in taxis and things like that.
F: The person he saw?
P: Yes, Lees wasn't ... Lees would do whatever he had to do.
F: So Lees was a bus man?
P: Yes. I like him actually. *(Pause)* I also could understand his frustration at not being believed.
F: Was he not believed because they thought he might be somewhere near the truth, or was he *really* dismissed as a crackpot?
P: It feels as though it's both.
F: How can it be both?
P: It was easy enough to dismiss him as a crackpot ... it was easy enough not to ... just to dismiss him, along with all the other rubbish that was talked about the case ... so that initially it was very easy to dismiss him as a crackpot. It was only by him being patient that he could be accepted. In essence I would have to say the story is true.

F: What, the story of him seeing somebody and following them?

P: No, he was consulted later.

(The sense was here that Lees had received impressions, and had later been consulted by the police, and had been of help to them.)

F: By whom?

P: By the police.

F: Did he come up with anything?

P: Yes.

F: Was it acted upon?

P: *(Pause)* Oh, don't do that ...

F: What? Don't do what?

P: ... He's not allowing me to see.

F: Which would go along with our theory some time ago that there is a psychic block.

(From a psychic point of view this was most frustrating, but at the same time totally understandable. When one works within the spiritual field, promises and vows of silence can extend beyond the grave, and a competent psychic recognizes these. This is what happened here. It was as though a blind had been drawn, and Pam was aware that it was not to be opened.)

F: Can you explain to him what we are doing and why? If that helps.

P: I have already done, and got told off for it.

F: Can you find out why he doesn't want you to know?

P: It's protecting the participants.

F: You mean us or the people who were around then?

P: It's both, actually.

F: Why does he feel that we, and they, need to be protected?

P: He gave his promise then and it can't be broken.

F: Who did he give his promise to and why?

P: He did what he had ... wait a minute, let me sort this one out. He did what he had to do; he led them to where he thought the problem lay, and that was it so far as he was concerned.

F: That was his part over?

P: That was his part over and done with.

F: And whether they acted on that information was down to them?

P: Yes.

F: And after that he wanted no further part.

P: He needed no further part in it. So in the sense that that was it, the promise in that sense was there. That was it, he had done what he set out to do, he had ... it's almost that the promise was to himself. He'd identified the person connected and that was it.

F: And whether it was acted upon was nothing to do with him?

P: Was nothing to do with him at all. The reason that he's protecting us, no ... the reason that we are being protected..... oooh ... he was a bit pedantic ... the reason we are being protected is that this is, and was, extremely 'big' in all sorts of ways.

F: Is it information that even if it came out now would still cause trouble and turmoil?

P: Particularly if it came out now.

F: Why?

P: I don't know, but that was his answer.

F: Are any of our thoughts anywhere near the mark?

P: *(Pause)* It would seem so. I'm fairly certain it's not Gull ... Doesn't feel like Gull at all.

F: Is there any relevance to 1863? *(This is a reference to what we have called the 'Mountford' session, see page 119.)*

P: From where I'm looking now, I'm almost certain we're right ... Yes, there is. OK, so what do we need to do? Can somebody tell me how old he was in 1863?

F: He was born in 1849, so he would be 13 or 14.

(This is probably about the time that Lees first became aware of his own psychic ability.)

P: *(Long pause)* I think we need to find out ... Let me see whether he will tell me. *(Pause)* His association with court is actually later.

F: You mean the Royal court.

P: The Royal court, yes.

F: Later than when?

P: Later than 1863. *(Pause)* This is frustrating, because you have the same feeling that he knows something without knowing that he knows it. He's picked something up somewhere. No, he hasn't, he hasn't picked up something somewhere - he's made connections which fit for him. *(It is difficult to convey the feeling Pam experienced at this time. It seemed that Lees had learnt some things clairvoyantly and drawn his own conclusions, which were in fact valid. Such information would, of course, be no more able to be revealed now than it would have been at that time, particularly if he had imposed a vow of silence on himself.)*

F: Would they fit for anyone else?

P: Not at that time, no.

F: Would they fit now?

P: Yes, they would, but they don't ... they don't need to be known.

F: Do they not need to be known, or would it cause trouble if they were to be known? Or is there no relevance to them now?

P: There would be relevance to them now ... *(Pam shows discomfort.)* He's giving me a heartache ... did he have a heart condition?

F: It's not known.

P: There is a connection ... it's got to do with the Royal family; he's not allowed to reveal it, and I shouldn't be asking him ... and the only way we can get the connection is by doing it ourselves.

F: Could I just ask, is it relevant to the Royal family then, or the Royal family now?

P: Both!

F: Is it relevant to members of the Royal family who are still alive now?

P: The answer comes back 'only marginally' ... it would have been a scandal at the time ... and it would have completely altered history.

F: Would he be prepared to guide us part of the way ... to point us in the right direction?

P: His answer seems to be we don't need it ... great!

F: We don't need his help or we don't need the answer?

P: I think we don't need his help.

F: Is there any truth at all in the Sickert theory?

P: Not as such, no. *(Pause)* The Cleveland Street thing would have been a scandal of itself, but it would have led to other things. It would have led to the revealing of other things.

F: What would it have revealed?

P: Manipulations that were going on.

F: Of whom?

P: What you need to look at is what Victoria was doing at that time. We need a history of that time. We need to look at what was happening with Victoria and what was happening politically at that time. We need to know what was happening with the Royal family and the manipulations that were going on.

F: *By* them or *of* them?

P: Both. It's the dynasty thing. That backfired on them. *(Pause)* There is a pattern to this ... there is plot and counter-plot. I wouldn't call it a conspiracy theory, but things went on which were difficult.

F: Any idea what they were?

P: No, all I'm getting at the moment is intrigue. I think it's going to need basic fact before we can put it together.

F: Which is finding out what was happening around that time?

P: Yes. The feeling is weird, and the feeling, if I can come back to Lees, is that he somehow or another had connected into that. He was quite powerful even then.

JAMES MAYBRICK - 11 NOVEMBER 1997

Present: Pam, Fiona, James

An unexpected and generous invitation from Camille Wolff and Loretta Lay of Grey House Books to view and handle the document known as the Maybrick Diary at a lunch scheduled for 21 November prompted us to hold a session with Maybrick beforehand. I felt it was important to contact Maybrick directly rather than through the diary because to have done otherwise carried a risk of contaminating the information I received about him.

At this stage I had viewed a video about the Maybrick diary - and been sceptical about that programme's contents - but I knew very little about Maybrick himself, most of the research on him having been done by James Eden. We hoped to prevent the risk of leakage between this session and the one scheduled for the 21st by delaying the transcription of the tape until after the day of the lunch.

It was quite difficult to make contact with Maybrick, and the considerable number of pauses are indicative of the care that had to be taken to be certain that the correct information was being received. Here is what happened.

* * *

P: We are attempting to contact James Maybrick and find out whether or not the diary attributed to him is, in actual fact, his and also to find out information about him. *(Pause)* The first thing I would say is happening is that my ears ... Does arsenic make your ears go funny?
J: No idea.
P: It feels as though ...
J: It's not one of the drugs I've tried *(humorously)*.
P: My ears are more sensitive than they should be. *(Long pause)* I don't particularly like the feeling ... the feeling of this particular person, although I do get the impression it's a projected image, its how he was then. *(Pause)* The energy is not clear, he's very arrogant ... it's not a clear energy. He wasn't a person who would put up with stupidity or anything he didn't consider was correct and proper. Rightly, he was a very jealous personality - but we know that from his chart anyway. *(Long pause)* He seems to be quite tall, he's also fairly stocky. *(Pause)* If I present him with the idea of the diary, he just laughs ... it's quite cynical.
F: Did he write the diary?
P: I think the diary we've got is a transcript.
F: Is it an exact transcript?
P: Let me describe what I'm seeing, then we might be able to make sense of it. I've got just a sheaf of papers - and it's loose papers - on one side of the desk ... and I've got what I take to be the diary on the other side. *(Pause)* It would seem that the diary is the transcript of the papers.
J: Did he write the papers?
P: Not all of them, no.
F: Was he writing the papers or the diary as something of a joke or was he writing what he felt?

P: You almost get that feeling ... joke would be the wrong word. It's this cynicism that keeps coming up. *(Pause)* There's a very cynical streak to him. I get two time-frames. It will be interesting to see what happens when we get our hands on the diary ... The diary is later than ... the diary is later than 1888.

J: Do we know how much later?

P: I would have thought 1910.

J: Didn't he die in 1891? *[Maybrick died in 1889.]*

P: This is precisely what I'm getting. I don't know ... I don't think he's the transcriber.

F: But he wrote the papers? When did he write the papers?

P: I don't get clarity on this at all ... it doesn't feel like 1888, but it doesn't feel very much later.

F: Did he write down the diary on the sheaves of paper as some sort of ... not joke, but some kind of trick?

J: Twisted fantasy?

P: It feels like ... I think twisted fantasy is the right word. It feels like he has done it for his own amusement to begin with.

F: But he actually wrote the diary but didn't commit the acts within the diary?

P: That's something else I don't understand because there's almost a sense of voyeurism. There's a sense of watching the acts being done ... No, watching one act being done. *(Long pause)* I think you'd have to look at the Stride-Eddowes murders. Can't get through the fog ... fog or fug? *(Occasionally, Pam queries her own use of words during a session for the sake of accuracy. Here she said fog, but 'felt' fug.)* I don't think he was the Elizabeth Stride murderer: he's not tall enough, he doesn't seem tall enough.

F: Did he murder any of them?

P: *(Long pause)* I have to say he doesn't seem evil enough for that.

F: Even though he was a very unpleasant man?

P: Twisted but not evil ... not 'evil' evil, do you know what I mean?

F: Manipulative.

J: A good businessman.

P: An opportunist ... I'm not very happy about him at all. I can't get a sense of the murders with him, but I do get a sense of him knowing...

F: Was he one of the group who may have known why the girls were murdered. Was he part of a larger group?

J: A cog in the ever-turning wheel.

P: *(sighs)* Is there *anything anywhere* that says he's a spy?

J: Not that I've read.

F: I don't know enough about him ....

J: But he did travel to various places, to and from London, America ...

P: Because the sense that I'm getting is he's on the periphery - to answer your question, Fiona ... he's on the periphery of something - and I don't know if that's the archetypal Jack the Ripper ... flitting around on the edges or whether he actually did it for information.

F: Did what?

P: Spied.

F: So you're pretty certain he was some sort of spy?

J: A spy for whom?

P: I didn't think they had industrial spies at that point ...

F: Yes ... so you feel it was more on a .....

J: You don't become a successful businessman without knowing a few things ...

F: Without knowing what the opposition was doing ... rather than being a spy in the sense of a James Bond spy ... he was ...

P: He was a carrier of information.

J: Carrier for whom?

P: Well, that's why I asked, because it feels like a foreign ... it doesn't feel to be carrying for Britain, if that makes sense ... and he knew the East End, and he knew some pretty seedy characters.

F: Did he have any connection with Russia?

P: Not obviously. When I asked that, Canada came up.

F: Why would he be spying for Canada?

P: It's got something to do with his own trade.

F: Cotton ... was cotton his trade or was that a front?

P: No, I think cotton was in that sense his trade ... but it's to do with industrialization.

J: Can any of this be related directly back to Jack The Ripper business?

P: Well, this is why I'm a bit puzzled, because it seems like he knew what was going on ... still can't get that he was a murderer, but he knew what was going on - he knew what was needed to be done.

F: Is he therefore guilty by association, in that he didn't put a stop to anything?

P: Yes, I would have said so. *(Long pause)* He didn't have anything to do with the Mary Kelly murder, nothing at all ... I can't say the same about Stride and Eddowes - there's knowledge there.

F: What about Nichols?

P: No, it doesn't feel as though he knew Nichols.

F: What about Martha Tabram?

P: I can't be certain. Nor can I be certain over Annie Chapman.

F: Did he visit any of the girls as a client?

P: That's the feeling.

F: So that was his only real connection?.

P: Mmm.

P: I can't put him together. I can't put him properly together with any except the double murder, and I don't know if that was both, do you see what I mean? Can we check what arsenic - or strychnine - does to your hands?

F: What do your hands feel like?

P: Well, they're not itchy on the outside, they're itchy on the inside.

F: Have you had that feeling before?

P: No, it's not the same as Martha Tabram.

F: More like pins and needles?

P: Mmm, it's the circulation. It makes you very aware of ... whatever he is, it makes you very aware of ... it doesn't numb you ...

F: It heightens your sense of reality?

P: It heightens your sense of your own body ... it's a very weird feeling.

F: Arsenic is a stimulant, so therefore it would affect the hands. *(Pause)* Is the watch a forgery or a fake?

P: My immediate reaction was No.

F: But why, if he hadn't murdered them, he didn't particularly know the girls, would he have scratched the watch with the initials. Was he trying to take the blame for somebody else?

P: I get this terribly twisted sense of ... not even a sense of humour ... just twisted.

F: Would he have got some sort of pleasure ...

P: Yes.

F: ... of actually having been thought of as Jack The Ripper?

P: No, because I don't think he particularly was at the time ... What was important were the two lives.

F: The one as the upstanding respectable merchant, and the other as the 'Canada' connection.

P: A 'perverted Canadian connection'.

F: You mean he was perverted, or it was a perverse connection?

P: It was a perverse connection. It's the deviousness.

F: In that sense that wasn't unusual for the time.

P: No, it wasn't unusual, but what was important was that it was because he was away for half the time that Florence *[Maybrick's wife],* in actual fact, fell in love with the other fellow. *(Pause)*

He just had the ability to live two lives and he expected each of them to go on without the other.

F: He expected them to be two completely separate entities?

P: He got very worked up when they weren't. I can't get hold of the diary properly. I think I need to wait till I can feel it. I don't actually properly understand the pile of papers.

J: How would he get information? The watch apparently had the initials of two women murdered in Manchester that very few knew about.

P: It was his hobby ... hobby? Wrong word! ... It was his *(Pam exhales)* ... I can't tie him in with the Ripper murders, I can tie him in with knowledge. We'd have to find out who his associates were ... When did he die?

F: 1889.

P: Does anybody know when exactly, or just 1889?

F: May 1889.

P: Were the Manchester women after the Jack The Ripper murders?

J: No.

P: Oh *(long pause)* I'm not getting very far with this. I have the same sense of frustration. When I ask about the Manchester one, his attitude is very much the cynic again, and it doesn't make sense ... If he was anything to do with Jack The Ripper then he continually felt at one removed from him, and that doesn't mean it's the same sense of disassociation [*sic*] that I had with Jack The Ripper, with the person we have called 'Jack the Ripper'. It's not the same sense of dissociation.

(During some of the other sessions Pam had been aware of the murderer's dissociation from what was going on around him. It was as though his actions did not belong to him. With Maybrick the feeling was very different, much more that of someone who does not belong to the real world and is essentially a very lonely character. Although difficult to describe, the two feelings are very different.)

I can't explain that, it's just a different feeling. *(Pause)* With Maybrick there's a sense of watching the whole time. That's why I asked about the spy. There's a sense of watching, watching, watching everything going on and in that sense being one removed from it. All I can say is that if he did do them he's not taking responsibility for them even now. Let's see if I can go in a different way. *(Pause)* I'm trying to approach it from a spiritual point of view and what was actually going on. It just gives me a headache ... No, I can't even get anything that way. All I can say is that he knows more than he's letting on. *(Pause)* If you took arsenic as a stimulant, it would eventually poison you anyway, wouldn't it?

F: Yes, it would build up.

P: That was taken to be aware ... to get rid of the pain ... to move into a different state of consciousness ... a more active way. I feel like I'm going round and round in circles on the outside. I don't like this - I can't get into the centre, I can't get into what's what ... I'm going to come out ... That's the first time I've felt I've been 'played with'.

F: That's the sort of thing Maybrick would do, though.

* * *

This session left us with a feeling of dissatisfaction which lingered until after I had handled the Maybrick diary (see page 143). The strongest feeling after transcribing this session was that Maybrick definitely had knowledge of the murders which others did not have.

It is interesting that in the very first session we held to review the area, on 8 July, I mentioned that one of the men associated with the women had earache. In this session I experienced the same sensation. This would lead me to believe that we had received an important piece of information. Maybrick also seems to have had a slight squint which would tie in with information gathered from the Elizabeth Stride session (see page 102).

TOUCHING THE EVIDENCE - 21 NOVEMBER 1997

The lunch hosted by Camille Wolff and Loretta Lay was an enjoyable but somewhat nerve-racking occasion. The experiment was essentially a gamble and I felt that I was putting my reputation on the line by taking part in it. As for everyone else, I sensed that even the doubters among the respected Ripper experts and authors present were uneasy at finding themselves in the position of not knowing what was going to happen.

Over the years I have learnt to be sceptical about articles presented to me for verification and about my own ability to successfully identify their vibrations. This is why I tend to check - and recheck - my findings and will not say something is the case unless I truly sense it to be so. This threefold checking consists of 'feeling' something to be so, 'believing' it and 'knowing' it. I am satisfied in my own mind that the information relating to the diary, the knife and the shawl is genuine.

Keith Skinner made his questions extremely clear, and also attempted to record the proceedings. As mentioned elsewhere, electro-magnetic energy is very sensitive to psychic energy and, unfortunately, at the end of the session it was discovered, much to everyone's chagrin, that the tape machine had malfunctioned. We have used the brief notes kept of the session and our memories to compile the following narrative of what happened. The technique for working out the timings was broadly the same as that used in the test session (see page 16), although on this occasion with a pendulum.

The Maybrick Diary

The diary - which was made available for the occasion by its publishers and owners, Smith Gryphon, and by Shirley Harrison, the narrator of *The Diary of Jack the Ripper* - consists of a book out of which - at the front - a considerable number of pages have been cut. The remains of these pages are stained brown in places, as are the endpapers, yet the pages on which there is writing are clean and clear. The writing is quite small and cramped and tends to alter in character in different parts of the document. I would suggest that this is partly due to tiredness on the part of the writer, but also to the fact that the individual was receiving a considerable emotional charge from what he was writing. While I am only an amateur graphologist it did seem that there were several inconsistencies that could not easily be explained. The upward or downward slope of a line of writing can show the state of mind of the writer. In three different parts of the book, the lines rose to the centre of the page and then fell away, finishing at about the same level as they began. This would indicate someone whose moods were changeable, but not depressive. As already stated, the writer's style was quite small and cramped initially. He did not seem to be particularly searching for great meaning to life, and would probably not have been looking for any particular motivation. Nor was he looking for spiritual enlightenment. At one point on the same page the word 'God' is written in two different ways - one more open and free-flowing as he asks for forgiveness and one very pushed together when the words indicate that the writer is angry at his fate. This indication of ambivalence is also reflected in the variation of the personal pronoun (I). In one style it is small and closed, showing a strong need - and desire - for privacy, while in the other it is again more open and flamboyant. This duality is sometimes seen when mind-enhancing drugs are used.

On one page where the writer seems to be experimenting with the word 'bastard', the feeling is of considerable anger. On another the writer has scribbled 'bitch' three times, and curiously has linked the words together. This is done in quite a flowing way, not erratically or jerkily as one would expect. It is almost as if the writer is trying to make sense of his feelings for the person about whom he is thinking.

On handling the book my first sensation was one of nausea, mixed with a very odd feeling of foreboding. It was not a sense of evil, but of a kind of broodiness - of waiting for something to happen. I dowsed over the remains of the excised pages to establish a date for these and to find out if it differed from the remaining pages. (This was done by working backwards in periods of ten years from 1940 and then ascertaining the actual year within the relevant decade.) The pendulum registered 1888 for the front papers, but 1891, 1892 and 1895 for the written pages. Interestingly, 1892 got a weaker response than did 1891 and 1895. This was confusing, because James Maybrick died in 1889. However, it would support my initial feeling that the diary had been copied into its present form. It does seem strange that the copying should have been done over such a long period, yet the fact that the handwriting for the poems and doggerel is much neater than for the rest of the contents would support the idea of various parts of the diary being copied at different times.

The vibration connected with the writer was not the same as that I had experienced when connecting with James Maybrick. I became confused when the pendulum registered that it had been transcribed by James Maybrick. This was actually clarified by a supplementary question when the pendulum indicated that the transcription was by his son, also called James. Since I did not know at the time that he had a son, we should be able to accept this answer as true. The question was also posed as to whether Michael Maybrick, James Maybrick's brother, was involved in the murders. The answer came across as 'No'. I had the distinct impression that there was disappointment at this.

A question was posed as to whether, on an individual basis, James Maybrick was associated with any of the murders. The pendulum gave negative answers to each name except that of Elizabeth Stride, to which the answer given was a definite 'Yes'. I rechecked this information in order to remove any personal bias.

Before this session I did not believe James Maybrick was implicated in the killings. The clear answers given to the questions asked changed my view and I came away believing that he was in some way connected with the murders and that the diary itself is more than probably a transcript of his thoughts and feelings.

The Knife

Thanks to Donald Rumbelow, on the same occasion I was also able to handle the knife that was believed to have been left beside the body of Annie Chapman. This is possibly one of a pair that may have been the Ripper's weapons. The knife I handled was given to Miss Dorothy Stroud in 1937 by a friend who said that it had belonged to Jack the Ripper. At that time, it was contained in a box lined with blood-stained velvet. Miss Stroud burned the box and used the knife for carving and later for gardening, at which time it got broken close to the hilt. The repairs to the knife are not particularly noticeable.

An early theory was that it was the type of instrument used in post-mortems, having a thumb grip designed for ripping upwards. The knife is now known to have been manufactured in the 1870s and to be of a type used by surgeons for performing amputations. The pointed end of this particular knife was ground down by a later owner.

Such a knife is described in Home Office files as possibly the type that may have caused Annie Chapman's injuries. There is no record in police files of such a knife being found.

On first handling the knife, I decided to attempt to date it using the pendulum. I began by asking if the knife was in existence in 1940 and then proceeded to count the decades backwards. Through dowsing it was established that the knife was not in use from the 1940s back to the

1890s, but that it was in use in the 1880s. When I reached 1870 a negative answer was given.

I felt that the knife had picked up some of the 'myth' as it were, but I could not be totally sure of its past. A question was asked as to whether the knife still retained an aura of evil. The vibration I experienced while handling the knife was not particularly similar to the vibrations of either suspects or victims I had experienced during the sessions. The only connection was that the knife was of a similar length to one I had seen psychically during a contact session.

My conclusion is that although the knife was certainly in existence at the time of the murders, it cannot be directly associated with Jack the Ripper. Indeed, until the killer has been positively identified, it may be impossible to establish a connection by psychic means.

It is perhaps interesting to note that surgical knives prior to 1892 had bone or ivory handles, but thereafter, with the coming of sterilization techniques to ensure aseptic conditions in operating theatres, such knives were made totally of metal.

The Shawl

In November 1997 I also took the opportunity to contribute to a television programme about Jack the Ripper. The programme began much as I had expected with the usual question as to whether I could identify the murderer. I gave my usual response: that in my view it would be morally wrong to ask the question directly since we would be making assumptions which in the context of the programme were not provable. If the question 'Who was Jack the Ripper?' was put it would increase the likelihood of an inaccurate response. I was not prepared at this stage to make any judgement whatsoever.

I used my normal method of dowsing with a pendulum to answer questions. Two questions put to me on that occasion are relevant to our investigation.

1, 'Will we ever discover who Jack the Ripper was?' The pendulum indicated 'No' in answer to this - a response which put us in our place in no uncertain terms.

2, 'Were there only five Ripper victims?' The answer was 'Yes'. This question was interesting in that it was somewhat ambivalent. Given my perception that Elizabeth Stride was possibly not a victim of Jack the Ripper, but that Martha Tabram was, we still have five victims. I suspect that my questioner meant the conventional five of Polly Ann Nichols, Annie Chapman, Elizabeth Stride, Catharine Eddowes and Mary Jane Kelly, but still the answer is the same - there were only five victims.

* * *

The most interesting aspect of the programme was that it enabled me to renew the acquaintance of Andy and Sue Parlour, who have written a highly informative book called *The Jack the Ripper Whitechapel Murders*. I am grateful to Andy and Sue for giving me one of the biggest surprises of my career, by offering me the opportunity to handle a shawl that was said to have belonged to Catharine Eddowes.

This shawl had allegedly been found by Police Constable Amos Simpson, the first person to reach the scene of her murder. The City Police, who had jurisdiction over Mitre Square, have no record of an Amos Simpson. However, he is shown on the Police Pension Register as having served in the North or Islington Division. It is therefore highly probable that he was one of the many officers from other areas who were drafted in at the time of the murders. Family tradition is somewhat vague about how he came to be in possession of the shawl. What is known is that the shawl had been kept safe within the family, for many years in an old sea chest. Pieces have been cut off - presumably parts that were stained with blood - but it is still in very good condition.

The shawl is not mentioned in any police reports, but it appears to match contemporary descriptions of Catharine's dress, which is described in the post-mortem report as being of 'tiny flowered patterns, containing the colours blue, pink, green, yellow and maroon'.

I confess that I had fully expected at best to pick up a negative reaction and at worst gain no information at all. Instead, I was most surprised, particularly in full view of a television camera, to feel that, without doubt, this shawl was the genuine article and that it belonged to the era of Jack the Ripper. The shawl called forth an almost electrical reaction in my hands, which for me is a sign that the article is what it is purported to be. Over the months I had become extremely aware of Catharine's vibration, and when holding the shawl I experienced the same feeling I had when we carried out the contact session with her. When I used the pendulum to check my findings, not only did it verify that the shawl was genuine, but it also gave information as to timings about the garment's ownership. Using the question 'Was this shawl Catharine's in ...', I received the following information.

1885 - I suspect the shawl did not exist. It had not been made.
1886 - The pendulum registered that the shawl belonged to Catharine.
1887 - The shawl did not seem to belong to Catharine. I suspect she had either lent or pawned it.
1888 - The shawl belonged to Catharine.

This information may indicate Catharine's financial state at various times in the years before her death. I would have expected such a luxurious item to perhaps have been pawned during her time hop-picking in Kent, given that she and Kelly had returned to London with so little money that they had to pawn his new boots. It is curious that on the night of her murder two days later, she should have been in possession of such an article. Another point to ponder is the good condition of the shawl. If indeed it had belonged to Kate for so long one would have expected it to be more worn or torn. She gave every appearance of being a vagrant and of wearing every item of clothing she owned. I wonder whether it had belonged to someone else, or perhaps it had been a treasured possession which was kept in one of the many calico bags that were found by Catharine's body.

FINAL CONTACT

One important factor emerged from the 'touching' sessions and this was the conviction that James Maybrick was responsible for the murder of Elizabeth Stride. If this was correct, then we were looking for not one murderer but two or possibly more. A link between the Ripper's victims has never been established, but all the way through the sessions I had the feeling - which was confirmed in both the Martha Tabram and Mountford sessions - that the women shared more than the hard fact that each of them was a chapter in the grim tale of the Whitechapel murders. We had to go back to the women themselves and see if through them we could not clarify some of the major outstanding questions. This we did in the session of 30 December (transcribed on page 151). However, just before doing this we investigated further what may be called the royal connection with the murders.

As we have already seen in the Gull biography the suspicion of the existence of this connection emerged in the early 1970s. Dr Thomas Edward Alexander Stowell (who, incidentally, was born only three years before the murders) first implicated Prince Albert Victor, the Duke of Clarence and son of the Prince of Wales, in an article in *The Criminologist* in 1970. When the article - heavily edited - was published, the suspect was simply designated as 'S' but sufficient details were given to make it apparent that Prince Albert Victor was the person in question. Stowell later denied that The Duke of Clarence was implicated, but sufficient damage had been done and it could be said that this was responsible for sparking renewed interest in the Ripper case.

In 1973 the notion of a royal connection was raised again when Joseph Gorman Sickert - who claimed to be the illegitimate son of the artist Walter Sickert - recounted the following story in a BBC documentary. He alleged that Prince Albert Victor had secretly married his grandmother Annie Elizabeth Crook, that the marriage was witnessed by Mary Jane Kelly and that the child of the marriage - Alice Margaret Crook, who was born in 1885 - married Walter Sickert. Also, according to Sickert, in 1888 there was a police raid on certain premises in Cleveland Street which resulted in the Duke of Clarence and Annie Crook being taken away and the latter being incarcerated in various mental institutions for the rest of her life.

Experts on Walter Sickert and Prince Albert Victor have not accepted this story, and Joseph Sickert himself later retracted it. However, it was subsequently investigated by Stephen Knight, who concluded that the Ripper murders were the result of a Masonic conspiracy designed to cover up the so-called Sickert connection.

There is very little evidence to implicate the Duke of Clarence in the murders - indeed, he is now known to have been out of London at the relevant times. His astrological chart shows a Mars/Uranus opposition, which, as we have seen in the charts of the prime suspects, can give rise to sexual inadequacy. In Albert Victor's case this opposition is probably due to an over-intellectualized approach to sex. There is shown - by both the Sun and the Moon being in Capricorn - a strong sense of guilt associated with his parents and his attitude to them, and also with his attitude towards women. Since he also has Saturn square the Sun, one could make the assumption that he was profoundly affected by his father's treatment of his mother. Incidentally, because Saturn is in Libra it is highly unlikely that he would have flown in the face of convention enough to have married outside legal jurisdiction, so the story that he married a common shop-worker without the permission of his family and had a child by her seems remarkably out of character and thus highly suspect. His chart shows the potential to idealize women but certainly not the capacity for murder, and it is doubtful whether he would have been party to it.

Prince Albert Edward

After drawing a blank here, we spread the net a little wider and quickly assessed other possible royal suspects astrologically. The chart of Prince Albert Victor's father, Prince Albert Edward, the Prince of Wales, later King Edward VII, shows an opposition to Pluto similar to that in Maybrick's chart. Like Maybrick, this would have given him the ability to 'play' with women in a somewhat cynical way, and of course this would mean that he had little respect for the women with whom he was associated. Taken to its absolute limits, this might give the potential for murder. He also had squares to both Pluto and Venus from Mars, showing that sexual relationships would carry a good deal of stress.

Despite being older than the norm, Bertie also fits the psychological profile of a serial killer. He had a bad relationship with his parents, had little to do which interested him, due to Victoria's dislike of him, and no doubt by that time had some physical ailments.

Bertie was a rake and a womanizer who disappointed his mother's hopes that he would turn out to be a man in his father's mould. In 1861, in an attempt to instil some personal discipline in him and to enhance his leadership qualities, he was sent to Curragh camp in a remote part of Ireland. His fellow officers smuggled into the camp a young lady by the name of Nellie Clifton for his personal use. She then proceeded to boast of her conquest. His misdemeanours became public knowledge and his father went to Ireland to bring him home in short order. On the return journey to England Albert became ill with typhoid and subsequently died. Victoria blamed her son for her husband's death and ever afterwards claimed that she 'could not look at him without a shudder'.

On 10 March 1863 Bertie married, taking as his wife a member of the Danish royal family, Princess Alexandra, thus fulfilling after death Prince Albert's aspiration to unite the royal houses of Europe. Bertie continued his philandering ways, and soon his behaviour was brought to the attention of a disapproving public. Bertie was named during the Mordaunt divorce case in 1869-70, one of the biggest scandals of the time, together with Lord Cole, who Lady Mordaunt named as the father of her new-born son. Lady Mordaunt was subsequently declared insane and her testimony invalidated. (Here, in common with the woman in the 'Mountford' session, we appear to have a case of post-natal insanity.)

Bertie's indiscretions surfaced again in 1876, when Lady Ayelsford's affair with Lord Blandford resulted in another scandalous divorce case. Bertie had written several risqué letters to her, the contents of which - fortunately for him - were not fully revealed in court. By 1885 his popularity had deteriorated to such a degree that, on a visit to Cork in Ireland, he was pelted with rotten vegetables. Throughout his 60 years as the Prince of Wales, Bertie seems to have had a love/hate relationship with the populace, sometimes being revered and sometimes reviled. By 1888 his standing within his own family had worsened to the point where the Kaiser, a relative of Bertie's, refused to visit Austria at the same time as him. His reputation as a thoroughly disreputable character presumably did little to enhance his relationship with his mother or the rest of the immediate royal family.

There is no evidence to implicate the Prince of Wales in the Jack the Ripper murders. The information we have about him in this regard is based solely on intuition and psychic faculties. If, as we suspect, the 'Mountford' baby was in fact Bertie's, is it not probable that its existence would need to be hidden in view of Bertie's recent marriage? We can think of no other reason for the birth to have been brought to our notice in both the Tabram and 'Mountford' sessions.

SESSION OF 30 DECEMBER 1997

Present: Pam, Fiona, James

In this our final session we attempted to clarify in our own minds what we had discovered and clear the ground for further research.

* * *

P: The first thing I become aware of is something that, in some ways, I have been aware of before- that's looking at it at two different levels. It's almost like looking down on the situation with the players all spread around, whilst also almost participating in that play. It's like watching a play, but also being part of it at the same time. It's actually quite a weird feeling. It's not that same feeling I had as being up in the corner when I was watching the Mary Kelly thing, but it's more being up above it looking down. *(Pause)* I'm trying to scan in on each of the women, and the first thing that seems apparent is there is a link between Martha Tabram ... there is some kind of link between Martha Tabram and Dark Annie. Polly Nichols at the moment seems to be standing almost to one side. Standing on one ... one side as though she's not actually part of what is going on ... Yet if I then introduce Elizabeth Stride and Catharine Eddowes, Polly Ann seems to have some connection with Stride, but I'm not sure about Catharine Eddowes; it's a very tenuous link, anyway, between those two. If you then introduce Mary Kelly into the equation, the best description that I've got is that you begin to be on very marshy ground: obviously I've got to be seeing this symbolically, but previously the ground was quite stable - it was just an inter-relationship. Then you put Mary Kelly in the equation and everything starts going slightly haywire. *(Pause)* Elizabeth Stride and Mary Kelly were much more of a type. They, if anything, had more in common than the others.
F: In what way?
P: Their backgrounds feel similar. Their experiences feel similar. *(Pause)* It's not that they come from a common background, but they've come through similar experiences. One wonders whether that's the prostitute, having been prostitutes rather than falling into prostitution. *(Long pause)* 'The Catcher' was somebody to be avoided.
F: Why?
P: The feeling is that 'The Catcher' was almost an authority figure. I think in one of the previous sessions, James asked whether he was a policeman - I don't think he's a policeman, but it's something to do with not being ... not being found out.
J: Explain.
P: I think he goes back to the contagion, the ... diseases thing.

F: So he was like a local rat catcher?

P: Yes, almost.

F: Was he someone who would go round and examine the people ... and if they had a disease would stop them from ...?

P: Well, this is why I'm a bit surprised because I don't get any sense of 'The Catcher' with Mary Kelly, which would mean that 'The Catcher' belonged to earlier on in the women's lives.

F: In all of their lives?

P: They all knew about it.

F: Had they all come across 'The Catcher' or was it just something they were aware of?

P: It's almost as though he was part of the neighbourhood.

F: Did they think he was the Ripper?

P: No, no that's not where it comes from. What seems to be important is that they are not actually known as prostitutes. You know I've said all along I didn't know whether they were prostitutes; if 'The Catcher' caught you then you were branded a prostitute.

F: How would he go about catching people?

P: It's information.

F: Was he a well-known figure, or just well known to the people of the area? Was he somebody who would have been recognized by anybody, or just people of the area?

P: No, I think he would be recognized by the women. He wouldn't necessarily be recognized by the community, but he'd be recognized by the women. *(Pause)* That's where you get the furtiveness, if you like; you know this thing about Jack the Ripper flitting in and out of the shadows, so to speak; that's actually very much as 'The Catcher' was. He would flit in and out of the shadows. Also, it was a good way of getting information spread around the area.

F: Who was he employed by, who sent him to the area?

P: *(Pause)* I keep coming up with just the authorities, but if I come out a bit I would have said it was the social purity lot.

F: You mean the 'do-gooders'.

P: The child prostitution and that type of thing.

F: You mean the Church?

P: I would have thought probably the social reformers. People like Josephine Butler, like William Stead. Because the important thing is, if you wanted information through the neighbourhood you actually made sure 'The Catcher' knew about it.

F: So, he was an information gatherer sent there by the social reformers, who was turned into a negative thing, who was seen as somebody who interfered and was someone to be avoided?

P: Yes, but they just used him. There was a double standard there because ... because the girls knew about him.

F: I suppose they didn't have telephones and it was cheaper than a stamp!

P: *(Laughing)* You are probably right. But as I say what's interesting is that he's either perceived, or was, a very small person - and I mean small ...

F: You mean physically small?

P: Yes, physically small, because he's small and he's furtive and tends to pop up all over the place.

F: A bit like the child kidnapper in *Chitty-Chitty Bang-Bang. [A small, wiry furtive man whom people tried to avoid.]*

P: It's quite weird.

F: Does he actually have any relevance to the murders or was he just somebody 'of the time'?

J: Surely it's a man? Is it definitely a man?

P: Yes, definitely. Definitely, but if I'm asking for dates ... that's why I think it's more with the social puritan thing, because it sort of predates ... it predates Jack the Ripper, because there is the same feeling about him ... Wait a minute, let me try and sort this out ... there is the same feeling about him as there was initially about Jack the Ripper.

F: What was that?

P: That he was a nuisance, and something to be feared. I suppose if you had been a 'Catcher', you would know the area, wouldn't you?

F: You would know all the little back alleys.

P: All the back alleys and things like that. I think that's where the suspicion came in, but I don't know if that was something necessarily brought up to the police. I think that was a community thing. He was a nasty piece of work anyway but it's *not* Jack the Ripper. It's not the way we've experienced Jack the Ripper.

F: Did he think he knew who Jack the Ripper was?

P: I don't get any sense of communication from him at all.

F: So he's not a major player.

P: No, I think he is just a suspicious character.

F: Just an unpleasant, suspicious character of the time.

P: Almost, though, the template for Jack the Ripper.

F: What do you mean?

P: It's like a mould.

F: Your archetypal Victorian villain? He was just a nosy old busybody who liked spreading rumours and information, misinformation?

P: Yes.

F: So we don't need to worry about him too much?

P: Only from the point of view that, as I say, it worked on both levels. If you wanted to get information *into* the East End then you told 'The Catcher'; if you wanted information spread ... and that's what they both used him for ... if you wanted information spread, you spread it via 'The Catcher'.

J: What do you mean both?

P: Both authority and the community ... Not very nice, though. One thing that I think did draw all the women together - and we have come across this - is their recognition that things would have to change.

F: Do you mean for them or for the area or for other people?

P: I think it was for both, for all of them. There's very much the ... there is a strong sense of community among all the women, anyway. There is a very strong sense of 'if you were a prostitute in the East End, you belonged to a community'. But there is also a very strong sense that there were those who were beginning to feel that things couldn't go on as they had done, that things would have to change.

F: Do you mean amongst the prostitutes, among the women themselves?

P: Yes. I mean, I do get this thing with Polly Ann ... this social reform thing. She wanted things differently. Was she a confirmed alcoholic? Because in some senses she seems to be clearer.

F: She was the one who ... her children lived with their grandfather and father. *(Pause)* She was the one who had the new bonnet. She was the one who said 'See what a jolly bonnet I've got now.'

P: Is she the one who went and slept in Trafalgar Square?

F: Yes.

P: I think that's partly what, for want of a better word, held them together. What held the prostitutes together. If in actual fact things weren't going to be changed for them, they would do it themselves. *(Long pause)* You know the theory that Mary Kelly is supposed to have known something and blabbed to her friends? I'd stand that on its head.

F: What do you mean?

P: *(Pause)* If ... Martha Tabram knew something, Martha Tabram had information ... Mary Kelly could get information ... it ... sounds like a spy story.

F: What does?

P: Mary Kelly going into the East End was like putting a detonator in a powder keg. Once she got there, it started waves of 'cause and effect'.

F: Was she put there, or did she go there of her own choice?

P: I think she landed up there as there being nowhere else to go, but in actual fact once she had landed there it caused problems. I think the Sickert story is a load of rubbish, but it's something that when you put Mary Kelly and Martha ... No, when you put what Mary Kelly knows and what Martha Tabram knows together ... then you've got a problem.

F: What did they know?

P: Mary Kelly knew how to get information from her clients ... we are going round and round in circles here, because Mary Kelly could not go back into the West End.

F: Why?

P: Because she should have been exposed.

F: As what?

P: Like I say, it's ... she had eyes, she had ears: she would pick up information and she'd squirrel it away and you never knew when she was going to bring it out. She'd been ill ... she'd been ill and that was why she had landed up in the East End and it was the information that she carried that was the difficult one.

F: Was that before or after she got to the East End?

P: Before she got to the East End, information that she had before she got to the East End.

F: Why did her being ill mean that she ended up in the East End and had to stay there?

P: Because she was no longer ... she could no longer work in the way she had done.

F: Gathering information?

P: Yes.*(Long pause)* I'm censoring this, and I don't know why I'm censoring it. I don't know whether it's Mary Kelly censoring it ... Let me shift it.

F: Obviously whatever you say is going on the tape, so therefore whoever is around is happy for it to go on the tape. Because otherwise you wouldn't be being told it. So whatever is coming in you should say.

P: Well, what I feel is that Mary Kelly was used as an information gatherer.

F: Was she 'The Catcher'?

P: No, she wasn't 'The Catcher' because 'The Catcher' was male, but she wasn't used for gathering information in the East End - she was used for gathering information *(prior to her moving to the East End)*. When she was no longer any good for that - because I think she had salpingitis *[inflammation of the reproductive system]* - there came a point when she couldn't be used. It was then that she landed up in the East End. She was a damn sight more astute than the others and it was she who began to put three and three together, so to speak.

F: What information was she gathering? Was it anything to do with the Fenian activities or was it just general information?

P: It was politically sensitive information. When she was working earlier as a prostitute, it was politically sensitive information.

J: Can the information not be revealed?

P: Well, I get that it was about people, it was about people's activities and this is where I tie it in with Bertie.

F: Could you give a date on the information?

P: *(Pause)* I think we are talking about 1884.

F: So she was collecting information, sensitive information in 1884, when she would have been about 21, which would tie in with the previous session where she didn't want to tell you what she was doing when she was about 21.

P: So she was collecting sensitive information, but then she was dumped. I think that's where Barnett came in.

F: Do you mean he would sort her out, he looked for her, or they just happened to get together?

P: *(Pause)* I don't think they just happened to get together; planning went into it somehow.

J: On his part?

P: He strikes me as a very weak individual.

F: Was it planned on his part ...?

J: Or was he approached?

F: Was he approached to get involved with her?

P: The feeling is that he was there by design, and it wasn't his design.

154

F: He was almost a fall guy, he was a patsy?

P: *(Long pause)* He ... took up with her, he ... took up with her in order to keep her off the streets.

F: Did he want to keep her off the streets or ...?

P: It was both; it was dangerous for her to be on the streets.

F: For her or other people?

P: Other people.

F: Do you know which other people?

P: I still come back to the Royal connection *(firmly)*. Too much could be revealed.

F: So to get her off the streets in a semi 'normal' relationship and lifestyle - i.e. her partner working and her - and then having a room as opposed to living in a hostel was as much getting her off the streets as could be done.

P: Yes. As *would* be done.

F: That was as far as people would go to protect her.

P: I want to find out what she was doing before she took up with Barnett, because there is stuff in there. *(Long pause)* It's what Martha Tabram knows and it's what Mary Kelly knows.

F: Can you find out what it is that they actually know, and if so why the other women were killed?

P: This comes back to something before, it's almost as though they were experiments.

F: So why was Martha killed first?

P: I think she made a connection ... made a connection somewhere. Now, when I say she made a connection I don't think that's just a mental connection - I think she actually may have recognized somebody.

F: Martha?

P: Yes.

F: Do you know who?

P: I think we are going back to our session. *(Pause)* This is all too tenuous, I cannot keep hold of it, there is still this ... this business of bluff and double bluff.

F: If Mary Kelly has allowed this information which was withheld last time, can you find out why she is prepared to give us this extra information now and if there is anything else that they are going to tell us?

P: *(Long pause)* Catharine Eddowes was killed because she knew who the killer was.

F: Who the killer of Martha Tabram was?

P: Yes. I *still* think Elizabeth Stride had nothing very much to do with it.

F: Was she a red herring?

P: I don't think she was a deliberate red herring.

F: So, why was Polly Nichols ... why was she killed?

P: *(Pause)* The phrase that comes to mind, and it scares the hell out of me, is to see whether it could be done. It's like I said with the Annie Chapman one - she was easy because she was sick, but Polly Nichols - that was almost like laughing at everything.

F: Who was, Polly Nichols?

P: Polly Nichols' death. It was almost a confirmation that it could be that easy. *(Pause)* If I were writing a fairy story, a spy story ... the month in between - the month of October - was because they thought they'd silenced the whole thing, when in actual fact it hadn't been silenced and that therefore meant that Mary Kelly had to be killed. And the only one who could do it then was Joe Barnett. *(Various parts of the jigsaw fitted perfectly within the altered state of consciousness in which Pam was working. However, viewed on a mundane level the information received - that Mary seems to have become a danger to herself and others - began to sound worthy of a Victorian melodrama with its own plot and counter-plot.)*

F: So that's why Mary Kelly was running scared, that's why she wanted to go ... to disappear, to go away, because she then thought she would be safe.

P: But by that time Joe Barnett was out of control anyway.

F: So he would have killed her anyway. Was he told to kill her?

P: That became inevitable.

F: It was inevitable that he was going to kill her. Was that a decision he made himself or a decision that was made for him which he then carried out?

P: No, I think that was a decision he made himself. *(Pam's feeling here was that Mary Kelly and Barnett had been caught up in a kind of dance of death which led to the final acts. It clarified the feeling coming from the murderer in the Kelly session. On a conscious level Pam confessed to finding this somewhat far-fetched.)*

F: But would she have been killed anyway?

P: I can't answer that: that's conjecture. It became evident in the middle of October that she was going to have to be killed. The reason that it stopped after the 'double murder' was that it became too dangerous. Catharine Eddowes ... with Catharine Eddowes' killing, and the realization that it was a mistake ... a) it was too dangerous to kill, but b) it was too dangerous to leave her alive. So they *were* gunning for Mary Kelly in the first place. You've got a politically/royally sensitive situation, you've got information that is coming out on Bertie, when in actual fact he's begun to recoup what he'd lost.

F: What do you mean?

P: His unpopularity, he was beginning to put that right. It had been very carefully engineered. Do you remember I said about the dynasty ... things had been changed so that he was becoming more popular? Had it been known what he was really doing ... I suspect his firefighting was as much an undercover thing as anything ... he got a buzz from his firefighting activities.

F: He may have been a pyromaniac - a pyromaniac enjoys setting fires and watching them.

P: No, he didn't set the fires. He enjoyed the fires and the camaraderie.

F: Did he know Mary Kelly?

P: No, not East End Mary Kelly.

F: Had he been with her in Knightsbridge?

P: She knew of his activities. I'm not going to say that she had actually been with him because I don't know, but she knew of the activities and that made it politically sensitive.

(At this point, Pam's hold on the information she was receiving seemed less secure.)

F: What relevance does that have to Martha?

P: Martha also knew of his activities.

F: What relevance does that have to 1863?

P: It was only when 1863 fell into place, as it were, that what she had seen began to make sense, that it began to become dangerous.

F: How did it become dangerous?

P: Could you trust a country to someone like that?

* * *

It was this question which led me to the conclusion that my own thought processes were intruding. I was no longer simply reporting what I felt and saw and what I said was probably contaminated to some extent by previous knowledge and personal opinion. In the interests of truthfulness, we made the decision to terminate the session.

THE END OF THE TRAIL

It is now time to make sense of the information and impressions we have gathered during the course of our investigation. As the contact sessions progressed we became increasingly aware of an underlying theme of intrigue and suspicion running through the whole of our enquiry. Primarily it was a feeling that everything was interconnected and that the theories - whether Royalist, political, medical or otherwise - were all relevant. It felt as though the information which others had accumulated was pertinent but that it had been put together in the wrong order. This was disturbing, because having deliberately set out not to create a theory we were now in the process of having to do just that in order to offer an explanation of our findings. The following is an attempt to do this as far as we are able - we feel there is enormous scope for further investigation because many unanswered questions still remain.

I feel that we must start with Martha Tabram, who, I believe, unwittingly played a key role in the mystery. Initially all the evidence pointed to her being a minor player in the Ripper drama, but this has proved to be far from the case. In the session with her it became clear that as far back as 1863 she had worked in a hospital-type environment, where she had been inadvertently drawn into some kind of intrigue which involved the birth of a baby boy whose existence had to be hushed up. My feeling was that it was not an appropriate place for the mother to be because it was an institution for the insane. The mother appears to have suffered quite badly from post-natal depression, and the baby was taken away from her. It is known that Sir William Gull had associations with such establishments and an interest in such cases. Martha must have been affected by her experiences in that place, otherwise the information would not have become available to us. The assumption must be that for some reason Martha's knowledge of the existence of the child put her in danger. One explanation might be to do with the parentage of the child. My feeling is that the Prince of Wales was involved in some way.

There is no evidence to link Bertie with the Ripper murders. However, there is a possibility that he had a stronger connection with the East End than was previously thought. It is known that he enjoyed fire-fighting and therefore seems to have had a fair degree of freedom. It is believed in some quarters that he kept a flat in Watling Street, which is not far from Whitechapel, and most of his fire-fighting was in the area now known as Docklands, so he may well have had the opportunity to associate with the 'unfortunates' of the East End.

Our findings suggest that the knowledge the victims held, whether in whole or in part, collectively or individually, put them in danger. It may have been that some of this knowledge came from Martha Tabram. We have not been able to establish whether the women knew each other, but given that they all lived within a relatively small area of London, this possibility cannot be ruled out. What is almost certain is that information or rumour quickly spread, and what was whispered in one place would find its echo in another.

Catharine Eddowes seems to have had information about the killer, since she is said to have been prepared to claim the reward for his unmasking. Our investigations show that she was in a hurry after she left the police station, as though she was going to meet someone. We have always found it slightly suspicious that her partner did not seem to be expecting her back that night, claiming that he thought she might have stayed at her daughter's. Is it feasible that he thought he would gain from whatever she was doing on that fateful night?

Long shadows of intrigue and suspicion hang over Mary Kelly's murder. Mary was obviously fearful prior to her death. We would venture to suggest that she was coming to the point where she realized that some knowledge or information she held was dangerous. We find it suspicious that she apparently took up with Joe Barnett so quickly after arriving in the East End. It has always been assumed that this was at her instigation, and yet one cannot help wondering whether Joe, with his knowledge of the East End, had not been put into the position of observing her and her cronies. In the sessions it became apparent that Mary Kelly's arrival in the East End coincided with a sense of growing unease. We believe that, although her murder was the last in the series, she was in some way a catalyst for the others.

In order to make sense of this we looked at some of the possible reasons. It may be recalled that in 'The Psychic Dimension' (see pages 62-8) we looked at theories about the murder sites. Early on in the investigation I had instinctively felt that they formed the shape of an arrow pointing to the seat of government at Westminster. How, we wondered, could the murders possibly be associated with matters of state? The conclusion we reached was that the women may have been caught between what may be described as two warring factions: an embattled establishment on the one hand and the forces for social and political change on the other.

The most divisive issue in British politics at the time of the murders was the Irish question, which had polarized opinion both in Parliament and the country. In 1886 Prime Minister Gladstone's Irish Home Rule bill had been defeated in Parliament by an alliance between members of his own party, the Liberals, and the opposition Tories. The Irish Republican Brotherhood, or Fenians as they became known, had been pressing for independence, using violence to achieve this aim. Acts of Fenian terrorism in London were rife between 1883 and 1885 and included the bombing of Scotland Yard in 1884.

The conflict between East and West London became part of the wider political struggle for freedom and justice. Bloody Sunday, which occurred just one year prior to the murders, on 13 November 1887, highlighted the gulf between the classes and the lengths to which the establishment was prepared to go to maintain the status quo. Socialist groups, the Metropolitan Radical Clubs and the Irish National League (later Sinn Fein), as the Irish Republican Brotherhood was now known, defied a ban by Sir Charles Warren ('a soldier in jackboots') against public meetings in Trafalgar Square. The protesters attempted to take over the square, and found their way barred by 1,800 police (1,500 on foot, 300 mounted) backed up by 600 soldiers. The Riot Act was read, and some 20,000 people were dispersed. Many of the organizers of the march - such as William Morris, George Bernard Shaw, Annie Besant and W.T. Stead - combined forces to form the Law and Liberty League in order to generate funds to pursue legal redress against the government for this action.

None of the women, apart from Polly Nichols, were what could be called political agitators. Mary Kelly is known to have Irish connections, as did Joe Barnett, but there is nothing to indicate that either of them were Nationalist activists. Could it be that an opportunist might have used the deaths to draw attention away from sensitive issues, such as indiscretions, sexual or otherwise, committed by Royals or politicians? If such action also silenced potential agitators like Polly Nichols, so much the better. All that was required was the right man for the job - a 'Jack'.

We feel that Joe Barnett has the profile and vibration which most closely fits the perception that all the women except Elizabeth Stride had of their killer. Again and again the murderer's coldness and dissociation while committing his crimes came across, and this dissociation was present when we made contact with Barnett himself. He is seen to be capable of anger which 'flips him out', as we called it. His astrological chart shows the ability to mutilate, and we came to the conclusion that he was the most likely candidate so far. There were obvious reasons to suspect him of killing Mary Kelly (his obsessive love for her, his impotence, the certain knowledge that she was having sex with other men), but no particular reason to link him with the other murders.

Throughout our investigation there has been a feeling, and it is only a feeling, that Barnett's activities were directed by someone else, perhaps someone who had nothing to fear from the law. If they are genuine, the original 'Dear Boss' letters purporting to come from Jack and received by the Central News Agency certainly show Jack's need to make a flattering statement about his cleverness. In poking fun at the police in this way Jack seems to be intimating that he is above the law. This could point to Maybrick, to D'Onston Stephenson, to Tumblety, to Bertie, and perhaps to Gull, all of whom had a high degree of arrogance in their make-up.

We believe that Maybrick is the man identified in the sessions as 'The Catcher' - this ubiquitous figure who seems to have kept his finger on the pulse of what was going on in the East End, who would know who could be manipulated and who could not. It is possible that 'The Catcher' was used by people in authority as a means of disseminating negative information in the area, so as to generate fear and panic among the population.

We feel that we can state with some authority that Maybrick was probably responsible for killing Elizabeth Stride, who was murdered on the same night as Catharine Eddowes. From the contact session we learnt that Elizabeth had been going to meet someone, and that she was angry. The sense was that this person would not co-operate. It is possible that she was trying to blackmail Maybrick with some information she had. We know from her astrological chart that she was a curious person, and the sense is that she, like Tabram, Eddowes and Kelly, knew something. According to his astrological chart, Maybrick was capable of murder. Evidence from the diary suggests that he was also fascinated by the death of prostitutes. If Stride was blackmailing him with information that was about Martha Tabram or that had come from her, he might have welcomed an opportunity to experiment.

James Maybrick was murdered in Liverpool in May 1889, allegedly poisoned by his wife, Florence.

My feeling is that with Annie Chapman's murder the pattern for the rest of the killings was set. The manner of her murder captured the interest of the public and perhaps gave the murderer the idea for how to conduct the rest of the campaign he was primed to undertake by Maybrick. Both she and Polly Nichols may have been part of the initial smokescreen to hide the motive for the Tabram murder.

The question we are left with is, why did the murders stop? Barnett seems to have disappeared after the inquest of Mary Kelly and did not reappear until 1906. Interestingly, his name does not appear in the censuses of 1891 or 1901. There is a gap of some five weeks between the murders of Stride/Eddowes and Kelly. It is possible that Barnett, knowing that Eddowes sometimes used the name of Kelly (that of her live-in lover), had murdered her in the hope of fooling those who were controlling or manipulating him. Only when his 'mistake' was discovered was he then forced to dispose of the woman he had loved, perhaps with devastating consequences for him. The 'autumn of terror' may have ended in the destruction of the façade he had so carefully constructed. In the session with Mary Kelly I felt that her murderer had stayed with the body for some time after the killing, as though he was waiting to be picked up by someone.

In the sheer ferocity of Mary Kelly's murder there is a terrible sense of finality, of the deed being done - perhaps of that boil being lanced.

* * *

When it was first suggested that I write this book I have to confess that my first reaction was one of incredulity. So much had already been written about Jack the Ripper - and so much disagreed upon - that I doubted whether a psychic investigation could add anything to the existing massive - and contradictory - body of evidence. Nonetheless, the idea intrigued me sufficiently to make me agree to the suggestion.

I began the investigation with an open mind and a quiet faith in my 'alternative' methods of enquiry. I leave readers to judge for themselves how much or little of the evidence presented here they can accept. However, I believe that we have come close to the truth behind the murders, although much valuable work still remains to be done. My fervent hope is that other investigators will follow the new leads we offer and finally bring this perplexing case to a satisfactory close.

I would like to end on a personal note, concerning our 'silent witnesses', especially the women. At the outset of the investigation, I made a promise that none of the spirit contacts would be disturbed by my actions. That promise was kept.

APPENDIX: ASTROLOGICAL CHARTS

Our intention in casting each of the following charts was to find out what sort of person we were dealing with. We were not trying to prove anything, simply to discover more about each subject.

The 'flat' or solar chart is constructed for the time of midday on the day that an individual is born, and it gives information as to how that person is likely to react to certain situations in life in the broadest sense. We have briefly explained below what each planet represents in an individual's character.

The Sun

The Sun sign shows how creative urges are expressed through conscious acts of will. It gives an understanding of an individual's 'public face'. The Sun 'rules' (is at home in) the sign Leo. If the Sun is strongly placed in the chart there is a need to express sexuality in the most definite and personal terms. A weak Sun can reduce physical vitality. If, for instance, Mars were very powerfully placed in a chart dominated by a weak Sun, then physical energy might not be equal to sexual desire. This might result in frustration and anxiety.

The Moon

The Moon's position in the zodiac shows unconscious emotional reactions to situations based on early childhood experiences and family training. It also gives information about relationships with the mother, and thus, by association, how relationships with women are perceived. The Moon rules the sign Cancer.

For a man with the Moon in a difficult aspect to Pluto and/or Mars, there could have been difficulties in his relationship with his mother, which would lead to sexual problems for him later on. He could also have fathered a child which was later aborted either wilfully or through natural miscarriage.

In women the Moon in a 'hard' aspect with Mars and/or Pluto may indicate that miscarriage and/or abortion has occurred.

Mercury

The planet Mercury's position in the zodiac indicates an individual's thought processes and how the ideas and decisions these engender are communicated to others. It also reveals how decisions are made and what is considered before a decision is made. The position of the planet will indicate what communication skills are available. Mercury rules the sign Gemini. In the fire or air signs Mercury works through the male (more aggressive) energy, while in either earth or water it operates through the female polarity.

Mercury's role in sexual activity is largely one of inventiveness in sex play. It is worth noting that the Ripper murders were more a statement to the world at large than a message to the women themselves. The letter received by the Central News Agency, if genuine, has an element of playfulness about it - for example, in the reference 'my funny little games'.

Venus

Venus's position in the zodiac indicates how individuals give of themselves and how they express their feelings for others. It also reveals the ways in which the good things of life, both the material and the spiritual, might be attracted. It suggests what need there may be for comfort and sensuality, and also what to those individuals constitutes beauty. Venus rules the signs of Taurus and Libra.

Venus is sensuality; Mars is sexuality. A strong Mars and an 'overworked' Venus often indicate a powerful sexual drive, but a difficulty in finding the right partner and/or setting to achieve consummation. Interestingly, Venus and Mars conjunct (placed together in a chart) can indicate bisexuality in a person; we found this in Catharine Eddowes' chart, and the astrological work we did regarding the Duke of Clarence reveals the same placing. (There were many rumours of the Duke's homosexual activities as well as his dalliances with prostitutes.) This aspect can also sometimes indicate a clinical, if not downright cynical, attitude to sex and sexual activity.

Mars

Mars' position in the zodiac shows how physical energies are used to express needs. It affects aspirations, assertiveness, courage, and sex drive. It gives an indication of how individuals express themselves in everyday life through their actions, rather than words. Mars rules the sign Aries.

Mars reveals the extent of an individual's need or ability to dominate and direct the course of his or her own life and the lives of those with whom he or she comes into contact. The nature of sexual drives, their direction, the limits of their reality, and relative strengths or weaknesses are all related to the position of Mars in the natal chart.

Jupiter

The planet Jupiter's position in the zodiac shows how the individual expresses the need to grow and expand. Jupiter indicates the ways in which life is enjoyed and the reactions to opportunities as these present themselves. It indicates a person's interest in the higher values of life and how this interest is shared with others. Jupiter rules the sign Sagittarius.

Jupiter of itself has little to do with an individual's sexual expression. However, when it has strong aspects to any of the other planets which do describe sexuality, it can serve to underline a tendency to seek pleasure and exercise desire. In certain positions it can indicate a potentially dangerous degree of self-gratification.

Saturn

The planet Saturn's position in the zodiac indicates the ways in which individuals may try to establish and then protect their position in life. It also shows how responsibilities may be shouldered and recognition sought for their efforts. Saturn rules the sign Capricorn.

Saturn modifies and can restrict, inhibit or limit sexual activity. When acting with the Moon, for example, Saturn can retard emotional growth to such an extent that full sexual maturity and emotional self-expression are severely compromised. In the horoscope of a man, it can make him very reluctant to respond to the vibrations of the women he meets in his life. When with Venus, for example, it can limit partnerships, perhaps to people of a particular type, or at least hamper the individual's ability to find fulfilment in personal relationships. This could manifest as a tendency to use prostitutes for sexual gratification instead of applying oneself to a monogamous relationship.

Neptune

Neptune's position in the zodiac influences the overall outlook of all those born within the same period of thirteen years during which the planet remains in one sign. Thus it can reveal the mystical and inspirational influences felt by each generation. Neptune rules the sign Pisces.

The positions of both Uranus and Neptune may be indicators of sexual imbalances; both give rise to variations in sexual behaviour. Neptune's modus operandi works through the female polarization of energy and is receptive and more subtle in its effects. The expression 'way out' might have been coined for Neptune. In a difficult aspect to Mars, Neptune will give a tendency to masochism. If Saturn or the Moon is involved there is likely to be some kind of domination in sexual practices.

Uranus

Uranus's position in the zodiac shows a great deal about the motivation, goals, and creative flair of those born in each seven year period during which the planet is in each of the signs. Uranus rules the sign Aquarius.

This planet indicates eccentricities in behaviour, sexual or otherwise. Uranus is very forceful, aggressive, and direct in its effects. It is very commonly found in very strong positions in the horoscopes of people who have a tendency to engage in the less understood aspects of sexuality. A difficult aspect to Mars is often indicative of sadism in the individual concerned. This tendency is especially exacerbated if Saturn is also involved in any way. If any of the other sexual indicators are in Capricorn and in aspect with Saturn and/or Uranus, there may be other forms of sexual deviance at play in the individual.

Pluto

Pluto's position in the zodiac influences the entire generation of people born within the same twelve to twenty-two year period during which the planet remains in one sign. It can reveal the need for regeneration and control in each generation. Pluto rules the sign Scorpio.

Pluto tends to emphasize the deeper psychological links between the individual's emotional framework and his or her sexual means of self-expression. Pluto when aspected with the Moon indicates a strong connection between the female aspect of an individual's nature and his or her maternal line. Tremendous upheavals often take place within the family and other personal relationships which may deeply affect the nature of the individual's sexual self-expression. This could be expected in, for instance, the chart of Joe Barnett; it is known that his mother deserted him when he was thirteen.

Pluto is the planet of destruction and transformation. A person who murders in order to rid the world of a contamination would show heavy influences from Pluto.

FOOTNOTE: Where more than two planets are closely grouped in a chart this shows a heightened intensity of feeling or emotion associated with those planets

JOSEPH BARNETT 1

Date: Tue, 25 May 1858

Time: 12 00

Zone: 00 E

Latitude: 51 31 N

Longitude: 0 6 W

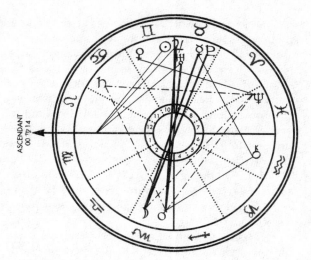

Joe would have had strong opinions, and his way of working generally appeared consistent. However, when under pressure he could slip into bigotry and a fear of change. He would often need help to keep his enthusiasm and inspiration going, though good powers of concentration and endurance ensured that his determination for those things he believed in always remained strong.

Joe had the Sun in Gemini and could at times have been accused of being two-faced and insincere. It also meant that he could be both versatile and adaptable. He had a good mind and knew how to use it: he had a knack for always being one step ahead of events. When it came to making a judgement, he possessed a good deal of common sense.

Being flexible, he was able to take all kinds of lifestyles in his stride. He had a tendency to change his mind frequently, which meant he was continually altering his objectives. Tolerance and a love of freedom could have allowed him to go further afield than perhaps others might want to do. He could also be restless, disruptive and unpredictable. There was often a flamboyance in the way he made his decisions which could confuse people.

Much of Joe's energy was spent trying to solve his need for partnership. He had a great need to be in a relationship. A loving relationship was one of the few ways in which he could find real fulfilment, feeling he and his partner to be like one soul in two bodies.

Joe's working life would have been very important to him, for it provided the routine and stability which he considered to be essential. He was probably over-conscious of health matters, believing that a good life and good nutrition were important. His work gave him the resources to build on what he had and, for that reason alone, he was prepared to put up with the daily grind in order to create something better.

Being naturally sympathetic, Joe responded to many things which others might miss. He could be very moved by others' misfortune. There was often an excess of emotion with him which would need channelling. This emotional intensity could, however, make him very possessive. The person he loved was also the manifestation of his need, and he guarded both of these with jealousy. Joe did not like others moving in on his personal territory.

Sometimes Joe could find himself fawning to authority, allowing them to intimidate him or take advantage. This aggravated him. One of his chief aims in life was to discover how to overcome this tendency. He would also frequently find himself bottling up and keeping his feelings to himself, because to express them could be exhausting.

Joe would often find himself swinging wildly between his instinctive feelings and his rational thoughts. They did not function in unison. It is more than likely also that Joe found that his partners were not necessarily the ones to give him the right amount of confidence. Joe loved exchanging and sharing ideas with a partner but had to be careful to avoid relationships with those whom he instinctively felt might deceive or betray him. When Joe was threatened or insecure, he would be inclined to return like with like.

Emotional confusion could lead to clouded judgement. He often did not seem to know which way to go, unsure as to whether he should be a leader or a player, or at times even just an observer. Joe was constantly in a state of flux, not knowing whether he was one of the manipulated or if he was doing the manipulation. Luckily, these situations were not permanent and often seemed to disappear as quickly as they arrived.

With Mercury in Taurus, Joe had an effective and competent intellect which took naturally to the more contemplative, or reflective, way of thinking. He would have tended to pick up someone in mid-sentence while his mind was turning over the information. In its negative form this could have manifested as the speech defect of echolalia, which shows this tendency. In Joe's case things tended to surface very slowly at the front of his mind.

Mercury opposed to Mars and conjunct with Pluto suggests that, at his worst, Joe could be extremely cutting and sarcastic. He could also use the same mental powers to great constructive effect, becoming incredibly forthright and far-seeing. He was somewhat distrustful, in that he could imagine all kinds of conspiracies and plots being hatched in order to catch him out.

Mars in Scorpio suggests that Joe had a passionate nature and that when he found someone he truly loved, he would fasten on to that person and not let go. He remained completely loyal to that intuitive, or 'gut', feeling, although at first he might show caution and reserve. He did not suffer fools gladly, remaining clearheaded about others' behaviour however much he might have wanted to join them. There were times, however, when he found this self-imposed regime too strict, and he would lash out and go off the rails for a while.

The angles of other planets to Mars suggest that it did not take much to turn Joe from a placid and normal person into a formidable and implacable enemy. He felt that his anger was nearly always justifiable and reasonable, but, while he did have the benefit of rational judgement in a crisis situation, when certain buttons were pressed he could explode into the most intense display of anger. He relied on such sensations for stimulation and more often than not would probably receive some kind of vicarious pleasure from the arguments which occurred. Joe often felt it would help him if he were able to decide why he felt certain things and what had caused those feelings. Such rationalization would not always have helped him, however.

Jupiter in Taurus meant that one of Joe's greatest dreams was perhaps that of letting loose the dynamism which would bring about major change in the structure of society as he knew it. Most of the time he would keep such ideas well in check, which might well have made him seem dour and non-caring. The ritual of religion did not interest him in the least, but he would have had some kind of personal belief.

Saturn in Cancer indicates that Joe would be particularly bound to his family, which formed the centre around which his life pivoted. He would not have liked to see too many changes in this sphere: departures and marriages upset him. For instance, he would have found it particularly upsetting when his father died and his mother disappeared. On the other hand, he was thrilled by births, for they gave him a sense of the continuation of what he held to be important.

Joe was sometimes tempted to change the pattern of his working life from one of structure and discipline to one of adventure and abandon, such as when he and Mary Kelly began to live together after only two meetings. His occasional desire for, and pursuit of, change and diversity could have given him a reputation for instability and novelty-seeking. Equally, normality was something which he needed in order to feel that his feet were on the ground.

Joe would put up with situations, even the most mind-numbing, far longer than most people, because he had the tenacity to see them through. Setting his heart on something gave him the necessary impetus to move forward towards a goal, and it must have been particularly galling for him to lose both his job and his partner at the same time. Without the security which they had afforded he would have been like a ship without an anchor and must have been very frightened. The disappearance of those tangible things which reassured him of his own validity may well have led him to touch in on a side of his personality which he did not understand.

168

JOSEPH BARNETT 2

Date: Sun, 23 Dec. 1860

Time: 12 00

Zone: 00 E

Latitude: 51 31 N

Longitude: 0 6 W

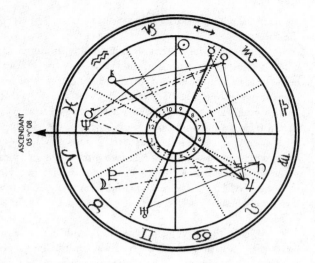

Joe Barnett 2 was good at coping with and understanding new experiences which were thrown at him, but he often found difficulty in expressing himself. If he genuinely did not understand something he could tie himself in knots and become stubborn and obnoxious. He needed proof.

With his Sun in Capricorn, Joe would have needed a basic structure which would enable him to create security for himself and those for whom he cared. He would have been fairly ambitious in his own way and would have used the experiences in his life to enable him to reach the top in whatever he was doing. In his need to be that little bit superior to everyone else he would probably have developed a good deal of perception and initiative, though at times of personal stress that perception and the ability to take the lead in any situation would have disappeared, leaving him tired and confused.

Joe would have had to be fairly conventional in what he was doing, and so the need to be gainfully employed would have been extremely important, not just from the financial point of view, but also for his own self-esteem. It was important for him to feel personally successful. He would have been fairly highly principled and would have had his own moral code. What he perceived as wrong-doing would have made him very uncomfortable. He would probably have been much respected among his own kind.

Joseph would have been demonstrative with his instinctive feelings and would not have experienced a problem in expressing them. However, he could find this boring at times and, having a great flair for drama, could go overboard and spill into imitation and exaggeration.

Although he had an instinctive feel for structure and order in both his personal and working life, what was orderly could become chaotic and structure could turn into bedlam. Sometimes it would seem that everything he attempted came apart in his hands, which meant that he would be overwhelmed by feelings of defeat and failure. Joseph perpetually battled with what he wanted to achieve in life and what actually happened. He would need to feel that he had his finger on the pulse of what was going on in the world outside.

With the Moon in Taurus, Joe's dependability was a virtue, and he would have needed to stand by his partner whatever the cost. Emotionally, he would play a waiting game and would observe and weigh the fundamental value of a person or situation before committing himself. His feelings were very deep, which normally meant he possessed good judgement and insight into the dynamics of his relationships.

The angles to the Moon indicate that Joe experienced feelings with great passion, though emotional harmony was sometimes elusive for him and he could over-react. Others felt that he was dependable and well-adjusted: all kinds of weird and wonderful folk would seek him out. He was something of a safe haven for drifters and hangers-on but would have had no difficulty in coping with this. On the other hand the Moon conjunct with Pluto suggests that he could often feel that he existed in a void. This would have arisen from his relationship with his mother, which led to a sense of loneliness. This feeling sometimes manifested as a fear of the future.

Joe had a quick adaptable mind, but sometimes, due to his Mercury being in Sagittarius, when it came to communicating his ideas his speech came out garbled and confused. He could be a 'Jack of all trades' but an authority on very little. He also displayed a cynical sense of humour which enabled him to talk his way out of trouble. The angles between Mercury, Saturn and Uranus show that Joe needed firm ground from which to operate intellectually. Today he would be what is known as a lateral thinker, developing many original ideas

Venus in Scorpio suggests that there was a tendency in Joe to strike out before he got hurt, which meant that his relationships could be highly volatile. Because of his emotional make-up it was difficult to judge his moods accurately, though few could be more passionate than he was. He was direct and up-front with his affections and could be sympathetic and sensitive when necessary, although he shied away from relationships where there was no sense of space.

Mars in Pisces suggests that Joe would have had an in-built fear of failure which would have made it difficult for him to make commitments. The anxieties that he felt could well have led him to use alcohol as a defence mechanism. He would rarely give himself permission to lose control in any way - it was highly spectacular when he did. Man's basic instincts fascinated and concerned Joe at one and the same time.

Joe loved a parade and all that was theatrical. His Jupiter in Leo meant that he enjoyed pomp and circumstance, and all sorts of displays. He could himself be personally demonstrative, dispensing his feelings generously, and with a touch of style, particularly in groups. Sometimes life seemed unnecessarily complicated to Joe when Saturn in Virgo came into operation and nothing seemed particularly straightforward. He needed clarity and order in his life if he were to succeed.

He did his best to co-operate with authority in his working environment, rarely wishing to upset the apple cart because he found change difficult to handle. Joe admired initiative in others but was often too apprehensive to demonstrate it himself.

ANNIE CHAPMAN

Date: Tue, 2 Mar. 1841

Time: 12 00

Zone: 00 E

Latitude: 51 28 N

Longitude: 0 36 W

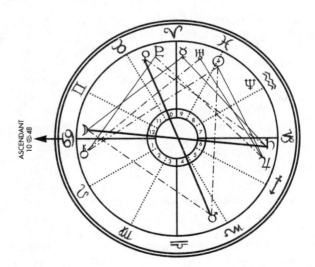

It has proved very difficult to pinpoint with complete accuracy Annie's actual birthdate. We chose this particular date as the most likely out of several after conventional research and then checking it out through the use of dowsing. The portrait that emerges from the following chart resounds strongly with the contact session we held. This lady also shows all the qualities that are demonstrated in what is known of Annie from witness accounts. More sophisticated astrological research will reveal whether we have succeeded in pinpointing Annie, but certainly her strength of character - and an endearing dreamy streak - shines through.

* * *

Annie was the kind of person who related to people through her feelings. She could be highly intuitive, and also could find herself taking on other people's problems, often getting heavily involved when there was no need to do so. This would often mean that her own life became messy and unhappy, and leave her unable to cope. This would have had an effect on her power to create stability in her life, and so the practical aspects of living would have been very difficult. Under pressure she found difficulty in expressing herself, although whenever she developed a proper structure she was fine. Then she was able to exploit opportunities and take advantage of what was round her.

Annie's Sun in Pisces meant that there were often two aspects of her life which appeared to take her in two different directions at the same time. If she learnt to go with the flow then everything worked perfectly. If she could not get things straight in her own mind then she would find herself buffeted by life and feel a bit like a boat on a stormy sea. It is perhaps this quality which meant that she could make mistakes at times of major life decisions - such as choosing to leave her husband. She would put herself in situations where she met new and interesting people for the sheer joy of it and then get scared and run for cover. Money as such meant little to her, except as an expression of the way she valued herself, and her financial state reflected this. In other words, if she was feeling good she found money, and if she was not then she became impoverished.

Annie would probably have relied fairly heavily on her own intuition, but would not have realized that those things which she took as omens were simply reflections of the way she was feeling. She had a wonderfully vibrant personality, but it took time for her to get into the position where she could express herself effectively. She usually knew what she expected of people but would get distressed and hurt when others did not want to co-operate. She could be quite dramatic at times, and sometimes that sense of drama could make her disruptive, almost as though she had to psych herself and others up in order to achieve her goals. One of the problems was that her objectives would often change in mid-stream as it were. This unpredictability could drive others to distraction.

Moon in Cancer suggests that Annie could be very receptive to atmospheres and the hidden qualities in people. She was very sensitive, and so when things were not going right for her she would disappear into her own private space and become very self-protective. Anyone, male or female, with Moon in Cancer also shows a strong need to 'mother'. The difficulties with her own children, and particularly the death of the eldest daughter, would have thrown her into complete confusion and turmoil. There would thus have been many conflicts between her own self-protectiveness and her need to protect others. If things got too difficult she would need to create both a physical and a mental space for herself.

One of the most difficult conflicts for her to resolve was that between her own need for independence and her sense of responsibility. She herself would have seen this as her own private battle and one which had to be continually faced. This often meant that she did not always understand her own motivation for the actions she took, or for the way she was thinking at any particular time. She could often see more clearly for others than she could for herself.

Mercury in Pisces meant that Annie was somewhat mentally disorganized. She did not have much in the way of self-discipline to allow her to stay with one interest for any length of time, but she did have the ability to assimilate a little information about a number of subjects. There was a curiosity in her approach to life which meant that she continually had her ear to the ground. She could, however, become easily exhausted by continually rushing around seeking mental stimulus. She could make mental connections which left others standing, but could also get lost in speculation and fantasy. At the same time she could be quite taciturn and get depressed if she was not sure of her ground. When she was on form, in an argument she could tie her opponents in knots and leave them wondering what had hit them.

Venus in Aries meant that in love relationships Annie could be quite forceful. She said what she meant, and meant what she said. If others could not handle this attitude, then tough.

She could strike out in passion, be far too intense within the moment, and end up destroying the very thing she needed most - to be loved. She had to be careful to control the fact that she could blow hot and cold, and therefore often ended up back in self-protective mode wondering how she had managed to get herself into a particularly tricky situation.

Mars in Scorpio shows that Annie was completely loyal to her own feelings. No matter how much others let her down, if she cared then she would allow many transgressions. She recognized that she was someone who needed to be fairly active sexually, and yet it would be one of the first areas where problems struck in a difficult relationship. When she was frustrated in any way, her volatility could take over, leading to moments of passion and explosive behaviour which frightened herself and others. Most of the time, however, because she knew what could happen, she remained level-headed and sensible.

Annie had a strong personal moral code, and Jupiter in Sagittarius would have meant that when she set out to enjoy herself that is precisely what she did. That need to take risks within the moment may well have led to her taking risks with her health, perhaps being a contributory factor to the tubercular condition revealed by her post-mortem. This condition was one which we ourselves encountered during our contact session with her.

She did not necessarily understand spirituality and religious issues as such, but it would have distressed her if she had felt life was not being lived properly. She would have recognized and appreciated that a common aim could draw people together, and would have liked the companionship that offered. At the same time such companionship would have imposed a strain on her sense of responsibility and correctness. Saturn in Capricorn shows that she would have preferred to use conventional means of achieving her objectives.

MONTAGUE JOHN DRUITT

Date: Sat, 15 Aug. 1857

Time: 12 00

Zone: 00 E

Latitude: 53 25 N

Longitude: 1 9 W

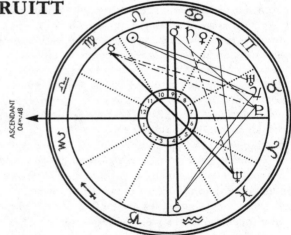

An emotional nature gave Montague a highly strung disposition. Working through feeling gave him an increased sensitivity towards intuition. His strongly sympathetic, compassionate nature meant that he was often attracted to people less fortunate than himself. This could create bewilderment and turbulence in his life and he could become moody and unpredictable. His protective reaction was an inclination to become reclusive and defensive. There was a tendency for him to become dogmatic and unwilling to make changes in his life.

Because he had the Sun in Leo he was a very proud person and did not suffer fools gladly. Public embarrassment would have been complete anathema to him, and whoever inflicted that kind of humiliation on him would have become his enemy for life. He guarded his personal dignity and self-esteem fiercely, and it may have been some such embarrassment which led to his suicide.

Montague's love of colour and parade drew him to such things as the theatre and to large-scale social occasions. He loved all the grandeur and energy and the flamboyant display of big emotions. It would have bored Montague to sit around and theorize for too long. He was full of ideas and had the confidence to translate them into action, recognizing the need for deeds of heroism. He could, however, often take action before having thought things through. Montague was exceptionally aware of all the grand display needed in being human, but this may have caused problems in his ability to handle close relationships properly. He would have found difficulty in expressing his deepest feelings. Others often thought of him as inconsistent, though in fact it was probable he had difficulty in finding an inner tranquillity.

Montague had a good sense of his own individuality. He liked to be noticed and was flattered when others singled him out for praise or attention. Nevertheless, he also had an equal need to be retiring and to withdraw into the safety of his own self-protection.

He could be extremely reasonable, adopting a rational and fair-minded approach to whatever issue was at hand. At other times he could be quite the reverse and become impassioned, even inconsistent. He had two levels to his personality which interchanged according to the force with which he reacted to circumstances. When his emotions were involved, it was his instinct which determined his reaction.

The combination of the Sun in Leo and the Moon in Gemini gave Montague a mind of high ability, with a great deal of determination. He was gifted and enthusiastic and also a very likeable individual. The Moon in Gemini also suggests that Druitt would have loved to have had someone with whom he could walk through life hand in hand. His friends gave him a strong sense of belonging, and it was this security which bestowed upon him his greatest emotional strength, for it made him feel part of something special. He needed intelligent conversation with others because this gave him a viewpoint from which to decide on his own course of action. The angles to the Moon suggest that Montague had a great need for relationships. If he was not actually in partnership with someone, he could make errors of judgement which would lead to deep depression. Fortunately, on the whole, these situations did not last long, and under normal circumstances he was able to recover his equilibrium.

Sometimes Montague created problems just to get his teeth into something. He probably developed a liking for the complexities and confusion that go with problem-solving. Mercury in Virgo suggests that he liked to study the detail of the difficulty, thus acquiring a working knowledge of the issue. He had a sensible rational outlook which meant that he could adapt easily to situations. He would sometimes feel the need for isolation, to be alone with himself and his thoughts: this was vital in order for him to maintain a clear view of things.

Mercury opposed to Neptune means that Montague was capable of developing considerable psychic ability. This would have given him the ability to be clairvoyant, and to have a greater perception of other people's motives. Mercury's angle to Jupiter meant that intellectually it was easy for him to understand the thoughts and emotions which gave rise to world events. Sometimes he might have found this faculty more of a burden than a blessing: being different was too much of a responsibility. He would have been familiar with the concept of mind manipulation in one form or another, and it may have been this that made him fear for his own sanity.

Venus in Cancer meant that Druitt's home was important to him. It was important that he had the security of knowing that he could create a space into which he could invite others. In that way he was able to assess how his partners would react to him. Each new relationship brought fresh insights and enabled him to make the adjustments to his own life which he saw as necessary.

Mars in Leo suggests that Montague had a good understanding of the need for action and was not likely to procrastinate in times of crisis. He would meet a difficult situation head on and deal with it with great efficiency. He had a strong belief in the power of one person to change the world in which he lived, and he had a great respect for an individual's own temperament.

Sometimes Montague was too rational about his feelings for others, particularly about those whom he considered special. His passionate nature was not the kind that ran away with him and dragged him into fierce arguments. There was no need for him to be too analytical, although others considered him to be reserved and mature when it came to handling himself in a crisis. The angle between Mars and Pluto would have caused Montague some difficulty, as he would have had a problem in being able to understand his own baser instincts. This side of his nature would have had some fascination for him.

Montague had a very fertile imagination, but he was capable of sitting on his own enthusiasm. This tended to make him pedantic at times, although this may well have been when he was in fact at his most anarchic, and most anxious to change his world. At the same time the world of spirit and religious feeling could remain an area of mystery for Montague. He would be reluctant to delve too deeply.

Saturn in Cancer would have forced Druitt to remain trapped in the past in some way. Family solidarity and responsibility would have been important to him and would have considerably shaped his beliefs and attitudes. After his father's untimely death the protection of his sisters' legacies before his own concerns demonstrates this quality. He would have conformed for the majority of the time but would have yearned for life to be different.

CATHARINE EDDOWES

Date: Thu, 14 Apr. 1842

Time: 12 00

Zone: 00 E

Latitude: 52 35 N

Longitude: 2 6 E

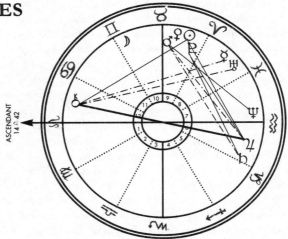

A chiefly fiery nature gave Catharine Eddowes a way of operating which meant that she was always very involved in what she was doing. She could fire up very quickly and would have had a lot of dynamic energy and enthusiasm. She had an enterprising, direct attitude and was quick to exploit chances. Kate, as most people knew her, might have found it difficult at times to relate to others on an emotional and instinctive level, since often she could be tactless and self-centred. She found it difficult to bear a grudge, however.

With her Sun in Aries, Catharine had a strong sense of her own individuality. The idea of living a life in the shadows would not have appealed to her at all. Her self-assertiveness was both her friend and her foe. It helped her when she was the only one with the nerve to speak out against injustice; but it worked against her when she could not keep her mouth shut.

There was an anti-social streak in Catharine. For instance, if someone set a time to meet, she would turn up late, which often caused arguments. She did not necessarily think she had done anything wrong. She tended to live in her own head. It was what she was thinking that mattered and she had the ability to make herself oblivious to her environment. She was probably an idealist, setting her own standards and living by them, regardless of opinion.

The angles to the Sun in her chart indicate that she was exceptionally aware of the whole gamut of human emotions. Sometimes, however, she would have difficulty in confronting emotional issues head on, and then they began to overwhelm her. She was most likely to have been superstitious and to have played around with 'black cats and lucky charms'. Catharine was fascinated by world events and very much wanted to be part of them. She would have liked to be involved in such a way as to feel that somehow she was actually helping to shape events, without necessarily being manipulated by them.

Catharine had a confidence in her approach to life which allowed her to enter easily into new projects. She had the potential for sweeping along all kinds of people in her enthusiasm, for she had little time for the difficulties that might lie ahead. Her sense of independence was strong. She would have been unlikely to spend too much time with those whom she considered likely to inhibit her freedom of movement.

Kate had an enormous sense of fun to which she often catered. This 'fun' side of her character meant that she liked to play jokes on people, although they were nearly always harmless pranks, not the malicious kind. She was described by her sister, Eliza Gold, as a 'regular jolly sort'. Her style was simple and direct, and she respected others who also laid it on the line rather than those who were devious and secretive. She found deviousness offensive, for when others started manipulating her it injured her sense of dignity and pride - it made her feel as if she was not being taken for the intelligent person she was.

Because her Moon was in Gemini, Catharine's friends would have given her a sense of belonging. It was this security which gave her her emotional strength - it made her feel part of something special. Her greatest dream would have been of being matched with someone who was totally committed to her alone.

It was very important for Catharine to have some kind of intellectual rapport with her partner. Words and conversation sparked certain thought patterns which gave her access to her emotional self. Understanding her inner nature gave her a way of overseeing others' actions. In clearing away her own difficulties first, she provided a haven for others.

The angles from, and to, her Moon suggest that Catharine found it difficult sometimes to let more positive and beneficial feelings surface. She may have had problems at times reconciling herself to what she considered to be her depressive phases and, equally, her recurrent sense of unease. In this state she could easily paint herself into a corner and develop an 'us and them' complex. She could find herself plagued and weighed down by emotional responsibility. Despite this she had the ability to put the past behind her and start all over again.

Kate did not have to strain for inspiration, although she would sometimes have found difficulty in formulating ideas that others could understand. Much of her mental energy seemed to disappear into a black hole rather than form coherent patterns. Once she got it right, there was no limit to the directness of her approach.

The angles to Mercury indicate that Catharine had a mind which could go off at all sorts of tangents. She made intellectual connections which astounded others, leaving them wondering where she got her flair and inspiration. She was nearly always on the go, even when she didn't have to be. Sometimes, however, she felt like escaping from the world. In other words, when things started grating, she got angrier and angrier, and this led to much frustration and depression.

She lived with the father of her children for more than 20 years. His name was either Thomas Conway or Quinn. While he did not drink regularly, it is known that when he did, he often beat Catharine. After the breakdown of this relationship, she met John Kelly, who was to be her companion for most of the rest of her life. When she took a shine to someone she meant it, and would stand by them through all sorts of difficulties. Because she had Venus in Taurus, Catharine could be trustworthy and devoted. Some people may have found her slow to make commitments - she herself may sometimes have regretted that she was not more rash in love. This is because, with Venus conjunct with Mars, Catharine's feelings were resolute, up-front and seductive. She would have been self-sufficient enough to know that she could do without a partner if necessary and therefore she would have tended to hold back in new relationships until she knew her feelings were reciprocated. Kelly said that they had 'got throwed together quite a bit, and the result was we made a regular bargain'.

Because others found it difficult to provoke Catharine, or to work her up to a pitch of excitement, they might have thought she lacked passion, or a sense of conviction. With Mars in Taurus and her Jupiter in Capricorn this was simply not true. When action depended on inspiration, her approach was often a considered and deliberate one. She would frequently appear not to be paying attention to anything around her. This was, in fact, part of her capacity for being able to keep her passions contained, although they simmered away but never quite boiled over. When they did, anything and everything was swept along with the force of her outburst.

The angles to Mars confirm that Kate was, indeed, a passionate person and one in whom there was little doubt about the intensity, or depth, of her feelings. Her volatile nature did have a way of working in tune with her instinctive reserve, giving her the benefit of rational judgement in a crisis situation. She was inclined to become involved with people or projects to an almost alarmingly intense degree. She always somehow came away from these experiences having used a degree of levelheadedness that was one of her greatest strengths.

Mars square to Neptune unfortunately shows that the best thing Catharine could have done when she went to a public house was not to drink alcohol. Her willingness to drink anything and everything alcoholic might have been funny at the time, but she really did not have the physical or emotional constitution to maintain such a lifestyle. It is known that neither her sisters nor her daughter approved of her drinking, and it apparently caused much distress. What was probably not realized at the time was that Kate had what is now recognized as the disease of alcoholism. Over-the-top enthusiasm takes people into all manner of extreme circumstances where judgement fails them and possible disaster ensues. When sober, Catharine had a kind of inner stop-cock which kept her from going as wild as those around her - or as wild as she would often have liked. In drink, the story was different.

By and large Kate worked well with the domain of religion and areas which expressed the spiritual quest. It was important to her to understand the meaning behind such a personal quest in the first place. She would have been aware of some quality missing in her own life. She would have treated religion and philosophy with some respect and with awe, although she disliked the manipulative power it gave those in authority. She felt that all those inner changes which were possible through involvement in spiritual matters were hers by right.

There was an anxiety which constantly nagged her - but really should never have been allowed to take precedence, for it could take her to the depths of despair. Her concern was that anything she worked hard for might disappear as if it had never existed. It seemed most often that nothing was secure, that nothing could be taken for granted. Even when she went hop-picking with John Kelly in the last weeks of her life it still seems that she came home with nothing, having to pawn his new boots for food on the way. She needed some kind of structure and organization in her existence, yet this disappeared when she was drinking. It is not known for certain that she was definitely a prostitute, although she may have solicited when she could not get money from her sisters or her children.

SIR WILLIAM GULL

Date: Tue, 31 Dec. 1816

Time: 12 00

Zone: 00 E

Latitude: 51 54 N

Longitude: 0 55 W

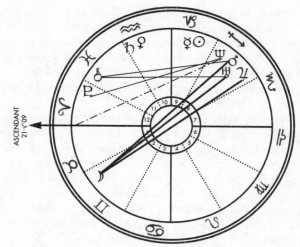

Sir William Gull had a multi-faceted, somewhat complicated psychology. His desire for, and pursuit of, change and variety may have given him a reputation for instability and novelty-seeking in certain areas of his life (he also remained loyal to Guy's Hospital for 25 years). He himself had a hands-on attitude towards personal and professional situations and crises, and this would have led to a degree of professional arrogance.

Anyone with the Sun in Capricorn can be compared to the mountain goat, continually striving to reach the top in whatever they do, and this was very true of Sir William. His ambition meant that he would achieve this by the most expedient method available, which usually involved taking the conventional route. By being in the right place at the right time he would have been able to move quickly up the ladder of success.

Gull had a strong sense of his own uniqueness, and would avoid situations in which he might become invisible. He forged his own personal path through life, despite often flying in the face of accepted wisdom. To succeed at everything he undertook was a challenge, for his successes were always of a highly individual nature.

Sir William was very principled, however, and would not sell himself short just to please someone else. Others frequently found much to learn from him. He offered not just information but also a set of rules by which to live. Sir William's mental agility led to versatility, and his cool manner and controlled emotional disposition earned him the respect of many as they saw in him evidence of the maturity they so often needed. The reforms he introduced into Guy's Hospital, which meant that medical students practised on real patients, show his far-sightedness. He could venture into intellectual areas where 'angels might fear to tread'.

Being naturally impatient, Gull would have been quick to anger, but just as easy to placate. He could be outspoken regardless of possible consequences. A touch of arrogance showed that there would have been many occasions when Sir William would be accused of being nothing but a downright troublemaker! However, he could often adopt a high moral tone. There would equally be times when he could seem to be unprincipled and anti-social, careering from one enterprise to another without a thought for those he trod upon in the process. He had an enterprising, direct attitude and was always quick to exploit opportunities. Sometimes, however, such persistent pursuit of power could overstrain Sir William's perception to the point where he could not see the wood for the trees. Opportunities could be right under his nose and he would miss them. In pursuing his goals he probably found it difficult at times to relate to, and appreciate, other people on an emotional and instinctive level.

It was important for Sir William to feel part of something special, and his greatest emotional strength came from his friends and the social circle to which he belonged. With his Moon in Gemini, it would have been very important for him to have some element of empathy with his partner, as this would be a source of emotional stimulation. Words and conversation sparked in him certain ideas which would lead him towards his own unique conclusions. The need to understand himself gave him a basis from which he could judge others. He could easily have taken as his profession accountant, consul, ambassador or public speaker.

There was a whole range of emotional energy within Sir William. He could be either passionate and enthusiastic or completely defensive, creating and seeking out conflict where there was none. Disruption and turmoil created a stimulating environment for him in which his emotional strength flourished.

Sir William had an independent mind, and any route he took was never arrived at accidentally, but was the result of careful planning and strategy. His Mercury in Capricorn meant that he was capable of tackling any problem without referring to others for reassurance - he intended to get to the top on his own merits and had the enthusiasm to do so. He had an inspired strain of optimism which pervaded his overall outlook and inspired others with enthusiasm. Jupiter in Sagittarius meant that he had a moral code to which he adhered, no matter what. He would not err from his personal canon of law.

Gull would have had a love of large social gatherings where people from all walks of life could come together on an apparently equal footing. Venus in Aquarius could suggest that others might have regarded Sir William as lacking emotional energy, although the angles to Venus suggest that this was not always the case. He would often rationalize his reactions rather than approach them from an emotional point of view. He could be very forthright, especially on a one-to-one basis when an intuitive response was important. His relationships, both professional and personal, would have needed to be quite structured, and his bedside manner would have been impeccable. He was no doubt good at telling his partner and colleagues of his feelings for them, but could also delude himself as to his own feelings.

Sir William would have had the potential for emerging as a real hero of the hour. Mars in Sagittarius gives the ability to be the one person who will say the unmentionable or do the impossible, and this task often fell to him. Equally, he could go to the opposite extreme, infuriating others when he was unable to commit himself. With the angles to Mars shown in his chart, Gull could be volatile and often disruptive, according to the circumstances around him. Often to protect himself he would refuse to get himself into a situation where he might lose his self-control.

Saturn in Aquarius dictated that Sir William needed to be a part of the general movement of human progress: his greatest fear was of not belonging. Part of his life-plan was to belong and so he could easily adapt and conform to society's strategies and organization, for this gave him security.

When it came to adapting to the normal patterns of life, Sir William could conform as well as anybody. Normality was something which he needed in order to feel that his feet were on the ground. However, he often had the feeling that things could be radically different. The angles between Uranus and Neptune and Uranus and Pluto suggest that Sir William would have been aware that society needed to be changed, but that the power and the energy to do this could be elusive and not easily usable. He may well have felt that it was his place to assist in this process of change.

MARY JANE KELLY

Date: Wed, 1 Apr. 1863

Time: 12 00

Zone: 00 E

Latitude: 52 40 N

Longitude: 8 38 W

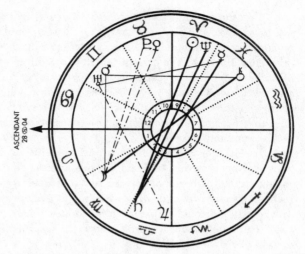

In the absence of any firmer information we have taken Mary's birthdate to be that recently discovered by John Morrison of the Cloak and Dagger Club, to whom we offer our thanks. To my mind this profile fits Mary's character better than any of the other possibilities we have investigated.

* * *

Mary was well equipped to manage life in its many aspects - she was balanced and versatile. However, to be truly successful, she would have needed to develop one of the qualities of intellect, emotion, will power or physical capability more fully. She had an enterprising, direct attitude and was quick to exploit opportunities.

With the Sun in Aries, Mary would have had a strong sense of her own individuality. The idea of living a life of obscurity did not appeal to her at all. Her self-assertiveness could be both a blessing and a curse. Some of her habits could be very anti-social. For example, she had no concept of timekeeping - she lived in her own personal time zone. In other ways she also lived in her own head - she could be totally oblivious to her environment. It was what she was thinking that mattered. She could also be an idealist, setting her own standards and living by them, regardless of opinion.

The angles to the Sun indicate that it was usually easy for Mary to convey her instinctive feelings to others, which meant they had no doubt as to where they might stand in her particular scheme of things. This could produce both positive and negative results. Mary had a vibrant, passionate nature, one which took provocation and adversity in its stride. The struggle between inhibition and freedom in her own life was strong, and often led to chaos and to her not knowing 'which side was up'. It sometimes seemed as if she sailed through life oblivious to all that was going on around her. This was not actually correct, since she could find herself very affected by the pain and difficulties around her, and would simply pretend that nothing moved her.

Mary had good intuition and a good appreciation of moral values, but she sometimes had trouble in putting herself forward or convincing others of her point of view, no matter how much she believed herself to be right. This is because of her difficulty in maintaining a high self-esteem, for in depression Mary could too easily be persuaded that the world was a horrible place and that the blame for this should fall on her. She had many special qualities.

The intuitive faculty is not something evident in many people. With that, Mary could have gone far. This was because she had the ability to identify with another person or thing and go through their experiences as if they were her own. It is perhaps this faculty which led to her create so many smoke-screens in her own personal life. She was able to make stories which she picked up seem as though they were her own. This same intuitive faculty would have been invaluable in Mary's dealings with society at large, for it allowed her to gauge others, to get a good appraisal of them without perhaps having to go through huge difficulties beforehand.

Emotionally, Mary kept herself to herself. A Virgoan Moon made her very private and self-protective, and she gave away very little in public or to people generally. Because she remained reserved in public, others often misjudged her as being aloof and detached, maybe even cold. But, with the chosen few, it was a different story altogether. Then, she would let down her defences and reveal just how generous and warm she could be. Angles to the Moon give the sense that Mary's affections and emotional life worked pretty harmoniously together, giving her the confidence she needed to express herself to her partner without the fear of misunderstanding or rejection. She loved attractive partners and would have been, to say the least, something of a flirt.

Emotionally, Mary often found difficulty in keeping herself in check. Emotional harmony was sometimes difficult for her, and she could over-react to others whose behaviour she might find offbeam. She would find it difficult sometimes to let more upbeat and positive feelings stay on top, and, while not intentionally provocative or aggressive, would often go overboard. She could drift into depression with great ease. This was likely to be due to her sense of being encumbered by emotional responsibility. She could create difficulties for herself where there was no clear way out, though this state never lasted for long. She tended to look for satisfaction in areas where others would not dare go.

With Mercury in Pisces, Mary always seemed to be chasing after one subject or another, no matter how obscure. She was often responsive to hidden meanings and undercurrents, which meant that she could have something of a scatter-gun approach to life. There were not many tricks that Mary missed. Her individualistic approach meant that she could shoot off into all kinds of unexpected areas with a degree of eccentricity. This could give her the ability to withstand a great deal of pressure, but when the façade gave way there could be problems.

Like so many of the women we have looked at, Mary was, on the whole, dependable and reliable. When she was in love with someone, she meant it, though when she fell out of love, she left her partner in no doubt of her change of heart. Venus in Taurus gives the individual the need for nice things and a lifestyle which 'feeds' the sensuous side of their nature. Mary would have loved the lifestyle that she originally seems to have chosen (that of the courtesan). With Venus conjunct with Pluto, she would often wonder what had got her into the relationships and situations in which she found herself, but had an equally strong ability to walk away from them.

Mars in Gemini can give an incredibly hurtful way of using words, and there were many who would have felt the cutting edge of Mary's tongue. As soon as she had said what she had to say, however, everything, so far as she was concerned, was back to normal. Her temper was explosive and often disruptive and at these times she was probably not disciplined enough simply to walk away from trouble.

As a rule, with Jupiter in Libra, Mary was fairly balanced in how she expressed herself. When she got obsessive over something, however, she tended to parade her feelings with much self-display, leaving others in no doubt as to the extent of her commitment. She also understood the need for a belief system and man's religious quest. She appreciated the meaning behind such a quest in the first place, and was prepared to make changes in her own beliefs if it suited her.

Things had a way of happening easily for Mary. Goals and opportunities which may have eluded others often came her way. With Saturn in Libra, this could be both good and bad. She might well have been able to save herself unnecessary difficulty, but she also had the facility to be complacent about her successes, which meant that they tended to be somewhat nebulous and disappear into the great blue yonder.

So, to sum up, Mary would have chosen a path in life totally of her own making. She would not have wanted to be conventional, though she would have been well aware of the problems which this gave her.

ROBERT LEES

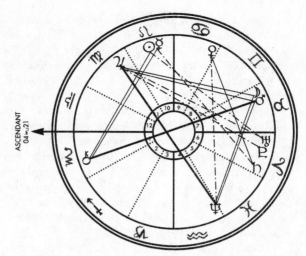

Date: Sun, 12 Aug. 1849

Time: 12 00

Zone: 00 E

Latitude: 52 39 N

Longitude: 1 9 W

Robert Lees enjoyed socializing and the escapism of social gatherings, although he needed to learn to take it in moderation. His love of colour and parade drew him to such things as theatrical display. Big emotions expressed by flamboyant characters, and the lofty speeches which often accompanied such performances, all fed his need for exhibition. His mental agility led to versatility and he could wander into high-brow territory where less able people would never dream of venturing. He was full of ideas and had the confidence to translate them into action. He needed to learn to sit down and think things through perhaps a bit more often. He would have found that this resulted in his plans being more effective and enduring. Public embarrassment was something he found difficult to handle, and yet he had the facility for inviting it upon himself.

Robert had a knack for attracting people who were perceptibly different or eccentric. It is as if he set out to draw towards him those who were like this, for there was a mutual fascination. The more unconventional they were, the more interest they had for him. He would sometimes find difficulty in expressing his intense feelings for his pet projects, but when he had got it right he was extremely eloquent.

The Moon in Gemini gave him a hold on all aspects of duality. He was able to differentiate between his emotional self and his more spiritual side. Because he understood this in himself, he was able to perceive what kind of healing and support others might need. It was important for him to be at peace within his close relationships, for he drew a great deal of strength from them. He felt things very intensely, and therefore his highs could be very high and his lows very low. This is because he took his responsibilities very seriously and could sometimes find himself overburdened. Emotional confusion could lead to clouded judgement, something about which he knew a great deal. There were times when it would have been better for him to have shut himself away from the world, because anything and everything could go wrong. These situations were never permanent, however, and often seemed to disappear as quickly as they arrived. This was because his faith allowed him to deal adequately with them.

Robert was mentally creative, often dreaming up all kinds of concepts that had not been thought of before, or thinking up new approaches to existing problems. He was capable of being totally spontaneous, but others could see him as arrogant and judgemental. His powers of concentration and foresight were well-honed. It was very important that Robert felt there was a place for him in the world and that he personally lent his own contribution to the structure of society as it was then. Without this, he would have felt redundant, as if he were not a part of any greater design, but consigned instead to total insignificance.

Robert could be too self-protective with his feelings, at times to the point of defensiveness. This was because he had a good appreciation of the finer, more feminine aspects of feeling. He may have taken his awareness of such qualities for granted, but he did need to be aware that he was one of the relatively few who actually was conscious of these qualities in the first place.

A sharp mind could give way to a sharp tongue, and both of these Robert had. He sometimes used them both without restraint, leaving others wondering why he should have been so cutting when perhaps the situation did not call for such an extreme response. He did not necessarily mean to hurt, simply to make a point. However, this quality sometimes was not disciplined enough, and he could wind up contributing in the wrong way with appalling timing. The lesson to be learnt was to think before he acted. The heat of the moment could catch Robert on the hop and, in an argument, he could lose his temper. This was probably due to the frustration that so often accompanied the inability to verbalize grievances. For this reason he would also have disliked the excessive use of stimulants, since that meant losing control.

Robert Lees could not help seeing a spiritual quality in everything, from the grandest down to the most trivial. His reaction was nearly always one of respect and deference to an overpoweringly unknowable energy: his concept of God. He was very aware of the connection between the movement of the spirit and the rhythm of music; thus he would often find a release for his inner feelings in the realm of music and dance. His own spiritual quest was a cornerstone of his existence, and because of this he always knew what changes were needed within his own life and also within that of others.

Robert worked well with the religious experience and, indeed, was very much in favour of the whole business of spiritual quest being propagated for the greater good. The whole point, as he saw it, was that, as there seemed to be some kind of inspired structure to the world at large, that same structure must exist within him; therefore he as an individual reflected the world, and it reflected him. He would not see it as any bad thing if society were to encourage a greater involvement with the more searching, interior life.

A man of high principle, he must have found being treated with derision very hard, but perhaps also saw it as part of his spiritual burden.

JAMES MAYBRICK

Date: Wed, 24 Oct. 1838

Time: 12 00

Zone: 00 E

Latitude: 53 25 N

Longitude: 3 0 W

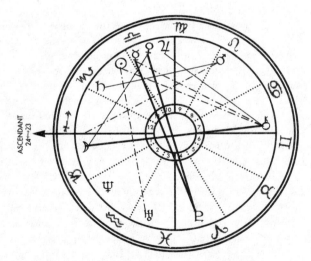

James Maybrick was amply equipped to manage life in its many aspects: intellect, emotions, willpower, and physical capability are all well represented in his chart. Thus he was balanced and versatile. His capacity for initiative, conviction, and perception combined well to enable him to cope with and understand the demands of experience. Money meant a great deal to him, and he required large quantities. A life of poverty would have been too much to ask of him.

With his Sun in Scorpio, James liked things to run according to plan. When he made up his mind to do something, then that is what happened. He persevered from beginning to end, whatever the project. Sometimes his single-mindedness could become too rigid, and he missed out on what was going on elsewhere. As a rule, he was fairly balanced in how he expressed himself, needing to walk the fine line between being purposeful and being obsessive. He could become completely fixated on one thing, going completely overboard, working up a fanaticism for some idea, concept or person. At times like these, he would parade his feelings with much self-display, leaving others in no doubt as to the extent of his commitment. Following the initial spurt of enthusiasm he would relax into more 'normal' behaviour. If such self-display did not occur, he could end up feeling repressed and frustrated, and then innocent people could suffer from the backlash.

The angles to the Sun suggest that Maybrick had a quick and perceptive mind. He could be incredibly versatile but at times could seem to be caught in a perpetual battle between what he wanted to achieve in life and what actually came to pass. Occasionally everything he attempted would fall to pieces, leaving him with strong feelings of defeat or failure. He could often make the wrong choices, sometimes having difficulty in deciding what was the right course of action. Maybrick did, however, have a rational and pragmatic mental approach which stood him in good stead when all around looked as if it were going to crumble.

Though he might have had some odd mannerisms, he would not take kindly to being laughed at. He would often find himself the centre of attention, a position he enjoyed, though at times he would tire of this. James remained loyal to those ideas or people on whom he had bestowed his attention. Fools, however, were not suffered gladly, and fidelity would have been an integral part of his make-up.

Maybrick's Moon in Capricorn suggests that he was highly sensitive - his feelings could be easily hurt. His reaction to this was to withdraw entirely and pretend to himself that he had not cared in the first place. He would decide it was just a difference of opinion. He needed constant reassurance to be able to express his emotions properly. As a partner, James would offer loyalty and devotion until he was rejected, and then he could become cold and vindictive.

The Sun in Scorpio coupled with the Moon in Capricorn intensifies the pride of Scorpio and makes the individual extremely self-indulgent. While there is a great amount of patience and endurance, there is also a hard nature and rigidity of opinion with some fixed habits. James could swing wildly between extremes of behaviour. It was this configuration which would have made him the able businessman he was.

The angles to the Moon indicate that James could often have found himself in danger of over-reacting to those whose behaviour he did not understand. He would not necessarily be overly aggressive but would find cause for argument when perhaps there was none. He could easily become depressed and feel that he was overburdened with responsibility. He also had the ability to bounce back from difficulty and was able to turn disorder into a productive outcome.

Mercury in Libra indicates a fair-minded approach to any problem. He would have had to have been under great pressure to have lost this. He would probably have often used the words 'On the other hand', since he would always wish to appear open in his judgements. He could handle disruptive or potentially threatening situations better than the majority of people because his comprehension allowed him to remain unflustered and therefore capable of warding off his enemies. He had a great appreciation of the way a fine mind worked and could use his own perceptions as a tool for understanding. He was well able to make what today might be called quantum leaps into the unknown. There was also a strong subversive streak in him which at times could verge on the anarchic.

Socially, James would have been fairly adept. Venus in Libra indicates that he liked good company and meeting new people because he had the tendency continually to re-invent himself in the light of the way he thought others saw him. It was very important for Maybrick to be in a relationship, for partners kept him emotionally balanced, though he would have needed someone who enjoyed social activities as much as he did. In contrast to this, he could also feel that his nearest and dearest were out to get him and he could shy away from personal involvement.

James had a good sense of action and was not likely to procrastinate too much in times of crisis. This is indicated by his Mars in Leo. It meant that he would meet a difficult situation head on and tackle it so as to wipe out his adversaries. He felt that a person should be respected for his or her individuality; and would therefore ally himself to all sorts of political and social causes if he felt this would bring about change.

The angles to Mars in Maybrick's chart indicate that he was a great believer in the world of intuition and passion. He would react sharply to anyone or anything which he thought was going to prevent him doing what he wanted to do. Fearing that others could not handle such a reaction, he could equally get very angry if he did not feel he was dealing properly with his own passion. He was drawn to the spiritual elements in life and would have been capable of using this area to express what was good in him.

The desire to make of one's life something different and unique is innate in most of us. James's preferred way was to follow his own emotional barometer and allow himself therefore to follow his own vocation. It would not matter whether it was deviant or not, he could be ruthless in its pursuit. If he thought his actions were correct, he would follow through with determination and energy. This is fairly typical of someone with Saturn in Scorpio.

MARY ANN NICHOLS

Date: Tue, 26 Aug. 1845

Time: 12 00

Zone: 00 E

Latitude: 51 31 N

Longitude: 0 6 W

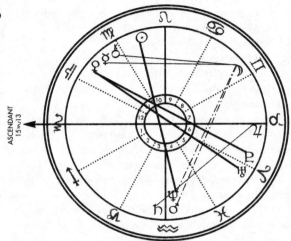

Mary Ann (or Polly, as she was known) was a good communicator and could be inquisitive. Most of the time she had a great deal of determination and endurance, but could at times slide into narrow-mindedness and intolerance. She had strong opinions and her ideas appeared consistent. Something would spring to mind and she would speak out. In fact, she reacted strongly towards any kind of restriction.

With her Sun in Virgo, Polly was usually good at handling the purse strings and ensuring that the little things were looked after properly. Happy to begin in a small way, she accepted that matters would often improve. She was someone who believed that life had to be as natural as possible, lived with the minimum of fuss. She could be quite shy, and would often seem to be isolated from the world. This could sometimes mean that she missed out on opportunities which came her way. These opportunities would often stare her in the face but she would not see them. Her mind would often be set on some far goal and future excitement rather than on the needs of the present.

With the Sun opposed to Mars, Polly would have managed to attract violence towards her. She would have met some fairly obnoxious people in her time. She usually succeeded in keeping her own emotional violence hidden, although at increasingly frequent intervals she found herself going over the top. The angle between the Sun and Jupiter confirms that she had a great flair for drama and appreciated the same quality in others. There were times, however, when this need for drama would become farcical. Polly was self-expressive and demonstrative with her instinctive feelings, and people knew her for her warmth and sense of occasion. She had a fairly good sense of her own individuality. She would have liked to be noticed, and was flattered when others singled her out for praise or attention.

Polly could be eminently reasonable, adopting a rational and fair-minded approach to whatever issue was at hand. At other times she could be quite the reverse and become heavily emotional, even irrational. There were two levels to her personality which interchanged according to the intensity with which she reacted to any situation.

Because she had the Moon in Gemini, Polly's friends gave her a sense of belonging, and it was this security which produced her greatest emotional strength, making her feel part of something special. She desperately needed partnership, but at the same time would not have wanted to be tied down by any kind of emotional commitment.

The angles to and from the Moon show that Polly's inner passions ruled her emotional life. Her partner was never left in doubt about how she actually felt. It was very important for her to have some element of intellectual rapport with her partner, although her responses would often be emotional rather than logical. She was instinctive and persuasively passionate. Understanding her own inner nature gave Polly a way of assessing other people's actions and reactions, and she would have had to learn to follow up on her own intuitive feelings. She could respond to all types of people and situations and others probably felt that Polly was a dependable and well-adjusted person emotionally.

However, Mercury in Virgo shows that Polly could create problems for the sake of having something to get her teeth into. She could develop a real liking for all the scheming that problem-solving requires. At these times, she again would feel the need for isolation. She would have been quite sensitive and creative and in this way she could work things through to her own satisfaction.

Venus in Libra and the angles to Venus indicate that Polly could tend toward being too self-protective with her feelings at times to the point of defensiveness. This could sometimes arise from feelings of guilt. Others did not always understand that this was because she felt things deeply and she was not prepared to be hurt. It was not always possible for her to see clearly in the heat of an argument, although she hated disharmony. In the cooler aftermath of an argument Polly would often explain away her own reactions. She would have sought people out in order to reassure herself that she was both needed and wanted, and also to ensure that she had the kind of support that she needed.

Mars in Aquarius confirms that she would have refrained from actual physical violence, feeling that there were other ways in which to make use of her more instinctive, even aggressive impulses. Her strong feelings about issues touching upon the welfare of her associates would have made her able to help almost anyone who might be in some kind of trouble, despite having prejudices of her own.

Angles to Mars show that Polly would have had to learn fairly early on in her life to handle her own mood swings. It must have taken a good deal of self-control to learn how to balance the argumentative side of her nature with the more sensible, reasonable side. She would therefore have learnt not to get caught up in situations where she ran the risk of losing her temper. Suppressing her innate power may well have caused problems with all aspects of her health, and sometimes with her appreciation of other people's motives.

Jupiter in Taurus suggests that Polly had a very fertile imagination, but one which on occasion she prevented from flowing into more uplifting areas. In other words, she could stifle her own eagerness. This might have made her rather prosaic at times, inclining her to keep her eyes on the ground when really they should have been scanning the heavens. She could also give the impression that her spirits too often seem dampened; but what is probably more correct is that they would be bubbling away deep below the surface where they were acquiring a compulsive force of their own. Polly would have loved to allow these forces to burst out in a backlash against the establishment.

Sometimes Polly would tell herself that the inner life did not really matter and that, in any case, it would somehow take care of itself. However, not even she truly believed this. Such a feeling usually results from a struggle to unite the internal and external realms, and from a sense of having failed to do so. She would have developed an antagonism towards the psychic and esoteric side of life, which never lasted for very long because at rock bottom she was fascinated by the 'other dimension', which was therefore somehow always striving to be acknowledged. Such a conflict would result in some wild swings between the polarities of the spiritual and the mundane.

Saturn in Aquarius meant that one of her greatest fears was of not belonging, of being on the outside looking in. She very much needed to be a part of the general movement of civilization, and exclusion from this would distress her. Polly would have felt some confusion over her perception that others needed to be different and the recognition that if things were to get better people must be prepared to change.

To find that she was an outcast from society would have upset her and she would have looked for ways, with greater or less success, to ensure that she belonged to some group of people, even though she would have done her best to retain her own individuality. She would often have attempted to change the pattern of her working life from the daily grind of poverty. She would long to throw it all overboard and to be different. She also had the potential, given the right support, to be so.

Polly seems to have used prostitution and alcohol to help her to manage her life. Of all of the Ripper victims she is the one who seems to have used prostitution most often as a way of getting what she needed. Hence a comment she made as she left the lodging house on the last evening of her life, 'I'll soon get my doss money.' She shows the same sterling character that epitomizes the other victims of the Ripper. She was well liked by those who knew her well, and though many of Polly's last years were spent in workhouses she seems to have coped tolerably well with that type of life.

ROBERT D'ONSTON STEPHENSON

Date: Tue, 20 Apr. 1841

Time: 12 00

Zone: 00 E

Latitude: 53 58 N

Longitude: 1 7 W

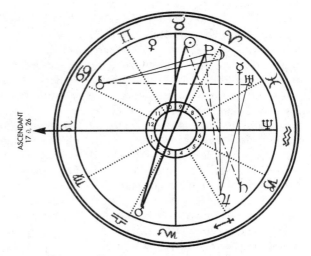

Robert D'Onston Stephenson had strong opinions and, while he was fairly consistent, he could at times slide into fanaticism and also be reluctant to change. He probably found it troublesome at times to relate to, and appreciate, others on an emotional and instinctive level. Inclined to be hot-tempered, he could lose control fairly easily. However, his attention would often be caught by something else, enabling him to move on quickly, for, like any would-be sorcerer, he needed to be in control to be really happy. Then his stamina ensured that his determination remained as strong towards the end as it was at the beginning.

Stephenson, with the Sun in Taurus, was no doubt fairly intense and conscientious. Roslyn D'Onston, as he called himself, would also expect these qualities in his partner: without them there would be no relationship. His home and his ability to nurture others would have been important to him, but there would also have been a very stubborn streak in him from which he could not be dissuaded. One of those people who always know they are right - because unfailing instinct told him so - he would always stand his ground when challenged, with little regard for personal danger. A strongly sensual man, Stephenson would have had to express his feelings physically by touching the things he loved and by surrounding himself with people and objects which called for affection. Money, for him, was simply a means for obtaining beautiful objects. By turns indolent and a whirlwind of activity, he accepted no half measures in his life.

APPENDIX: ASTROLOGICAL CHARTS

Even if he had been a calm person, D'Onston had a habit of attracting some very strange people into his personal space. There would have been in him a streak of emotional violence which could not easily remain hidden. This might well lead to eccentric behaviour. In his case it led to an interest in the occult.

He would have had at times an intuitive feeling for structure and order and would have wanted to make everything run according to patterns and rules, preferably his own. Frequently order and chaos would become confused, and he would land up in a complete muddle. Just when he had everything worked out was the time when it would most likely degenerate into problems.

Stephenson had a confidence in his own approach to life which allowed him to enter into new projects without even considering the pitfalls that might lie ahead. He had the potential for sweeping along all kinds of people in his enthusiasm. D'Onston would be unlikely to spend much time with, or effort on, those whom he might consider would inhibit his freedom. He had an enormous sense of fun which needed to be catered for on a continuous basis, and this could make him something of a dilettante and sensation-seeker. His style was uncomplicated and direct, and he had a great deal of respect for others who laid it on the line.

Being naturally persuasive, with the Moon in Aries, he could easily draw others into his circle, giving himself a perhaps false feeling of power. When this was transposed into an emotional context, he could end up believing he was irresistible to women. Stephenson reacted quickly to emotional stimuli, but always seemed to have the stamina to extricate himself from troublesome situations. Others liked his directness and his single-mindedness. Stephenson was volatile and touchy, but genuinely demonstrative, too, which gave others a sense of being in fresh and exciting company. The Sun in Taurus and the Moon in Aries would have given him the persistence to continue with his studies of the occult, beyond the norm. He would have needed the strength of personality to keep him focused on and organized towards the task in hand. This could sometimes land him in very weird relationships, for his partners were not necessarily the ones to give him the feeling that he had chosen well. He would then tend to look elsewhere for satisfaction.

D'Onston would have found it relatively easy to maintain good feelings in his dealings with people. He had much to give and usually responded positively and quickly to those same qualities in others. He responded intuitively to atmosphere and the subtle vibrations which create environments and situations. The Moon conjunct with Pluto sometimes meant that his emotions left him feeling as if he existed in some kind of a black hole. Often this was of his own making: everyone else was having the enjoyment he craved. He would seem to be losing out in a way he did not quite understand.

Mercury in Aries indicates that new ideas always seemed to be coming up for consideration. Mentally active, he did not have to search far for inspiration. If, however, that inspiration later proved unworkable, there was a tendency to suffer from a sort of mental paralysis. The angles to Mercury suggest that he would need to have found himself something in which he could invest his intellectual abilities: he would be good at debating, or at playing 'devil's advocate' in any argument. He may well have had the ability to get people arguing for the opposite view to the one they really believed in.

With Venus in Gemini, he would be devoted and loyal to his partner at the time - even if a little fickle on occasions! He would always need a love interest, since this would be one of the few ways in which he would feel totally fulfilled. Part of this need would have been the communion of minds and ideas. His greatest pleasure would come from friends and family, though he would find it difficult to make a full commitment to anyone. Mars in Libra shows that he would have had to consider every side of the situation before committing himself, and then he would often decide it was not worth the effort involved. He would struggle with the necessity to be objective and yet go with his feeling at the same time: this balance, when handled well, can give the ability to be clairvoyant. Handled badly, it can lead to arrogance and perhaps pomposity.

Stephenson had a religious belief which needed irrigating frequently, whether or not he would be involved in organized religion. Sometimes a devil, sometimes a saint, he nevertheless had a moral code to which he adhered consistently. With Jupiter in Sagittarius, he would simply respond to his private inner voice and would have huge enthusiasm for things which he considered brought joy and fun to everyone. He would live very much in the here and now, in the hope that he was doing the right thing, and would try to pass that belief on to others. He very much believed in the idea of a spiritual quest and would use his Saturn in Capricorn to help him manage that quest. He would have worked out his own methods of self-development, and would adhere to them quite strongly. He could thus reject what to others seemed normal and follow his own star. He would easily accept the esoteric, feeling that it should be used for the betterment of mankind.

ELIZABETH STRIDE

Date: Mon, 27 Nov. 1843

Time: 12 00

Zone: 00 E

Latitude: 57 43 N

Longitude: 11 59 E

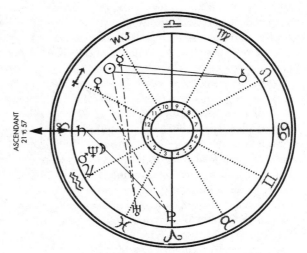

Elizabeth had a mind which was inquiring and intellectually alive. Ideas came easily to her and, just as easily, she could communicate them to the nearest audience. (She was known to speak several languages, and 'spoke English like a native'.)

Elizabeth would not always have found it easy to establish stability in her life, especially on a material level. She needed a structure which allowed her to be organized and methodical. Saturn in Capricorn shows that she would have had an admirable amount of self-control and discipline; and others will probably have been envious of her ability to stay on her chosen path. It was her capacity to adhere to a system which would carry her through in the end. Living by whatever system she chose was second nature to Elizabeth, for it allowed her to move through life by a proven method. It would have been this ability to make use of the system which would have enabled her to go into (and come out of) the workhouse when necessary, and to apply for loans or charity from the Swedish Church, as she did. She needed structure and organization in her existence and, if the way to these lay along conventional paths, so be it. They gave her the results she wanted.

What worried Elizabeth was the tendency for all that she worked so hard for over the years to vanish as if it had never filled any place of importance in her life. It would have seemed sometimes that nothing was stable, that nothing could be taken for granted. It was an anxiety which constantly nagged her but which really should never have been allowed to dominate, for that meant an almost certain route to depression.

A vivacious, social creature with a quick perceptive mind, with her Sun in Sagittarius, she was the kind of person who would go to a party and take over the proceedings. 'Long Liz,' as she was affectionately known, would enjoy conversation and would often make a spirited contribution to any discussion. She instinctively responded to humanitarian issues and had a passionate belief in freedom on all levels: physical, mental and spiritual. At times Elizabeth would have been moved by the feeling that a greater power was watching over her, that there indeed might be something 'out there'. This might well have brought her to the doorway of religion. She is known to have applied for poor relief several times to the Swedish Church in London; the last occasion was a few days before her death. On the other hand, a witness at her inquest is said to have overheard someone say to her, 'You would say anything but your prayers.' It mystified Elizabeth, for instance, how others could be so gullible so far as religion was concerned, yet the whole idea of life being a journey to be undertaken may well have intrigued her. She would probably have felt that religion was something which others needed, whereas she could take it or leave it. Elizabeth would, however, have had a highly developed sense of morality and principle, even though others might not appreciate how she arrived at her conclusions.

If anything made Elizabeth feel claustrophobic, she would make a dash for freedom. Her live-in partner, Michael Kidney, claimed that it was her drunken binges which took her away from him, and she is known to have quarrelled with him in the days prior to her murder. (However, Michael himself liked a drink, so although he claimed drink took her away from him there had to be other reasons as well.) It is more likely that her drinking habits were a way of escaping from a sense of constriction.

The angles to Venus, for instance, show that Elizabeth could go out of her mind in a relationship in which she felt confined or hampered. This is perhaps above all the main discovery about her. Emotionally, she felt suffocated if she thought her freedom was being threatened. No matter how fond she was of someone, if they did not respect that side of her, no permanent good could come from a partnership with them. Kidney is reported as saying, 'I think she liked me as well as anyone.' She did not have any qualms about being direct or forthright regarding her affections. She just came out with whatever she wanted to say and everyone else could think what they liked.

Elizabeth would often seem to be wrapped up with the powers that be, whether those powers were the government, the police, or the vigilance committee. What mattered to her was that, by virtue of their position, these powers had authority, and it was the very concept of institutionalized authority which seems to have intimidated Elizabeth and led to many skirmishes with the law. She is said to have been arrested numerous times for drunkenness, or for what she called her hysterical fits.

In astrological charts the Ascendant indicates how individuals express themselves in the world in which they live. Elizabeth had her ascendant in Aquarius, which means she had an open-minded view of life, and a broad appreciation of people to go with it. Her social circle reflected this. She had a knack for attracting people who were recognizably different, even eccentric. Fascination with the unconventional would have satisfied a streak of wildness and rebellion in her. Provided that she thought of herself as the centre of attention she could handle anything. Jupiter in Aquarius additionally indicates that she had a positive approach to all that brings pleasure to mankind, from music to religion, from literature to love.

Elizabeth related to people and situations by using her intellect as the judge, not instinct or feeling. She could be incredibly rational but at the same time had a strong sense of humour. Curiosity continually drew her into the outside world for new experience, although when sober she rarely ventured into situations where she felt she might let go and completely lose control.

With her Moon in Aquarius, Elizabeth would have discovered that a good social life was the key to her emotional balance. Without this, she had a sense of withering up. At the same time, others sometimes considered her to be emotionally detached and undemonstrative. She would have had a reputation for remaining uncommitted and somewhat stand-offish, but this may have been due to a cautious streak and a dislike of being let down. Having such a lot to give, but not always being able or in a position to give it appropriately, meant that when she did let go, she did so whole-heartedly.

In a good relationship, her ability to love and her emotional needs would work fairly harmoniously together. She would have had the confidence to express herself to her partner without fear of being misunderstood or rejected. The angles to the Moon suggest that it would have been surprising if Elizabeth did not try to use her physical appearance to the best possible advantage. Indeed, it is known that she was proud of the fact that she was often taken for being at least ten years younger than she truly was. Michael Kidney actually thought she was some years younger than the 45 she proved to be.

With Mars in Aquarius there were many ways in which she would have channelled her more instinctive assertive impulses, and one was to divert them into the sphere of mind power - or perhaps fantasy. Elizabeth would refrain from actual physical violence - she would normally recoil from it except in drink - and instead would use her mind to fight her battles. Her emotional life was one of intensity and passion. She would sometimes find it hard to tap into the source of her feelings and wonder if there was ever anything there at all. But when she did feel deeply about something she would make an unequivocal commitment. Her strong feelings about issues touching on the well-being of her fellow humans would make Elizabeth help almost anyone who might be in some kind of trouble, despite her own possible prejudices towards a particular person. She was able to respond to all kinds of people and situations which might have passed others by. She would empathize with people in a way that could be quite disturbing to others. If she let her mind rule her instincts she might have sometimes lost sight of the deeper source of her feelings, that private place within each of us. This would lead to a degree of frustration.

Mercury is the planet which highlights our ability to communicate effectively, and with this planet in Scorpio, Elizabeth would have had the power to sustain any goal for as long as she liked; she would remain true to an idea once it became fixed in her mind. Thus, once her mind was made up, she did not change it easily, and it may have become almost an obsession with her to see an idea through to the end. Thus she was often unwavering in the face of opposition. She could at times slide into dogmatism and an unwillingness to change.

Elizabeth had a strong and resilient constitution, which gave her great physical stamina but, if the warning lights were not heeded and acted upon in time, she would go under very quickly. She could fall into a kind of emotional no-man's land from which it would take considerable strength to emerge. For instance, it is not known how she came to be quite so poverty stricken in the East-End of London, but it is known that she was considered to be fairly resilient and kept her life together by sewing for local Jewish tailors and by cleaning.

Inspiration would come easily to Elizabeth. At times her individuality of mind would have led to some of the fabrications about her life, such as the death by drowning of her husband and children in an accident on the Thames. There is proof that there was indeed such a disaster in 1878, when the steamship the *Princess Alice* was sunk with the loss of 527 lives, but no proof that any of those lost were related to Elizabeth. (Her husband actually died in 1884 in the Poplar Union Workhouse.)

Venus - the planet which indicates how we show our affections - in the sign of Sagittarius meant that Elizabeth was sometimes seen as the life and soul of the party - a 'good time girl'. There are so many aspects of her chart which show she enjoyed a good time that it must have been hard for her not to be able to do so. While the witnesses at her inquest presented her as quiet and industrious, this is likely to have been in order to present her in the best possible light, so that others would think well of her. Even in death she would have wanted that perception maintained.

Notwithstanding this love of riot and fun, Elizabeth was usually completely loyal in a relationship, with a highly developed sense of morality. In the last few years of her life she always went back to Michael Kidney, even after an argument. Indeed, Elizabeth lived by her principles more than most, because the moral code she set herself could not be compromised. Elizabeth expected from her partner the same degree of honesty and constancy. Elizabeth did not double-cross, nor did she deceive those whom she truly loved.

MARTHA TABRAM

Date: Thu, 10 May 1849

Time: 12 00

Zone: 00 0 E

Latitude: 51 53 N

Longitude: 0 6 W

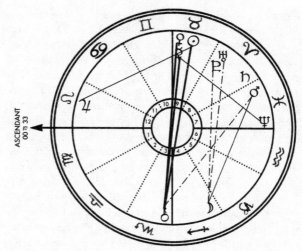

An assessment of Martha's astrological chart shows her to have been shrewd and loving. She was strongly sensual and would have needed to express her feelings through touch and by surrounding herself with people and objects which allowed her to show her affection. She would have worked at gaining a reputation for being available to her friends, although she was not good at expressing herself verbally.

Martha had a great deal of enthusiasm for life but was also inclined to be short-tempered. In the heat of an argument she could boil over, and instead of expressing herself through hugs and kisses she could physically lash out and cause a great deal of alarm to others. The angles to her Moon show that she often found herself emotionally fraught. She was not intentionally provocative or aggressive but, because emotional harmony was sometimes elusive for her, she would over-react to others whose behaviour she might find somewhat odd. Diplomacy was not her strong point: she would not have any qualms about being direct or forthright. However, others considered her to be reserved and mature when it came to handling herself in a crisis, and her nature, though passionate, did not allow her to be dragged into conflict.

Martha was loyal and able to remain in all sorts of difficult situations, although she would never allow herself to become bogged down. She expected a similar kind of loyalty from others and would not have made a commitment to anyone unless they showed the same qualities. She blended devotion and independence, which she often used as a shield. She had the vision and sensitivity to stand by those in whom others had no faith at all and would be convinced that they could succeed at whatever they were doing.

In the home Martha would have been very able, creating meals out of almost nothing, and making others feel welcome whatever the conditions. Money, for her, would mean that she would buy the best quality she could afford. She would have been very proud of this skill. Being what she considered to be gainfully occupied was very important to Martha - it provided her with routine and reliability. She would not necessarily have liked the activity, but needed to feel that there was a meaningful system and structure to her everyday life. She would often do things from habit rather than necessity.

Martha had a complicated personality and a quick perceptive mind. This was shown by her unpredictability and her nervous temperament. Her desire for, and pursuit of, change and variety might well have given her a reputation for instability and novelty-seeking. There was, for her, no middle way. She would either be extremely active or thoroughly lazy. She took challenge and adversity in her stride. Intellectual concepts would have to be explained in a logical, practical way. When they were not, or she did not understand, she showed her objection by becoming stubborn and unco-operative. Believing always that she was right, she stood her ground when challenged, with little regard for personal danger.

Martha was always capable of changing her direction in life quite dramatically. She would have sudden flashes of inspiration which would push her to try new experiences. She could be an incurable romantic, and like so many of her generation, could find herself driven by whatever idea she became fixated on. This could be quite overwhelming for others. For instance, she was probably something of a hypochondriac, paying a great deal of attention to her own health and that of others.

There were times when Martha could adopt a rather subservient attitude to people, appearing to allow them to intimidate her. While this secretly infuriated her, she could use it to her own advantage, and it is probably this aspect of her character which allowed her to ply the trade she seems to have followed. One of her chief aims in life, therefore, was how to overcome her tendency to be submissive and to find her self-assertion.

Martha responded to all kinds of people and situations which might not have made any impression on others: she reached out as far as she dared. She was fortunate in being able to turn emotional anguish into something positive. That inner disturbance was the key she needed to be productive. Martha could thus handle disruptive or potentially threatening situations better than most people, and so in many ways she was an unlikely victim.

Her mental strength normally allowed her to remain unflustered and therefore capable of warding off her adversaries. There was also a streak of deviousness in her and she could trip up unsuspecting opponents, easily leaving them not quite knowing what had happened. She used strategy and intrigue to get the better of her opponents. In the process she might well have struck a few raw nerves and hidden secrets along the way. She tended to attract the unconventional type, whether she wanted to or not.

Martha also had an intellect which was largely introspective. She would mull things over before giving an opinion. This process could be quite slow and may often have been mistaken for disinterest. She did, however, have the ability to change her outlook after some deliberation. There was a tendency towards anxiety. Often, she would feel that other people were conspiring against her and manipulating her fate. Her reaction would be to tend towards intrigue and manipulation herself.

With her Venus in Taurus, Martha would have had to make a strong commitment to whoever she was in love with at any particular time. It may well have taken her quite a while to admit to loving someone, but when she did she would not want to let go. It is perhaps unfortunate that it seems to have been the men in her life who left her, including her father, who separated from her mother and then died when she was sixteen years old.

However, Mars in Pisces indicates that she had a real difficulty when she was being asked to make a commitment - she disappeared somewhere and got thoroughly drunk. It was not that she could not face the issue: rather that often she would be apprehensive about backing herself to win. This kind of reaction would usually be due more to a lack of respect for herself rather than to an inability to succeed. A passionate and deeply devotional nature meant that an almost religious belief in people and causes sometimes led to a fear of her own forceful emotions and feelings. This could also have led her to drown her difficulties in drink.

Martha loved all sorts of lavish display, rituals and melodrama. She was personally very demonstrative, sharing her feelings generously and not without flamboyance. She was what is traditionally called big-hearted; thus she would always respond most favourably to those who possessed similar gregarious qualities. Religion for her would have a degree of superstition attached to it, but from a spiritual point of view she would actually have had some very firm beliefs. She would have believed, for instance, that one learnt through experience, and that only then could the lesson be passed on.

Martha would have liked all the familiar sights and sounds of her own home, as the presence of her nearest and dearest gave her emotional stability. From them she ultimately gained the strength required to face life with confidence. It must have been difficult for her in the three weeks before her death to find herself in a common lodging-house. It was very important that she felt there was a place for her in the world, that she personally made her own contribution to life. Without this, she would have felt superfluous, as if she were not a part of any greater design, but consigned instead to complete insignificance.

BIBLIOGRAPHY

Begg, Paul, Fido, Martin and Skinner, Keith *The Jack The Ripper A-Z* , 3rd edition. Headline Book Publishing, 1996

Bosanquet, C. B. D. *Handy Book For Visitors Of The Poor,* 1874

Cawthorne, Nigel *Sex Killers.* Boxtree, 1994

Corbett, Joseph *Essays Of London.* 1886

Cullen, Tom A. *Autumn Of Terror: Jack The Ripper, His Crimes And Times* . Bodley Head, 1965

De Courtais, Georgine *Women's Headdresses and Hairstyles.* BT Batsford 1973

Hammerslough, B. F. *Forecasting Backward and Forwards.* Llewellyn, 1994

Knight, Stephen *Jack The Ripper: The Final Solution.* Harper Collins, 1994

Langhorne, William Henry *Mission Life In East London.* 1876

McLaren, Angus *A Prescription for Murder: The Victorian Serial Killings of Dr Thomas Neill Cream.* University of Chicago Press, 1993

Mitchell, Susan *Victorian Britian: an Encyclopaedia.* 1997

O'Donnell, Kevin (from research by Andy and Sue Parlour) *The Jack The Ripper Whitechapel Murders.* Ten Bells Publishing, 1997

Oken, Alan *Astrology: Evolution and Revolution.* Bantam Books, 1976

Paley, Bruce *Jack The Ripper: The Simple Truth.* Headline Book Publishing, 1996

Pearson, Michael *The Age Of Consent: Victorian Prostitution And Its Enemies.* 1972

Poore, George Vivian *London Ancient And Modern.* 1889

Rumbelow, Donald *The Complete Jack The Ripper.* Penguin, 1988

Ryder, Stephen P. *Jack The Ripper Casebook* (available only on the Internet)

Sugden, Philip *The Complete History Of Jack The Ripper.* Robinson Publishing, 1995

Watters, Barbara H. *The Astrologer Looks At Murder.* Valhalla Paperbacks, 1969

Wilson, Colin and Odell, Robert *Jack The Ripper: Summing Up And Verdict.* Corgi, 1988

Wolff, Camille (compiler) *Who Was Jack The Ripper?* Grey House Books, 1995

Wood, Anthony *Nineteenth Century Britain 1815 - 1914.* Longman, 1972

INDEX

ACKNOWLEDGEMENTS

My personal thanks go initially to Andrew Ball, Fiona Ball and James Eden without whose support, encouragement, hard work, research (and a place in which to hold our contact sessions) this book could not have been written. Gallantry medals for their patience and understanding must go to The Bancroft Local History Library (particularly Chris and Malcolm); staff of The British Library and the British Newspaper Library, Colindale; The Cloak and Dagger Club; Family Records Office; National Fishing Heritage Centre, Grimsby; Grey House Books; Hulton Getty Picture Library; Live TV; London Metropolitan Archives; Museum of London; Museums of the Royal College of Surgeons; Newbury Library; Jeremy at the Patent Office; Public Records Office, Kew; Science and Society Picture Library, and Smith Gryphon Publishers.

We would have had even more difficulty in completing our project without the vast experience and knowledge of those who have 'gone before' and researched the Jack the Ripper phenomenon over the years. Special thanks should go to Paul Begg, Professor David Canter, Paul Daniel, all of whom were at the Grey House Books lunch on 21 November 1997, Shirley Harrison, Loretta Lay, John Morrison, Andy and Sue Parlour, Donald Rumbelow, Keith Skinner, and Camille Wolff.

In addition we would like to thank Paul Daniel, Andy and Sue Parlour, Alex and Jim Hodgson, Sean Tuomey and Smith Gryphon for use of their photographic images. Using The Electric Ephemeris astrological programme rendered our astrological research much simpler.

Finally, the help we received from the 'other side' must be acknowledged and our appreciation of the efforts made recorded.

PICTURE CREDITS

Bancroft Local History Library: page 3, (bottom); page 4, (top and bottom); page 5, (top and bottom); page 10, (bottom right).

Hulton Getty: page 1; page 7; page 10, (bottom left); page 12, (bottom left); page 14, (bottom right); page 16, (top); page 23, (top); page 24; page 28; page 30.

Courtesy of Public Records Office: page 8, (MEPO 3/140); page 10, (top), (MEPO 3/3155/1); page 11, (MEPO 3/3155/2); page 13, (MEPO 3/140); page 14, (top), (MEPO 3/140); page 17, (top left), (MEPO 3/140); page 18, (MEPO 3/141/167); page 20, (MEPO 3/3153/2); page 22, (MEPO 3/142/329); page 25, (top), (MEPO 3/142/195); page 27, (top), (MEPO 3/142/106), (bottom), (MEPO 3/142/10).

Courtesy of *Punch* Magazines Ltd: page 6; page 19.

London Metropolitan Archives: page 16, (bottom left); page 21, (bottom)

NOTE: PAGE NUMBERS REFER TO ILLUSTRATION SECTION.